# ANCIENT NUBIA

*Jar from Karanog grave 566*
*Meroitic Period.*
*E 8183*

# ANCIENT NUBIA

## Egypt's Rival in Africa

David O'Connor

The University Museum
of Archaeology and Anthropology
University of Pennsylvania

Editing
    Publications Department, The University Museum
Design and Production
    Bagnell & Socha
Printing
    Cypher Press

The logo of three birds and an alligator appearing
on the cover and title page of this volume was taken
from the engraved bezel of a Meroitic ring (p. 151,
pl. 116, E 8068).

**Library of Congress Cataloging-in-Publication Data**

O'Connor, David.
        Ancient Nubia : Egypt's rival in Africa / by
David O'Connor.
                p.  cm.
        Includes index.
        1. Nubia—History.  I. Title.
DT159.6.N83025  1993   939'.78—dc20   93-4769 CIP
ISBN 0-924171-28-6

Publication of this volume was made possible
through generous grants from The Pew Charitable
Trusts and the National Endowment for the
Humanities, a federal granting agency.

# Table of Contents

# Table of Contents

# Figures

*T*his book is a study of ancient Nubia written in conjunction with the exhibition of the same name, "Ancient Nubia: Egypt's Rival in Africa." As a discussion of the evolution of Nubian culture and history through the Bronze Age, and the Napatan-Meroitic Period, the volume forms an independent entity of value in its own right, developing the themes found in the exhibition; it also documents every artifact in a compendium of black-and-white photographs.

The two earliest known African civilizations are those of Egypt and Nubia. Over the very long span of time represented in this book, the two civilizations interacted in many ways, sometimes collaborating, for example, in trading relationships, but often competing with each other for territory or other advantages. Despite these interrelationships, Egyptian civilization and Nubian civilization differed from each other in many important ways, each showing a strong inner vitality of its own. Even in Napatan-Meroitic times, when many aspects of Egyptian culture were integrated into Nubian civilization, the latter still differed strongly from that of Egypt.

This book is about ancient Nubia, rather than about Nubia and Egypt, and in it the author describes the important aspects of each phase of Nubian civilization and discusses the many mysteries that still remain to be solved about Nubia. Some of the ideas he presents are controversial, and differ from more customary scholarly notions about Nubian history and culture; but he always bases these new ways of looking at Nubia on a careful consideration of the evidence, and always describes theories that differ from his own.

That this book and the exhibition with which it is associated should be produced by The University Museum of Archaeology and Anthropology of the University of Pennsylvania is very appropriate, for two reasons. First, The University Museum has had a long institutional involvement in the archaeological exploration of Nubia—two of its curators, David Randall-MacIver and Leonard Woolley, were among the archaeological pioneers in Nubia (1907-1910), and William Kelly Simpson directed a combined expedition of Yale University and The University Museum during the last great campaign of salvage archaeology in Nubia, in 1962–1963. Randall-MacIver, Woolley, and Simpson made some of the most important archaeological finds in Nubia, revealing distinctively Nubian cultural developments in both the Bronze Age and Napatan-Meroitic periods.

Second, much of the archaeological material recovered by these projects was allotted to The University Museum through the generosity of the Egyptian and Sudanese governments, and as a result The University Museum has one of the finest collections of ancient Nubian art and archaeology in the United States, indeed in the world. This collection has recently been further strengthened by an exchange of representative Nubian artifacts with the Museum of Fine Arts, Boston, which has a Nubian collection different in character from that of The University Museum.

As a result, The University Museum not only has an enduring interest in Nubia, as this book attests, but also the resources to develop a fine exhibition on ancient Nubia, which has received considerable attention nationally, and which, after being exhibited at The University Museum (October 1992–October 1993) will travel to eight other venues in the United States. Dr. David O'Connor, Curator of the Egyptian Section, The University Museum, curated this exhibition, "Ancient Nubia: Egypt's Rival in Africa." His curatorial assistants were Stacie Olson and Josef Wegner, graduate students in Egyptology at the University of Pennsylvania. Pamela Hearne, Coordinator of Museum Services, oversaw the exhibition's organization, and Jack Murray, Exhibition Designer, oversaw and designed the installation. Karen Vellucci, Coordinator for Publications, and her staff prepared the book of the same name for publication. The "Shabtis," the volunteers in the Egyptian Section of The University Museum, whose tireless efforts greatly facilitated the selection and documentation of the artifacts, also played a particularly important role.

Both the exhibition and the book were made possible in part by generous support from the Pew Charitable Trusts, Philadelphia, and the National Endowment for the Humanities, a federal granting agency.

Robert H. Dyson
Charles K. Williams II Director
The University Museum of
Archaeology and Anthropology

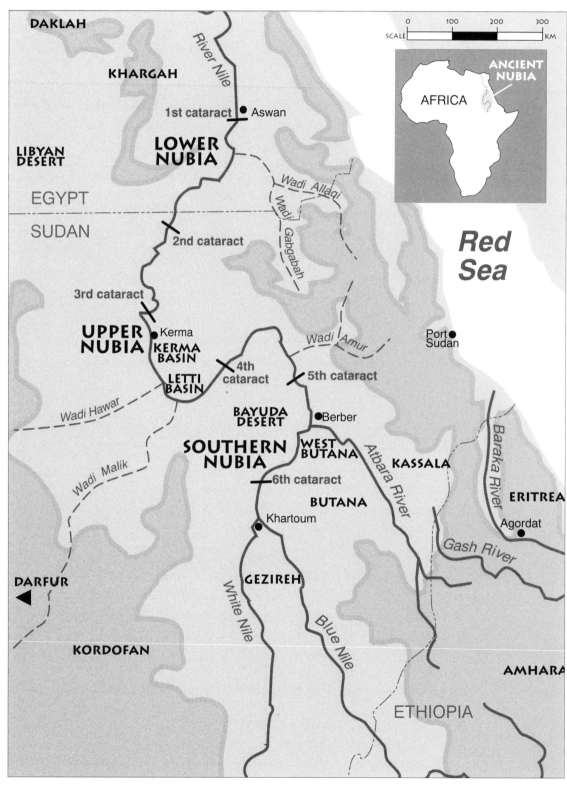

**Fig. Intro.1**
Map showing principal regions and significant sites of
Nubia and contiguous regions. Inset: Nubia and Africa.

# An Introduction to Ancient Nubia

*Nubia and Egypt*

*T*he Nubian and Egyptian civilizations are the two oldest yet known in Africa. They shared the same river, the Nile, and a common frontier over which contact and interaction ebbed and flowed for thousands of years. Inevitably, Nubian and Egyptian history are closely intertwined, but, in the final analysis, the two civilizations were very different from each other. Both the Nubian world view and modes of cultural expression were always unique, even when Egyptian art, language, and concepts became part of the cultural vocabulary used by the Nubians. Moreover, Nubia was typically the rival, rather than the dependent, of Egypt, as the two powers competed endlessly for territory and trade routes in what I call below the "Lower Nile" river system.

This book is about ancient Nubia, during its Bronze Age (ca. 3000–1000 B.C.) and Napatan-Meroitic period (ca. 1000 B.C.–A.D. 350). One point this book makes, with which some scholars would disagree, is that Nubia had a civilization—that is, was in "an advanced stage of social development"[1]— throughout most of the Bronze Age, as much as in Napatan and Meroitic times. This does not mean that either Nubia or Egypt always displayed political unity and cultural uniformity; on the contrary, political fragmentation and cultural diversity extending over long periods occurred in both lands, yet each represents a civilization.

Geographically (Fig. Intro.1), Nubia extends from the Sixth to the First Nile cataracts,[2] and Egypt from the latter to the Mediterranean. Internally, Nubia consists of Southern Nubia; central, or Upper, Nubia; and northern, or Lower, Nubia; and Egypt, of Upper (southern) and Lower (northern) Egypt. The Nubian Nile is often called the "Middle Nile," but historically it is more useful to see Nubia and Egypt sharing a single environment, the "Lower Nile," from Khartoum to the Mediterranean.

Most Nubians and Egyptians lived on the narrow floodplain, but their powerful riverine civilizations influenced, and often controlled, much of the vast deserts flanking them. With some exceptions, the Egyptian deserts were empty of people; but the semideserts flanking much of Nubia supported substantial nomadic populations, which played important roles in Nubian history.

"Nubia" and "Nubian," for the periods covered in this book, refer only to geographical locations, not to the ethnicity or language of the peoples involved. Nubia is a word of uncertain origin. By 1400 B.C., Egypt was already known as *Aigyptos* to Greek-speakers, and as *Misr* (its modern Arabic name) to the Semitic world; but Nubia, as a country's name, does not occur before the third century B.C.[3] The Christian Nubians (A.D. 540–1500) spoke Nubian, and hence were "Nubians," and the language itself does go back into the Bronze Age. Nevertheless, many, perhaps most, of the "Nubians" discussed in this book may not have been Nubian speakers, and their precise ethnic status is unknown.[4]

## The Discovery of Nubia

Ancient town and cemetery sites attest to Nubian civilization, as do written records of the Nubians and others. However, European scholars knew little about the monuments of far away Nubia until, in the nineteenth century, travelers and scientific expeditions published the records of their visits to that land.

Most of Nubia lies in the modern Sudan, and after the Sudan came under joint control by Egypt and Britain in 1898, research into ancient Nubia developed along two very different lines. Lower Nubia, shared between Egypt and Sudan, became a periodically expanding reservoir for the Aswan dam and hence experienced several major campaigns of salvage archaeology. Its archaeology is now the best known in the entire Nile Valley.

In contrast, Upper and Southern Nubia have been much less thoroughly explored. Numerous foreign projects have worked at individual sites, encouraged first by the British and then, after 1956, by the independent Sudan; but large-scale archaeological surveys have begun only in relatively recent times. Of the projects, George Reisner's were the most important. He established the basic, hitherto unknown archaeological sequence for Lower Nubia. Later, for the Boston Museum of Fine Arts, Reisner excavated at Kerma, perhaps the most important Nubian Bronze Age site; and he explored the royal cemeteries of the Napatan and Meroitic kings, establishing the basic chronology and historical outline for these rulers.

Many other archaeologists have worked in Nubia, but in the context of this book, the pioneering excavations (1907–1910) of David Randall-MacIver and Leonard Woolley in Lower Nubia are notable. This work, undertaken for The University Museum of the University of Pennsylvania, produced most of the artifacts illustrated in this book, and the sites they excavated are prominent in it because they were especially significant in Nubian history and culture.

Randall-MacIver was an important figure in African archaeology, having suggested in 1905 that the great stone buildings at Zimbabwe (thirteenth–fourteenth century A.D.), in Rhodesia (modern Zimbabwe), were built by Africans, not "superior" foreigners. White supremacists disliked Randall-MacIver's suggestion, but it has proved to be correct. In Lower Nubia, Randall-MacIver and Woolley studied a major Bronze Age Nubian settlement at Areika (chapter 4); only one other comparable in size and complexity has ever been excavated. They were also the first to excavate on a large scale at one of the fortresses (Buhen) implanted by Egypt in Nubia during ancient "colonial" times (chapter 5). Finally, at Karanog, Randall-MacIver and Woolley excavated a town (and its cemetery) that was the capital of the Meroitic governors of Lower Nubia in the second and third centuries A.D. This site is unique among excavated sites in Nubia (chapter 7).

Many important discoveries remain to be made about ancient Nubia, more so than in better-explored Egypt, but the evidence available already suggests many ideas about early Nubian history and culture. However, current theories disagree in two, most important ways. Was Bronze Age Nubian society tribal and small in scale, or were large-scale chiefdoms and states typical? And was the Napatan-Meroitic kingdom socially complex but weakly structured, or was it more strongly unified than many scholars think?

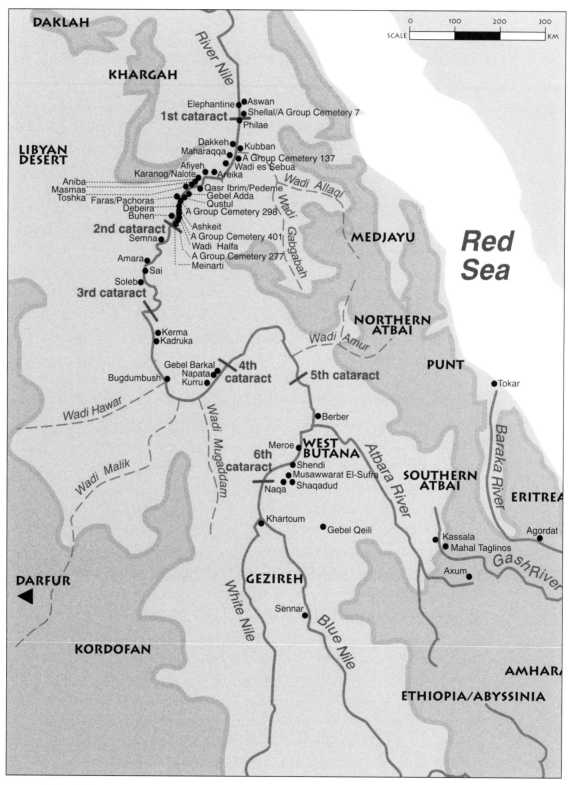

**Fig. 1.1**
*Map showing all sites referred to in the text.*

# Understanding Ancient Nubia

*Approaches to Nubia*

The questions asked in the introduction give this book its basic structure. For ancient Nubia, from 3000 B.C. to A.D. 350, there is much information. The archaeological record is rich, if incomplete. Egyptians, Greeks, and Romans wrote about the Nubians and depicted them in art. The Nubians left us their own written records, some in Egyptian, most in Meroitic—the written, as yet largely untranslatable language of Nubia from 180 B.C. to A.D. 400. From the evidence we can evoke something of Nubia's human reality, but will do so within the framework of two major and debatable issues.

Most scholars today argue that Bronze Age Nubians were organized into relatively small, simply structured chiefdoms, except for a comparatively short-lived state centered at Kerma. However, I propose instead that for most of the Bronze Age Nubian political systems were strongly centralized, covered large territories, and were akin to states and kingdoms rather than chiefdoms. For later times, some scholars suggest that the Napatan and especially Meroitic kingdoms were large but very loosely organized states. Other scholars (with whom I agree) argue that these kingdoms were relatively highly centralized, and cohesive and stable.

My predilections aside, I will always indicate where scholarly opinion about important topics differs. In fact, it is this continuing debate about Nubian history and culture that brings our inert sources to life.

Our impressions about ancient Nubia have to some extent been overshadowed and distorted by the impressive, better-known history and culture of Egypt. If Nubia is seen as dwarfed by "that great colossus on the north,"[1] Nubia does indeed look peripheral. From this perspective, tribal Bronze Age Nubia can be imagined as heavily pressured and even manipulated by powerful Egypt. Later—in this same perspective—the independent Napatan and Meroitic kingdoms appear to derive their culture from Egypt, becoming merely barbarian variations of a superior model.

This perspective on Nubia is flawed. It exaggerates the political and social stability of Bronze Age Egypt and underestimates that of contemporary Nubia. Instead, we should see two major powers competing for resources and lands of the Lower Nile. Later, Meroitic Nubia and Ptolemaic, later Roman, Egypt are stalemated so far as territorial expansion is concerned. But the Meroitic kingdom may have been highly centralized rather than loosely "feudal" in structure, and its culture a subtle blend of Nubian and Egyptian elements rather than an awkward mixture of the two.

This book, then, presents a more positive or dynamic version of Nubian history and culture than some other studies. Nevertheless, Nubian culture was not "ideal," and superior to others, although some Greek and Roman writers said it was (others disliked the Nubians). The Nubians, it was said, were "the first of all men and the first to honor the gods whose favor they enjoyed."[2] Some even suggested that the Egyptians were originally emigrants from Nubia and Egyptian culture Nubian in origin. Because some Greeks also thought that their own science, art, and religion derived largely from Egypt, one could argue that Greek, and ultimately West-ern, civilization had Nubian as well as Egyptian roots.

These ancient ideas have influenced modern studies such as Martin Bernal's *Black Athena*,[3] but they are not historically well founded. Such theories were invented in antiquity to explain the origins of the Greek and Egyptian civilizations, which otherwise seemed mysterious. Moreover, by praising the supposed nobility of the Nubians, Greek and Roman writers were able, by comparison, to criticize aspects of their own cultures that they found distasteful. A similar phenomenon occurred in sixteenth- and seventeenth-century Europe. To point out deficiencies in their own society, critics invented type figures of supposedly superior qualities—"Wise Egyptians," "Good Savages," and "Chinese Sages"—with little reference to the realities of the three cultures involved.[4]

In fact, no people enjoyed a "Golden Age;" human history is full of light and shadow, good and bad. Ancient Athens is admired as an early democracy, but most of its population (women, foreigners, and slaves) were excluded from voting. Egyptian art, religion, and social organization are striking, but conditions were often oppressive for most of the Egyptians. Like Greece and Egypt, Nubia reveals both achievement and failure; but, like them, its civilization was a major one and its history fascinating in its diversity.

### People, Places, and Things

We get our knowledge of ancient Nubia from three sources—its peoples, places, and things.

The peoples and places are those named in texts about ancient Nubia, in ancient Egyptian, Meroitic, Greek, Latin, and other languages. Often, the people or place involved is obscure to us. Are the people named the entire Nubian nation or those of a subregion, or even a small village? Is the place all Nubia, part of it, or a single site? And which people are to be located in which place?

These questions can puzzle scholars, but a few names at least are reasonably clear in meaning. The Bronze Age Egyptians called the Nubians "Nehasyu," a word including nomads as well as riverine Nubians, and even the Puntites, far away on the Red Sea coast. However, the nomads east of Lower and Upper Nubia were also called the "Medjayu." *Ta-Nehasyu* then meant simply "Land (*ta*) of the Nubians," and was used as such into the Roman period.

After 1550 B.C. Egyptians also often called Nubia "Kush," a name originally applied only to some or all of Upper Nubia. During the first millennium B.C., however, Kush was the preferred name for all Nubia in Egyptian, Assyrian, Persian, and Hebrew.

The Greeks and Romans gave Nubia yet another name, Aethiopia or Ethiopia. Ethiopia was applied to other parts of Africa as well. Eventually, Ethiopia became identified with the land of Abyssinia, which had only slight historical connections with nearby Nubia.

The third source of information, the things of the Nubians, are those that make up the fabric of their archaeology—cult-places, houses, graves, artwork, and artifacts. In each phase of Nubia's history these things display a distinctive typology, characteristic of that phase and no other; they are said to form the archaeological assemblage typical of that phase. In fact, even within the same period of time, the assemblages of different regions can be markedly different from one another. For example, in the Bronze Age, and in Meroitic times, the archaeology of Lower Nubia was usually different from that of Upper Nubia.

The archaeological picture of Nubia as a whole is very incomplete. We know this because we can reasonably predict where in Nubia and its hinterlands people would have lived in the past; yet often we know little or nothing about the archaeology of the regions involved.

Thus, we can reasonably guess that in the Bronze Age and later there was a more or less continuous ribbon of agricultural villages along the Nubian Nile (and the downstream end of its tributary, the Atbara). The ribbon was broken only twice, by stretches of the valley between Lower and Upper Nubia, and Upper and Southern Nubia. Along these stretches the environment was very harsh, and settlement sparse or absent.

East and west of Southern Nubia nomadic pastoralists covered large areas on a seasonal basis. A significant number may have been riverine peoples taking herds out into the semi-desert; others were nomads coming up from the south, to which they returned as the grass withered every year. The delta of the river Gash, east of the Atbara, is "anomalous, with the silts providing good grazing as well as good agriculture following the annual flood."[5] The nomadic belt once stretched farther north, when the climate was marginally better, and included part of Upper Nubia; but after 1300 B.C. only Southern Nubia lay within it.

Another important nomadic population, known as the "Medjayu," was based on the Red Sea coast; every year they followed the rains back into the Red Sea hills and onto the plains east of Upper and Lower Nubia.

Throughout the regions listed above we would expect to find archaeological remains, except when historical circumstances (rather than environmental change) led to depopulation for a time. For example, Lower Nubia was largely empty of settlement from about 2900 to 2350 B.C., and 1000 to 300 B.C. However, if we look at the columns in Figure 1.2 that represent the various parts of Nubia and its hinterlands likely to be occupied by settled peoples or nomads in ancient times, we see that they often are shaded, so as to show that their archaeology is unknown. It is true that the archaeology of nomads is more elusive than that of settled peoples, but the basic reason for the archaeological gaps is that the regions in question have not been subject to comprehensive archaeological surveys.

Lower Nubia has received such surveys and hence is exceptionally well documented archaeologically. Elsewhere, individual sites have been excavated and limited survey undertaken in some regions (others are almost completely unexplored). But only large-scale archaeological surveys can reveal the full range and extent of ancient sites within a region. This is particularly true for Bronze Age and Napatan sites, which are rarely discovered in any other way. Sites of these two periods along the valleys suffer from erosion, burial under silt and intrusive sand dunes, and overbuilding by later sites,

namely, the many Meroitic, post-Meroitic, and medieval towns and villages that have already been located by archaeologists throughout Upper and Southern Nubia. Numerous ancient cemeteries also flank Upper and Southern Nubia, representing literally hundreds of thousands of graves. Many are Meroitic or later, some probably Bronze Age; few have been systematically excavated.

On the semi-desert and desert plains, settlements were probably small, and cemeteries not very conspicuous, because the ancient inhabitants were typically nomads, often on the move. However, careful surveys could recover many such sites, as recent work in the southern Atbai has demonstrated.

The Nubian archaeological picture is, then, tantalizing and frustrating, yet also full of potential and excitement. In terms of Nubian history, future discoveries will lead to great increases in basic knowledge and understanding, which is no longer the case in better-explored Egypt.

## Discovering the Nubians

Excavating sites and deciphering texts provide evidence that must then be interpreted if we wish to discover the living reality of Nubian society, but in so doing scholars can reach very different conclusions. One area of debate, already mentioned, is the political status of Nubians—were they organized into chiefdoms or states? The issue is difficult. Small, simply structured chiefdoms are clearly not states, but large complex chiefdoms and early states have much in common.

A chiefdom and a state both have a single, paramount ruler. However, a chiefdom's population does not exceed about one hundred thousand people, but a state's is in the hundreds of thousands, or millions. Moreover, the governmental systems are very different. A paramount chief rules through subchiefs, whose functions replicate, on a smaller scale, those of the chief. And in a chiefdom kin-relations are all-important; people are appointed to government and allotted income and status because they belong to important families or lineages, with claims on offices and resources. But a state ruler heads a centralized government, serviced by regional ones that are narrower in function; and officials are appointed, salaried, and rewarded not so much for reasons of kin, but because they are efficient and loyal.

We shall return to Nubian political systems later. Generally, it is difficult to evaluate the political, economic, and cultural status of any community on the basis of archaeology alone, all the more so when "Western" ethnocentric bias effects our decisions. We tend to overvalue developed societies with material cultures similar in important ways to our own, and undervalue others with material cultures more alien to us.

Thus, ancient Egypt, with its monumentally scaled, stone-built, and rectilinear pyramids and temples (akin to our own monumental architecture) seems to us "superior"; yet other complex societies found different, less familiar modes of expression. The "Great Enclosure" at Zimbabwe in Southeast Africa, for example, was built by local peoples between the thirteenth and fifteenth centuries A.D. Massive,

stone-built, and monumental, it compares well at 6300 square meters with the Egyptian temple of Amun at Karnak (about 8400 square meters) in the earlier 18th Dynasty. But at Zimbabwe oval and circular forms are preferred, and the interior has a convoluted complexity very different from the axial regularity of the Egyptian temple plan.

In Nubia, the material culture of Napatan and Meroitic times integrated much from Egyptian art and architecture; we instinctively see it as valuable and civilized. Earlier, Bronze Age Nubians preferred much less grandiose modes of expression in material culture, but this does not mean their social organization was simpler and more primitive than that of the Egyptians, as examples from other African cultures show.

For example, the great Zimbabwe monuments—products of a well-organized society—were actually part of the capital of a state or a very large complex chiefdom; but the large town (about 100 hectares, or almost 1 square mile) surrounding them consisted of clay huts with thatched roofs. Later, nineteenth-century Buganda was also a highly organized state, with a well-laid out capital city several miles in extent. Yet its palaces and houses were all built of grass and wood.

Archaeology can be supplemented by written records reflecting a society's degree of complexity, but Bronze Age Nubians were not literate. This does not imply cultural immaturity, for many complex chiefdoms and even states have functioned well with little or no literacy. The Inca state in Peru, for example, used a system of knotted string (*quipu*) for its records.

Egyptian texts refer often to Bronze Age Nubia, but they say little about Nubian society or politics. Most surviving texts are from temples, and present pharaoh as a conquering hero for the benefit of the gods; Nubians, like all foreigners, are rendered simplistically as emblems of the cosmic chaos the gods empower pharaoh to overcome.

To some extent we can "read between the lines" of such texts to learn more about Nubian society, but even here scholarly biases creep in. For example, Egyptians called both Near Eastern and Nubian rulers *heka* or *wer*. Scholars translate these words as "ruler" or "king" for the Near Eastern rulers, but as "chief" for the Nubian, although nothing in the Egyptian texts warrants the differentiation.

As for Egyptian art, it contrasts half-naked Nubians and their simply built villages with robed Near Easterners living in fortified, mud-brick towns. This contrast, however, reflects long-established conventions, not reality. For example, Middle Bronze Nubians at Kerma with a highly developed culture lived in a large, fortified mud-brick town at that site, and perhaps did so elsewhere as well.

After the Bronze Age, written sources are more revealing. The Napatan rulers made use of Egyptian and its writing system, although the surviving texts focus on religion and royal victories, not Nubian society as a whole. Later, the Meroites invented an alphabet for their own language, but the many surviving texts—rich in social as well as historical information—remain largely untranslatable, although some valuable insights have been recovered.

## An Introductory Outline

Despite the large archaeological gaps noted above, a partial outline of Nubian archaeology and history can be sketched, as an introduction to the more detailed chapters that follow.

Before the Bronze Age the Nubian archaeological map looked very different from its later phases. The climate was more favorable, and vast areas that later became desert supported many hunting and gathering people. From 9000 to 4500 B.C. the archaeology typical of the phase is labeled Khartoum Mesolithic. Later, from 4500 to 3500 B.C. the climate deteriorated, and for much of Nubia human activity was restricted to the river valleys. Archaeological characteristics differ from one region to another, but the basic economy was neolithic, involving "in some cases . . . cultivation of domestic plants, and herding of domesticated animals."[6]

Toward Bronze Age times the archaeological picture becomes more sharply differentiated. After 3500 B.C. Lower Nubia was occupied by sedentary agriculturalists with a distinctive material culture, labeled A-Group. They were brought to an end by Egyptian aggression in about 2900 B.C., and Lower Nubia remained empty of Nubians for almost 600 years.

Contemporary with the A-Group is the as yet poorly known Pre-Kerma culture of Upper Nubia. Farther south, the Berber-Shendi Reach (Southern Nubia), well settled in Neolithic times, is an archaeological blank for 2000 years. Some suggest that it was empty of settlement, but possibly its Bronze Age archaeology remains to be discovered.

| B.C. | Lower Nubia | Upper Nubia | Southern Nubia | Western Butana | Butana | Eastern Desert/ North Atbai | South Atbai | Red Sea Plain | Kordofan |
|---|---|---|---|---|---|---|---|---|---|
| 3100 | Classical A-Group | Pre-Kerma | | | | | | | |
| 3100–3000 | Terminal A-Group | Pre-Kerma | | | | | | | |
| 3000 | Hiatus | Pre-Kerma | | [Shaqadud] | | | Early Kassala, Butana Group | | |
| 2400 | C-Group IA, IB | Early Kerma | | [Shaqadud] | | | Middle Kassala, Gash Group | | |
| 2050 | C-Group IIA, IIB | Middle Kerma | | | | | Middle Kassala, Gash Group | | |
| 1700 | C-Group III | Classic Kerma | | | | | Middle Kassala, Gash Group | | |
| 1550 | Egyptian Occupation | Egyptian Occupation | | | | | Middle Kassala, Gash Group | | |
| 1000 | Hiatus | | | | | | Late Kassala, Mokram Group | | |
| 750 | [Napatan] | Napatan | [Napatan] | | | | Taka, Hagiz Group | | |
| 250 | Meroitic | Meroitic | Meroitic | Meroitic | | | Taka, Hagiz Group | | |
| 250 | | | | | | | Taka, Hagiz Group | | |

**Fig. 1.2**
*The principal regions of Nubia and contiguous areas, illustrating the variable degree of archaeological coverage we have for each. Hatched columns or segments represent areas that are archaeologically unknown, mainly because the necessary intensive surveys and fieldwork have not yet been carried out.*

7

Throughout the Bronze Age nomadic herders lived east and west of Southern and even Upper Nubia. Their archaeology is almost unknown, except at Shaqadud, and in the southern Atbai and the deltas of the Gash and Baraka rivers. By 3000 B.C. a fairly uniform material culture, the Gash Group, existed in the last three regions, and lasted until 1500 B.C.

The Upper Nubian Pre-Kerma assemblage developed into the Kerma Group, typical of the region from 2400 to 1500 B.C., or even later. Lower Nubia was resettled by Nubians in about 2400 B.C.; its archaeological assemblage until 1700/1500 B.C. is labeled C-Group.

Egyptians were active in Nubia. They controlled empty Lower Nubia, and raided Upper Nubia, through the 4th to 6th Dynasties. Then, after a period of withdrawal, Egypt conquered Lower Nubia in about 2000 B.C., although Upper Nubia remained independent, developing into a powerful Nubian kingdom. This "kingdom of Kush" gained control of Lower Nubia in about 1680/1640 B.C.

Contemporaneously (2400–1500 B.C.) the Gash Group underwent important developments: many of its settlements were permanent, and one (Mahal Teglinos) had a town and cemetery occupying 17 hectares (about 42 acres). Some suggest that the Gash-Baraka region was included in Punt, a coastal land vis-ited by Egyptian trading expeditions, but this is doubtful.

Egypt began a new drive for empire after 1550 B.C., and ultimately controlled Lower and Upper Nubia until about 1000 B.C. The population continued to be mainly Nubian; and the Egyptians both traded and fought with the independent people of Southern Nubia as well.

Thereafter Egypt weakened internally and abandoned Nubia, while Nubia rapidly grew strong and expansive. After 900 B.C. rulers arose in Upper Nubia who conquered Egypt and ruled it *and* Nubia as the 25th Dynasty for almost a century, creating perhaps the largest state ever to develop along the Nile. Egypt was lost after 650 B.C., but Nubia continued as a wealthy, independent kingdom, centered first at Napata, then (fourth century B.C.–A.D. 350) at Meroe, farther south.

The Meroitic kingdom eventually disintegrated. Lower Nubia became divided into the two kingdoms of the Blemmyes and the Nobatai, while in Upper (and Southern?) Nubia Meroitic culture was transformed into the Tanqasi culture. By the end of the sixth century A.D. Nubia had become divided into three kingdoms—Nobatia, Makouria, and Alwa—which converted to Christianity, opening yet a further and fascinating chapter in the diverse history of the Nubians.

# Chiefs and Kings in Early Nubia

*T*he story of Nubian civilization opens with a challenge. Most scholars see the Nubians of the earliest Bronze Age (ca. 3000–2900 B.C.) as divided up into small, simple chiefdoms. But a few argue that Lower, or northernmost, Nubia at least was already organized as a kingdom, in which the form and traditions of pharaonic kingship arose. Egyptian kingship, then, would actually have been derived from Nubia.

This challenge to orthodoxy really involves two separate issues: was there an early state in Nubia, and was the institution of pharaonic kingship created in Nubia? The latter notion has little factual support, but the former raises an important question: by the end of the fourth millennium B.C. was Nubian society already so productive and dynamic that it could generate a state?

This question is discussed later, but at the outset we can assume that, whether organized into chiefdoms or states, these early Nubians had ideologies and organizational systems different from those of the "proto-states" (in scale more comparable to complex chiefdoms) developing in Egypt a little earlier. During the later fourth millennium B.C. Egypt and Nubia were very different in material culture and did not share a common language, to judge from the later linguistic situation in the Bronze Age. Their world views must have been quite different, and it is a society's world view that shapes its ideas about the cosmos and its gods, and about social and political organization.

At this time, Nubia as a whole was certainly varied in material culture and could not have formed a political unity. However, the apparent unity of Egypt by about 2900 B.C. was a very recent development and probably not very stable. All Egyptians then shared a common material culture and language, but only shortly before had been highly fragmented, divided up into proto-states competing for territory and power. National unification of a sort was achieved under the pharaoh Narmer (ca. 2900 B.C.) or even earlier (3100 B.C.?), but still required a long period of consolidation. And culturally important features such as burial customs show that ideological differences between northern and southern Egypt continued even after unification.

Indeed, if we consider the Lower Nile as a whole, the prehistoric background to the rise of chiefdoms and early states in both Egypt and Nubia can be seen to be quite complicated. This probably generated different kinds of social and political systems, not only "Nubian" as compared to "Egyptian," but also in both Nubia and Egypt.

## A Regional Perspective on the Lower Nile in Prehistoric Times

To understand this prehistoric background better, we can focus on 3500 B.C. and see, as if from a satellite, that throughout the Lower Nile system the archaeological and cultural picture is varied and complex. Some areas—Upper Egypt and Lower Nubia—are better documented than others, but almost all provide some kind of information.

We tend to think of ancient Egypt as a cultural unity, but in 3500 B.C. it was by no means homogeneous in material culture. The Nakadan culture was typical of southern Egypt (and itself exhibited regional variations), but the vast Delta displayed a distinctly different culture, the Maadian. This broad distinction is important, although recent work suggests that gradually, and primarily through trade and other peaceful contacts, the two cultural regions melded into one, by the time of what is called the Nakada IIC period. Differentiation in political and social systems, however, may well have persisted longer, and remained significant even after the national unification described above.

Contemporaneously, a single continuously evolving culture can be traced in Lower Nubia, namely, the A-Group (3800–2900 B.C.). Recent work shows that A-Group culture was long-established in Lower Nubia, but within the second cataract region and northernmost Upper Nubia was a different material culture, the Abkan. It ended about 3500 B.C., but its ceramic traditions may have influenced those of the southern A-Group.

The A-Group consists of three phases. The Early A-Group, falling on either side of 3500 B.C., lasted a long time; it antedates the Bronze Age. The next two phases, Classic followed by Terminal, were both relatively short. Although A-Group material culture is quite different from that of contemporary Nakadan Egypt, many Egyptian pottery vessels occur in A-Group contexts. They were containers for imported liquids and solids (e.g., beer or wine, oils, and cereals) and equate the Early A-Group with the late Nakada I and Nakada II phases in Upper Egypt. Classic and Terminal A-Group are coeval with Nakada III, the Terminal phase ending abruptly early during the 1st Dynasty of Egypt.

So far as the rest of Nubia is concerned in 3500 B.C., both Upper and Southern Nubia had large areas of farm and grazing lands, hence probably large populations. Upper Nubian material culture has recently been defined as a regional variant of an archaeological assemblage, the Khartoum Neolithic (very different from the A-Group), typical of southern Nubia and extending into the (then) savannah lands of the Butana.

The later phase of these Neolithic cultures was particularly interesting. The economy was largely pastoral and few if any permanent settlements developed; yet people formed into large communities, generating large cemeteries (some with as many as 1000 burials). Differentiation in grave size and burial goods within these cemeteries reveal a socially complex society, and even indications of centralized government in some form.

In these early times, there were likely to be nomadic cattle herders in what later became deserts or semi-deserts east and west of Upper and Southern Nubia (Lower Nubia was already too far north for such a possibility). Their archaeology, however, is unknown. Communities of hunters and gatherers (rather than herders) are attested to at some sites in the western Butana and throughout the southern Atbai. The material culture of the western Butana was similar to the Khartoum Neolithic, but that of the southern Atbai (labeled the Butana Group) was more distinctive. Large settlement sites here (up to 10 hectares, or 25 acres) suggest an unexpected social complexity, given the relatively simple economic basis of the communities in question.

The preceding survey shows that, in 3500 B.C. and later, the Lower Nile was characterized, from north to south, by a series of distinctly different material cultures—Maadian, Nakadan, A-Group, Neolithic (Upper and Southern Nubia, the western Butana), and Butana Group. Economies also differed: in Egypt and Lower Nubia sedentary agriculture based on flood irrigation was the norm; elsewhere in Nubia, pastoralism; and in southern Atbai, hunting and gathering. This variety in material culture and economy, less marked in earlier periods, was due in large part to climatic change. Semi-desert and savannah lands capable of supporting nomads, and creating a more interactive relationship between river valley and open plain, once extended far north, and included much of Upper Egypt. Over time, rainfall diminished and the savannah lands retreated southward, while regional communities (e.g., those of 3500 B.C.) became increasingly confined to specific stretches of the river, and increasingly different from one another in material culture, and implicitly in social systems and ideology.

Yet the Lower Nile— a vast, traversable oasislike corridor crossing the expanding deserts—did permit continuing contact and interrelationships. And these in turn did exist, because of a strong trading desire on the part of the various regional communities described above. However, trading contacts (and hence cultural interactions) took on a very structured form. Because of the ribbonlike arrangement of these regions, each one tended to become a trading middleman between two of the others, but was much less in contact with the other, more remote regions. It is also likely that each

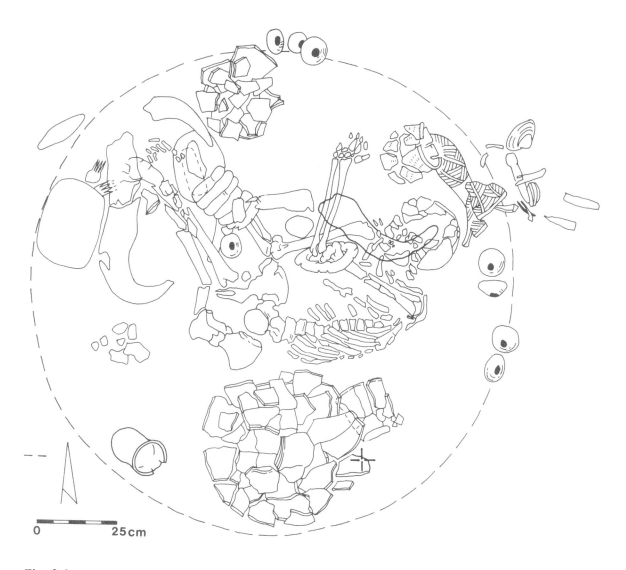

**Fig. 2.1**
*A late Neolithic burial, perhaps of a chieftain, at*
*Kadruka. Drawing by Nicole deLisle Warshaw.*

middleman tried to monopolize the trade flowing through it, and discouraged the development of direct contact between its two trading partners.

Thus, Maadian northern Egypt and Nakadan southern Egypt traded extensively with each other, while the north also transferred goods from the Levant to Upper Egypt, and Upper Egypt sent north exotic southern products derived from Nubia. In Nubia, Lower, or A-Group, Nubia was the chief trading partner of southern Egypt (as many Nakadan imports show) but had virtually no contact with the Maadian north (its artifacts do not occur in Nubia).

However, the typical artifacts of Nakadan Upper Egypt, abundant in the A-Group, are not found farther south, so the A-Group people presumably monopolized trade with Upper Nubia. The only partial exception is the occurrence of incised bowls and chalice-like beakers in black ware in southern Egypt; these are akin to Upper Nubian Neolithic types but are relatively rare.

Although little direct proof has yet been found, A-Group Lower Nubia must have traded with Neolithic Upper Nubia. The latter was the natural route for ivory, ebony, and other southern products (desired by both the A-Group people and the Egyptians) to move north; while the pastoralists of Upper Nubia probably also traded off animal products such as leather, and desired the cereals produced by Lower Nubia or imported from Egypt by the latter. Where Southern Nubia fitted into this trading system is not yet clear.

Within this general picture of inter-regional trade and growing regional economies it is noteworthy that social complexity and political developments were not restricted to Egypt and Lower Nubia. For example, at Kadruka in Upper Nubia a late Neolithic cemetery was clearly divided into higher-status and lower-status graves, while at the topographically highest, most "eminent" point was a unique grave, perhaps that of a ruler (Fig. 2.1). Its male occupant had unusually rich and elaborate grave goods. They included a massive ivory bracelet, nine well-made stone mace-heads, two stone palettes, and, among other pottery, an elaborately decorated chalice-like beaker.[1]

## A-Group Communities of Lower Nubia

As the best documented for the period, the A-Group people of Lower Nubia are the focus of this chapter. They provide our best insight into cultural and political developments in Nubia at the beginning of the Bronze Age, although circumstances in other parts of Nubia must have been different. The A-Group also brings us back to an important issue discussed earlier. Some scholars view them as a people with simple, small-scale political systems. However, the general evidence, on the later A-Group at least, indicates considerable social complexity, and one site suggests a high degree of political centralization.

Technology and economy are intimately linked to social complexity, but unfortunately our knowledge of them for the A-Group is impressionistic rather than specific. Settlements would have provided the best detailed evidence, but have almost never been excavated. Archaeologists in Nubia have usually concentrated on cemeteries, which contain many of the same kinds of artifacts as settlements did, but in different proportions.

Pottery, the graves show, was an abundant product of A-Group Nubia. Typical wares included brown coarse or smooth fabrics; red-polished wares, often black-topped; and very thin brown-and-black cored "eggshell" ware, its beige surface painted with bold red designs. Incised and impressed decoration also occurred. Beakers, bowls, and cups are common in graves, but jars are rarer and were probably commoner in settlements.

Other items included stone cosmetic palettes, different in shape and material from the slate palettes imported from Egypt; jewelry made of stones, ivory, and shell; and bone and stone tools. Metal was rare, and apparently always imported.

Overall, A-Group material culture shows slight influence from contemporary, Nakadan Egypt despite many imports from the latter. Maadian and Nakadan Egypt had enough in common to meld into a common material culture; Nakadan Egypt and A-Group Nubia did not.

On the economic side, the available evidence suggests that A-Group people were usually sedentary farmers practicing flood irrigation agriculture and raising substantial animal herds. They were probably self-sufficient in food, and because they supported an elite stratum, probably produced a food surplus as well. Foreign trade was another important source of wealth but, as we shall see, was apparently monopolized by the elite.

A-Group cemeteries reliably indicate the geographical distribution of the population, concentrated within the three fertile zones of Lower Nubia, zones centered in recent times at Dakkeh, Aniba, and Faras-Wadi Halfa. However, these same cemeteries are not fully representative of social complexity, and do not provide reliable data on overall population size.

Excavated A-Group cemeteries all lie on the low desert (easily accessible to archaeologists) adjoining the floodplain. Like those of later periods in Nubia, as in Egypt, they display statistical peculiarities indicating that they contained only part of the contemporary population. No doubt, some desert cemeteries were destroyed in the past or missed by archaeologists; but it is also likely that the settlements, always in the floodplain and virtually never located and excavated, had adjacent, floodplain cemeteries.

The A-Group cemeteries we have, then, represent special (not socially representative) segments of the population, namely, people of high and relatively high status and selected lower-order individuals privileged enough to be buried in the same cemetery. These poorer people included relatives and dependents of the elite, as well as servants whose services the elite required in the afterlife.

These circumstances also mean that estimating overall population size is difficult. Conservative archaeological estimates seem too low (about 5000), modern figures—reflecting better health and nutrition than enjoyed in antiquity—too high (about 50,000). A good working compromise could be an A-Group population of about 20,000 or 25,000. In late prehistoric Upper Egypt, with its larger floodplain, comparably sized regions supported 100,000 to 150,000 people.

The few A-Group settlement sites excavated suggest that small huts built largely of perishable materials were typical; but this may be misleading. One settlement at least, at Afiyeh, included large houses of rough-cut stone masonry and occupied at least 1.2 hectares (almost 3 acres). Its location was peripheral, and more centrally located ones may have been considerably larger. In later A-Group times sizable towns of mud-brick, fortified with a town wall, could have existed. In late prehistoric Egypt this was certainly true, yet virtually none have been located and excavated; the same may be true, on a smaller scale, in A-Group Nubia.

Chiefdoms and early states are centralized political systems that can only be generated by socially complex societies. Social complexity means that the relevant population is divided up, in terms of power, status, and wealth, into upper, middle, and lower classes or levels. Specialization is also typical of social complexity; many persons are farmers or herdsmen, but some are more or less full-time administrators, priests, soldiers, and artisans.

At least in their Classic and Terminal phases, the A-Group people display considerable social complexity, implying that their political systems were centralized to a substantial degree. Settlements nearly always provide the best and least ambiguous evidence for social complexity, but for the A-Group we must use the less representative yet nevertheless compelling evidence of the cemeteries. In some cultures, it is true, the social complexity of the living society is *not* represented by their burial archaeology and customs; but in the A-Group cemeteries considerable social and economic differentiation is evident.

Several features of cemetery archaeology are useful in analyzing social complexity. Graves with large pits or superstructures required a greater investment of labor, time, and resources, and their owners were therefore of higher status and probably greater wealth than those of smaller, more modest graves. Moreover, burials of elite and middle-class people may have more and richer grave goods than those of lesser folk, and may also display unusual burial customs.

All these kinds of evidence are relevant to the A-Group, as we can see in two especially well-excavated and recorded cemeteries that are typical of the later A-Group as a whole. Labeled Cemeteries 277 and 401 by their Scandinavian excavators, they lay in southernmost Lower Nubia. About 17 kilometers apart, the two cemeteries were at either end of a self-contained floodplain and were probably generated by a single community, first in Classic and early Terminal times (277) and then in the developed Terminal period (401).

In both cemeteries grave size is a good indication of status and wealth; 277 was largely unplundered, so its grave goods also provide an unusually reliable index to social complexity. However, although the two cemeteries combined were used for 150 or 200 years, they are both small (66 graves in 277, 33 in 401),[2] indicating, as noted earlier, that they represent only elite people and selected middle- and lower-order individuals. Most people were disposed of in other ways (e.g., in a floodplain cemetery).

In both 277 (Fig. 2.2) and 401, the differences in grave size and wealth of grave goods are subtle and relatively small in scale, but they are distinct and consistent, and best interpreted not as random variations but as the result of social complexity.

Originally, in Classic A-Group times, 277 consisted of two adjacent but separate "sub-cemeteries." Both contained elite burials, so perhaps they represent two different "lineages" or clans, each claiming descent from a prestigious ancestor and enjoying special rights to land, wealth, and status as a result. The southern sub-cemetery, on higher, more "eminent" ground and having the largest elite graves, may have represented the more prestigious or powerful lineage.

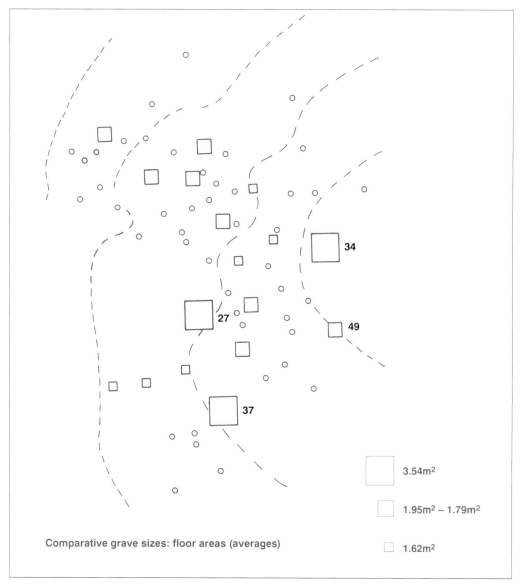

3.54m²

1.95m² – 1.79m²

Comparative grave sizes: floor areas (averages)

1.62m²

*Fig. 2.2*
> *The A-Group Cemetery 277; a schematic representation*
> *illustrating the variability in average tomb size, as defined by the*
> *floor area of each tomb. Tombs with floor areas less than 1.62m²*
> *are shown as circles. Drawing by Nicole deLisle Warshaw.*

As to social complexity in general, and using the floor size of the grave pits as an index to socioeconomic variability, two of the Classic A-Group graves were exceptionally large, on average 3.54 square meters. A few others were still comparatively large, but distinctly smaller than the largest; their floor sizes averaged 1.79 to 1.95 square meters. A third, even smaller "grade" of tomb had floor areas of 1.61 square meters on average; and the majority of the graves had even smaller, if variable floor areas. These patterns of variation continue into the later phases of 277, and into the latest cemetery, 401 (developed Terminal). Overall, they indicate that throughout its history this particular A-Group community was divided into at least four socioeconomic levels, quite a high number for an early society.

It is clear from Cemetery 277 that elite members of the community enjoyed special economic advantages and monopolized objects reflective of wealth. One of the two largest graves, 277:34, contained a necklace of forty-six gold beads, and gold was found (as a small object) in only one other grave of this largely unplundered cemetery. The other large grave, 277:37, contained two copper awls, Egyptian imports that were rare in the cemetery. In general, access to valued Egyptian imports, such as copper objects and the liquids and solids imported in Egyptian jars, seems to have been tightly controlled by the elite. Only 20 percent of the graves in 277 contained Egyptian pottery, and only 10 percent imported copper objects. Usually, the graves in question were the larger ones (of an average floor area of 1.43 square meters or greater), reflecting a close link between relatively high status and access to imports. A few smaller graves had valuable objects like metal axes and adzes; these graves were perhaps for servants assigned the material by a wealthier person whom they would continue to serve in the afterlife.

Although social complexity is associated with centralized political leadership, it can also be reflected by other factors, as Cemetery 277 demonstrates. The three largest and hence most "important" tombs (277: 27, 34, 37) contained only female burials, except for one secondary male burial. These women are not likely to have been political leaders, yet clearly they had higher status than any leaders that might have existed. Some of the children were also clearly of elite status, and were buried in graves like 277:7 (1.49 square meters floor area), much too large for the child's physical size. Incidentally, some children here and elsewhere in the A-Group were buried with an ostrich egg, rarely found with adults. Perhaps the egg represented an abundant food source suitable for a child, or even symbolized the child would mature, or "emerge from the egg," in the afterlife.

However, it is possible the political leaders or "chiefs" of the community are recognizable in Cemeteries 277 and 401. Grave 277:49 (of Terminal A-Group date) was the fourth largest in the cemetery, and placed—like the female's grave 277:34—on the highest and hence perhaps most prestigious ground. The first internment in 277:49 was a male, heavily wrapped in hides, and supplied with an ostrich leather fan and perhaps a stringed leather cap. A later burial, in the same grave, was also a hide-wrapped male with a feather fan. Later, in Cemetery 401 the third-largest tomb, 401:49 (floor area, 1.80 square meters), contained a male on a plaited reed mat (a rare item), with a stringed leather cap and ostrich feather fan (Fig. 2.3). Ostrich feather fans occur with other elite burials (including women and children) in the A-Group, but the combination of special features in the three burials discussed here suggests that they might represent three chiefs who had ruled the community in succession.

The social and economic, and perhaps political, ramifications of the A-Group community discussed above are typical of patterns seen throughout many cemeteries of later

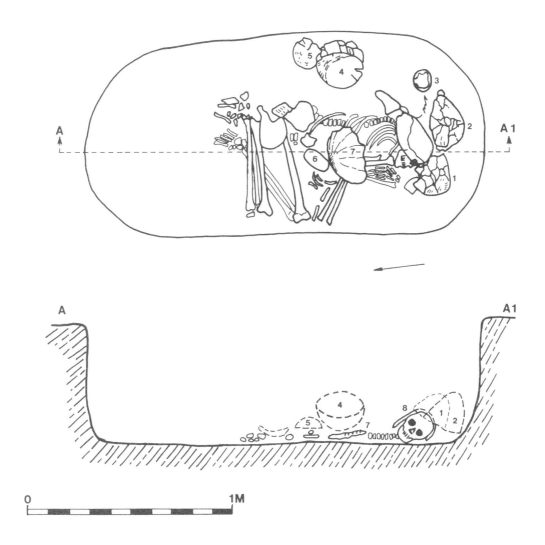

*Fig. 2.3*
> *The burial of a possible ruler or chieftain in the A-Group*
> *Cemetery 401 (Grave 49); note the leather cap on the head of*
> *the burial, and the ostrich feather fan (labeled 7). Drawing*
> *by Nicole deLisle Warshaw.*

A-Group Nubia. Elite and lower-order graves can be distinguished in about 30 percent of known A-Group cemeteries,[3] and the close association between desirable Egyptian imports and elite or higher-status graves is often seen. Even when the proportion of graves with Egyptian imports is higher than in Cemetery 277, this probably means that the cemetery had a higher proportion of elite graves than Cemetery 277. Thus, in Cemetery 298 (excavated by the Scandinavians) about 50 percent of the graves had Egyptian imports, but the cemetery was small and filled mainly with elite graves. In 277, the elite and/or middle-class graves with imports usually had a floor area of 1.43 square meters or more, and in 298, 1.58 square meters or more.

The community represented by Cemeteries 277 and 401 was *not* one of any obvious special importance in the A-Group, and the same holds true for many of the other A-Group cemeteries. We must conclude, then, that a relatively highly developed social complexity was typical of the entire A-Group people in later A-Group times. This in turn implies that some forms of centralized political control also existed then, but, as we have seen, the archaeological evidence directly reflective of chiefs or leaders over A-Group communities is not very sharply defined.

It is therefore not surprising that scholars have suggested that the A-Group people were politically fragmented, with power divided up among "local leaders" answerable to no higher authority. Even then, Adams has suggested: "If any individual or lineage wielded more formal authority than that of the 'institutions of kinship' it was probably authority of the highly restricted (and frequently elective) sort which we are apt to find among Neolithic farmers or herdsmen."[4] Despite these opinions, however, it may be that the later A-Group people were organized into a much more structured entity, a complex chiefdom, a type of polity that is larger in scale, and more elaborate in organization, than a simple chiefdom. In fact, there were A-Group rulers of such pretensions we might reasonably call them kings. The evidence for this idea was found in a cemetery excavated by the Oriental Institute of Chicago in 1962–1964.

## The Royal Capital of Qustul

Labeled L, the cemetery was near the modern village of Qustul. Dating to Terminal A-Group, the cemetery was small, with only twenty-three graves, but their types and especially size showed that they were very unusual in A-Group terms. The dominant type (60 percent of the graves) was a trenchlike open pit, with a subterranean side chamber; this type is very rare elsewhere. The other graves were open pits, but *all* graves were extraordinarily large, as defined by the floor area of each: 30 percent, at 19.30–34.34 square meters, were 1.3 to 2.3 times larger than any other known A-Group grave. All other graves were also notably large: 39 percent had floor areas averaging 15.97 square meters, 10.83 square meters, and 7.82 square meters, and even the smallest were, on the average, about 4.00 square meters.

These data alone indicate that those buried in Cemetery L were of unique status for the Terminal A-Group, and this impression was strongly reinforced by the lavish and rich grave goods. The cemetery had been severely plundered, and the timber roofing of each grave, thrown down or collapsed into the grave pit, had been fired. Nevertheless, many artifacts survived, although often broken and burnt.

Imported Egyptian artifacts had been numerous and of high quality. Copper and gold objects were rare, but probably had been especially attractive to the robbers. Most tombs contained well-made Egyptian stone vessels, in high numbers not recorded elsewhere for the A-Group; 123 were recorded and originally there were more. The amount of Egyptian pottery (at least 271 examples) was extraordinary; and 11 vessels originating from Syria or Palestine are otherwise unknown in the A-Group.

However, this was not an "Egyptianized" cemetery. The grave types were typically A-Group, and there was an abundance of A-Group artifacts, of exceptional quality. There were at least 800 examples of fine "eggshell" pottery painted with elaborate designs, and the cosmetic palettes, typically A-Group in form, were made of rare materials—"amethyst," milky quartz, and rose quartz.

There were also a few most unusual artifacts that prompted Bruce Williams, who published the information about the site, to propose a challenging theory, mentioned at the opening of this chapter. He suggested that Cemetery L was the earliest royal cemetery in pharaonic "Egyptian" style in the Nile Valley. The Nubian pharaohs not only dominated Lower Nubia, Williams argued, but also conquered much of southern Egypt. Soon after the earliest recognizable royal graves of Egypt (dated to Dynasty "0") occur at Abydos; these pharaohs of Abydos and their successors were, Williams suggested, the ideological and cultural heirs, perhaps even the actual descendants of the Nubian pharaohs of Qustul. The final unification of Egypt, and fully developed pharaonic kingship, would then be of Nubian origin.[5]

Williams' theory is exciting but the evidence for it is not convincing. At the time his theory was published, the Qustul "royal" tombs antedated the earliest royal tombs of Egypt, of Nakada phase IIIB. But recently an Abydos royal tomb of IIIA has been found,[6] so Qustul loses chronological primacy.

There are unusual objects in Egyptian style at Qustul, but they are all likely to have been imports from Egypt, not products of Nubia. Two vessels, for example, have painted designs recording, according to Williams, the conquest of southern Egypt (*Ta shemaw*) and of Hierakonpolis, a town of that region; but the worn signs may be misread, and in any case would refer to conquests of Egyptians *by* Egyptians, since the vases are of Egyptian origin.

A stone incense burner is of special importance. It was carved with motifs Egyptian in style and content (including a depiction of a pharaoh in a traditional crown), yet incense burners are typical of Nubia, not Egypt. Surely it, and therefore its pharaonic iconography, are Nubian in origin, Williams argued. But it is more plausible (because of the thoroughly A-Group or Nubian character of the Qustul cemetery) to suggest that the incense burner was made in Egypt, or decorated by Egyptian artisans, as a special gift for the ruler of Qustul of the day (Fig. 2.4).

The real importance of the Qustul cemetery is that the size and richness of the graves indicate rulers (possibly three to eight; Williams suggests ten to twelve) were buried there, together with their high-status kinfolk. Moreover, because no other Terminal A-Group cemetery approached the importance of the Qustul cemetery, its occupants likely controlled all of Lower Nubia, which would have formed a unitary political unit. In geographical and population size, this entity would have been a com-

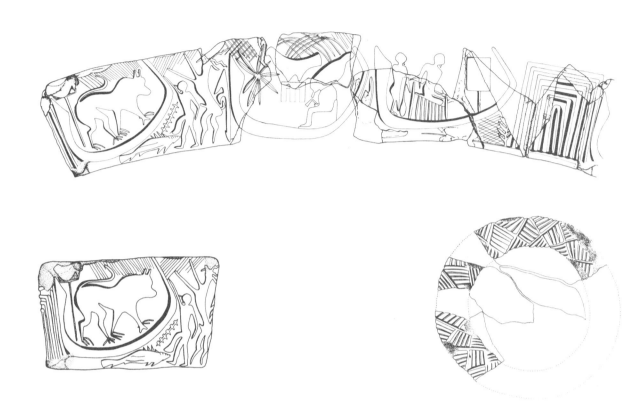

Qustul incense burner, L 24—1. Scale 1:2.

**Fig. 2.4**
*The incense burner from the Terminal A-Group Cemetery L
at Qustul. Above, the decoration of the burner, shown
extended; below left, the incense burner from the side and
right, from above.*

*(From: B. Williams,* The A-Group Royal Cemetery at
Qustul: Cemetery L. *Chicago: The Oriental Institute of
The University of Chicago (1968), Pl. 34. Courtesy of The
Oriental Institute of The University of Chicago.)*

plex chiefdom and not a state, but its rulers were sufficiently high in status to be called "kings."

Already then, early in the Bronze Age, at least one part of Nubia was on its way to statehood, and was a "proto-kingdom" like those found a little earlier in Egypt. Moreover, earlier—in the Classic A-Group—there were also rulers, like the one buried in an elite cemetery labeled 137, with two maces—symbols of kingly power imported from Egypt. Their handles were sheathed in gold and decorated, in one case, with rows of animals.[7] Whether such Classic A-Group chiefs ruled only parts of Lower Nubia or all of it, they indicate that political centralization was becoming a feature of Nubian society prior to the development of the royal cemetery of Qustul.

## *The End of the A-Group*

Early in the Egyptian 1st Dynasty, the A-Group ended and the Nubians were driven from Lower Nubia, not to return for about six centuries. This can only have been due to organized Egyptian aggression, intended to place this trade corridor, and the source of valuable stones and gold (in the flanking deserts), under direct Egyptian control.

The Egyptians not only prevented Nubian resettlement; early in their 4th Dynasty (ca. 2500 B.C.) they founded in Lower Nubia several strategically placed towns, such as Buhen. These improved Egypt's access to Lower Nubian mineral sources and perhaps reflect an increased volume of trade with Upper Nubia. However, some 160 years later Egypt abandoned these towns, and Nubians began to resettle Lower Nubia. A new chapter in Nubian history was beginning.

# The Lion and the Crocodile

*I*n this chapter the story of ancient Nubia becomes more complicated, but also much richer in detail and broader in scope. Until the rise of the Egyptian Old Kingdom, in about 2570 B.C., we necessarily had to focus on Lower Nubia and the A-Group, for little is known about contemporary circumstances elsewhere in Nubia. After 2570 B.C. our field of vision greatly expands: Upper as well as Lower Nubian archaeology is known (although the archaeology of Southern Nubia remains unknown until after 1000 B.C.), and Egyptian texts refer to Nubia more frequently and more explicitly than before.

Because the story is more complex, a brief historical and archaeological introduction to this chapter is necessary. The framework for this is provided in part by Egyptian dynastic chronology, in part by the Nubian archaeological sequence.

The relevant Egyptian historical phases include the Old Kingdom (4th–6th Dynasties; 2575–2134 B.C.) and the First Intermediate Period, a time of internal disunity and then reconsolidation in Egypt (2134–2040 B.C.). More broadly, these phases represent the Early Bronze Age. The Middle Bronze Age is made up of the Middle Kingdom (12th and 13th Dynasties; 1991–1600(?) B.C.) and the Second Intermediate Period (the largely contemporaneous 15th and 17th Dynasties; 1640–1532 B.C.). The obscure 14th and 16th Dynasties are not relevant to our discussion.

The archaeological sequence in Early and Middle Bronze Age Nubia is fairly well established, except for its earliest phases: my treatment of the latter, therefore, is largely hypothetical, and future discoveries may lead to its revision.

Upper Nubia was certainly a settled region during the 3rd to 5th Egyptian Dynasties (as it was earlier), but its material culture, labeled "Pre-Kerma," is as yet poorly defined. As for Lower Nubia, its A-Group people were expelled in about 2900 B.C. Some continued to live in the Second Cataract area (and here a transition from A-Group into a later culture, the C-Group, can be traced). Others settled in northern Upper Nubia, where their culture—now labeled C-Group—co-existed with a Kerma Group culture that had evolved from the Pre-Kerma phase. A so-called B-Group culture, placed between A and C, has been shown to be invalid.

Eventually, the bearers of the C-Group culture began to resettle Lower Nubia, late in the 5th Egyptian Dynasty (ca. 2400 B.C.); C-Group culture remained typical of that region until about 1650 B.C., and is divided into five developmental phases (IA and B, IIA and B, III). Eventually, the Lower Nubians became "Egyptianized" in material culture. In Upper Nubia the C-Group element remains visible for a while, but fades away by about 2000 B.C. The Kerma Group culture is the dominant one, apparently for all Upper Nubia. It too is divided into developmental phases (Early, Middle, Classic, and Recent) and persisted to at least 1550 B.C., and perhaps later.

Archaeological evidence in Nubia and Egyptian texts show that over the period 2900–1550 B.C. relationships between Nubia and Egypt were continuously changing. The story of this long period is often presented as that of the gradual, long-drawn-out conquest of Nubia by Egypt. In reality, it is one of alternating success and failure on the part of both lands, as they competed for control of a key segment of the Lower Nile.

During the 2nd to 5th Dynasties Egypt dominated Lower Nubia (empty of indigenes) and periodically raided Upper Nubia. More typically, it and Egypt were trading partners. Egypt remained active in Nubia in the 6th Dynasty but, as Lower Nubia was resettled by Nubians, Egyptian dominance eroded. Through the First Intermediate Period a disunited Egypt was militarily inactive in Nubia, although trading and other links continued. Once reunited, Egypt conquered (with some difficulty) Lower Nubia, and held it from about 2000 to 1700 B.C. Upper Nubia, however, remained independent and increasingly powerful, and soon after 1700 B.C. replaced Egypt as overlord of Lower Nubia.

Egypt soon after became divided between an intrusive Canaanite Dynasty (the 15th, or "Hyksos") in the north, and an increasingly independent Egyptian or Theban Dynasty (the 17th) in the south. At about the time the Thebans defeated and expelled the Hyksos (ca. 1550–1540 B.C.), Egypt regained Lower Nubia and then, after a long period of repeated campaigning, conquered Upper Nubia for the first time. This "colonial" period in Nubia lasted until about 1070 B.C., but in the long term was but one phase in its chequered history. In a spectacular reversal, Nubia by 712 B.C. would be in control of all Egypt, which thus became a dependency of the Nubian state.

These last events however take us far beyond the Early and Middle Bronze Ages, which are the focus for this chapter. It is during these periods that desert Nubians also became important in the historical record. They were eastern desert folk, included under the Nehasyu, or Nubians, but specifically called the Medjayu. These warlike nomads were interacting with the equally aggressive riverine Nubians and with the Egyptians, by the 6th Dynasty and probably earlier.

The Egyptians clearly respected the warlike capacities of both riverine and desert Nubians. For example, Amenemhet I, first pharaoh of the 12th Dynasty, initiated the conquest of Lower Nubia soon after 2000 B.C. In a literary text, he is made to say: "I subdued lions, I captured crocodiles, I suppressed the people of Wawat (i.e. Nehasyu), I captured the Medjayu."[1] Here, the riverine Nubians, or Nehasyu, are identified with the powerful, menacing crocodile and the Medjayu with the threatening lion.

However, these Nubian warriors of river and desert were not simply aimless hordes, reacting to Egyptian aggression. Rather, they represented the "organized violence" of the complex chiefdoms and even states that in the Early and Middle Bronze Ages were rapidly developing in Nubia and its desert hinterlands.

This conclusion goes against most scholars' current opinions, which hold that from about 2600 to 1700 B.C. the Nubians were divided up into a large number of simple chiefdoms, with the partial exception of Upper Nubia in the Middle Bronze Age. Simple chiefdoms by definition are small in territory and population, and hence vulnerable to the aggression of a large-scale state like Egypt. Moreover, some argue, the Lower Nubians (but not the

Upper) were peaceful and submissive to the Egyptian advance.

However, there is evidence suggesting an alternative model of interpretation. In this, the rise of complex (i.e., large-scale and powerful) chiefdoms—and even their transformation into states—begins much earlier in Nubia than is generally thought. Moreover, this process may have included the combining of Upper and Lower Nubia, at least for a period, before the Egyptian conquest of the latter after 2000 B.C. In this alternative model, the Lower Nubians are not submissive, but rather a militarily aggressive people the Egyptians found difficult to control and dominate.

Which of the two models is correct cannot yet be conclusively proved; but the very different implications of each are most significant for the interpretation of Nubian history.

## Mysteries of the Early Bronze Age

These chiefdoms, and perhaps states, have a mysterious prelude, for throughout the 2nd to 5th Dynasties Upper Nubia remains fascinatingly obscure. Its secrets wait to be revealed by future archaeological discoveries.

Lower Nubia, as we saw, was empty of indigenes at this time. A few of its graves are dated between the 2nd and 5th Dynasties, but their relative wealth makes this dating unlikely, since no other contemporary Lower Nubian graves have been identified. Buhen was one of the Egyptian-founded towns referred to earlier; its inhabitants were mainly Egyptian, and its abundant broken pottery therefore Egyptian in

**Plate 1** Two painted eggshell ware bowls. These bowls were usually made in a very thin ("eggshell") ware of little functional value, and presumably were indicative of the prestige of their owners.

*Deep Eggshell Ware Bowl, Terminal A-Group, ca. 3000–2900 B.C., Nag Wadi, Cemetery 142, Tomb 9, Archaeological Survey of Nubia, 1910–1911, 92-2-5, H: 16.4; D: 19.8 cm, Ceramic*

*Conical Eggshell Ware Bowl, Terminal A-Group, ca. 3000–2900 B.C., Nag Wadi, Cemetery 142, Archaeological Survey of Nubia, 1910–1911, 92-2-2, H: 18.6; D: 16.7 cm, Ceramic*

**Plate 2** Two stone palettes, normally intended to be used for grinding minerals into powdered cosmetics for the face and eyes. 92-2-8 (right) is of standard form and material (white quartz), but 92-2-9 (left) is much more unusual in shape and composition (speckled porphyry).

*Grinder, A-Group, ca. 3400–3000 B.C., Sayala, Cemetery 137, Tomb 1, Archaeological Survey of Nubia, 1910–1911, 92-2-9, W: 7.5; L: 15.0; T: 2.8 cm, Speckled porphyry*

*Rhomboid Palette, A-Group, ca. 3400–3000 B.C., Nag Wadi, Cemetery 142, Tomb 1, Archaeological Survey of Nubia, 1910–1911, 92-2-8, W: 7.3; L: 14.8; T: 0.6 cm, White quartz*

**Plate 3** Three C-Group vessels. The pottery of C-Group Lower Nubia was distinctive in fabric, form, and decoration. 92-2-17 (left) is typical of a large class of roughware incised jars. 92-2-14 (center) is a red-ware, black-topped bowl with incised exterior, characteristic of phase IB. It is weathered, because pottery was often placed outside the tomb superstructure, and hence exposed to the elements. 92-2-12 (right) represents another kind of fabric, a burnished, gray soft ware often embellished with complex incised and impressed designs, sometimes picked out in colors.

*Roughware Jar with Incised Decoration, C-Group, phase IIA/B, ca. 2000–1600 B.C., Dakkeh, Cemetery 101, Tomb 360, Archaeological Survey of Nubia, 1909–1910, 92-2-17, H: 17.5; D: 16.0 cm, Ceramic*

*Incised Black-topped Bowl, C-Group, phase IIA, ca. 2000–1800 B.C., Dakkeh, Cemetery 101, Tomb 451, Archaeological Survey of Nubia, 1909–1910, 92-2-14, H: 6.0; D: 13.1 cm, Ceramic*

*Polished Incised Bowl, C-Group, phase IIA, ca. 1900–1700 B.C., Dakkeh, Cemetery 101, Tomb 51, Archaeological Survey of Nubia, 1909–1910, 92-2-12, H: 8.5; D: 11.0 cm, Ceramic*

**Plate 4** Fine red-polished, black-topped bowl (reconstructed, and partially restored). Its rim decoration is typical of the Early Kerma phase in Upper or Central Nubia.

*Black-topped Bowl with Incised Rim, Early Kerma, ca. 2300–2000 B.C., Kerma, Cemetery N, Tomb 173, Boston Museum of Fine Arts Expedition, 1915–1916, 92-2-21, H: 19.0; D: 32.2 cm, Ceramic*

**Plate 5** Two beakers, probably drinking vessels. Thin-walled, flaring beakers, red-polished and black-topped, and often highly burnished, are typical of the Classic Kerma phase. The gray and purple line below the black top was an intentional decorative effect. Both come from Tumulus K IV, at Kerma, which belonged to one of the Nubian kings known to Egypt as "rulers of Kush;" Grave 425, cut into the tumulus, was probably for one of the king's courtiers or retainers.

*Black-topped Red-polished Beaker, Classic Kerma, ca. 1650–1550 B.C., Kerma, Cemetery S, Tumulus KIV, Grave 425, Boston Museum of Fine Arts Expedition, 1912–1913, 92-2-44, H: 12.1; D: 14.4 cm, Ceramic*

*Black-topped Red-polished Beaker, Classic Kerma, ca. 1650–1550 B.C., Kerma, Cemetery S, Tumulus KIV, Grave 425, Boston Museum of Fine Arts Expedition, 1912–1913, 92-2-35, H: 12.3; D: 14.2 cm, Ceramic*

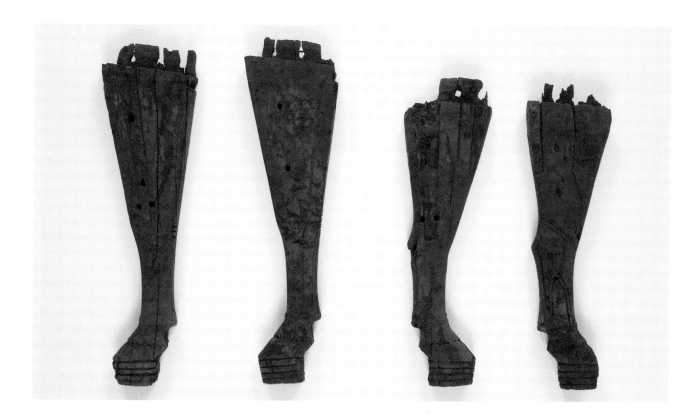

**Plate 6** Four wooden legs—representing the legs of a quadruped—belonging to an otherwise decayed bed. Elite members of Classic Kerma society were often buried lying on beds like this.

*Bed Legs, Classic Kerma, ca. 1650–1550 B.C., Kerma, Cemetery S, Tumulus KIV, Grave 425, Boston Museum of Fine Arts Expedition 1912–1913, 92-2-48 A, W: 11.1; L: 36.7; T: 4.1 cm, 92-2-48 B, W: 10.4; L: 36.4; T: 3.4 cm, 92-2-48 C, W: 12.4; L: 41.4; T: 3.5 cm, 92-2-48 D, W: 12.3; L: 40.8; T: 3.8 cm, Wood*

**Plate 7** Fly emblem, Classic Kerma Period. Kerma society included many warriors; the grave of one such was excavated by Randall-MacIver and Woolley, for The University Museum of the University of Pennsylvania, at Buhen in Lower Nubia. Dating to Classic Kerma, the burial goods included two ivory flies, with electrum (silver rich gold) heads, of which this is one. Such flies were emblems of military valor along the Nile, for Nilotic flies were tough and tenacious, just as soldiers were expected to be!

*Decorative Fly, Second Intermediate Period/Classic Kerma, ca. 1650–1550 B.C., Buhen, Tomb J33, Coxe Expedition 1909, E 10347 A, W: 6.0; L: 11.5; T: 1.6 cm, Ivory, bronze, and electrum*

**Plate 8** Classic Kerma sword. This type of short sword was carried by many Kerman warriors. The blade was bronze, and the handle or pommel ivory; the grip, joining blade to pommel, had decayed, but the bronze pins that had once held it in place survived. These swords were based on an Egyptian prototype but were probably made in Nubia.

*Sword, Second Intermediate Period/Classic Kerma, ca. 1650–1550 B.C., Buhen, Tomb J33, Coxe Expedition 1909, E 10341, Blade: W: 3.4; L: 31.2; Handle: L 14.1, W: 6.8; Studs: D: 1.3, H: 1.8 cm, Bronze with riveted ivory handle*

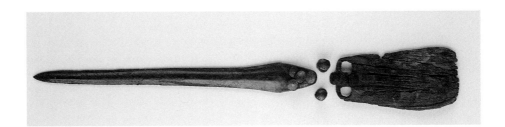

**Plate 9**  Shawabti, or funerary figurine, of pharaoh Taharka (690–664 B.C.) from his tomb at Nuri in Upper Nubia. It is made of syenite, a hard, resistant stone. Shawabtis, intended magically to relieve the deceased of laborious tasks they had to perform for the gods of the afterlife, were long established in Egypt; and their use here reflects the strong Egyptianization manifested by much of Napatan culture. Taharka was a member of the 25th Dynasty (780–656 B.C.), Nubian pharaohs who for a time combined Egypt and Nubia into a single, enormous state. In this case, the figurine seems to be a true portrait of this pharaoh, and has a distinctively Nubian cast to its features.

*Shawabti of King Taharka, Napatan Period, 690–664 B.C., Nuri, Pyramid 1, Harvard University–Boston Museum of Fine Arts Egyptian Expedition, 92-2-67, H: 32.7; W: 10.2; T: 7.3 cm, Syenite*

**Plate 10**  Shawabti of King Anlemani (623–593 B.C.) from his tomb at Nuri. He was one of the later Napatan rulers, reigning after Nubian control of Egypt had ceased. Well made of greenish blue faience (an artificial compound taken over from Egypt), it bears a spell intended to ensure that the shawabti replaces the dead pharaoh whenever labor has to be carried out in the afterlife.

*Shawabti of King Anlemani, Napatan Period, 623–593 B.C., Nuri, Pyramid 6, Harvard University-Boston Museum of Fine Arts Egyptian Expedition, 92-2-70, H: 26.0; W: 8.6; T: 5.7 cm, Faience*

**Plate 11** Alabaster canopic jar lid. This lid once sealed the canopic jar of a Napatan queen. Canopic jars contained the mummified internal organs of the deceased, and represent a custom of Egyptian origin. The finely carved features may reflect the queen's actual appearance.

*Canopic Jar Lid of Queen Alakhebasken, Napatan Period, 690–664 B.C., Nuri, Pyramid 35, Harvard University-Boston Museum of Fine Arts Egyptian Expedition, 92-2-92-2, H: 13.2; D: 10.5 cm, Alabaster*

**Plate 12** Green faience amulet . Its owner was perhaps a queen of the pharaoh Piye (747–716 B.C.) who had established the basis for the Nubian control of Egypt exercised throughout the 25th Dynasty (780–656 B.C.). The amulet represents the sun-god in the form of a scarab beetle (emblematic of the rising or resurrected sun, and hence a magically powerful object for the deceased, who sought to be reborn like the sun). The two rosettes represent both the dung ball, in which the beetle laid its eggs, and the sun-disc itself. Above the beetle, set in a cornice-like feature, is the winged sun-disc (protected by cobra or uraei), the form taken by the sun-god as he traversed the sky.

*Amulet, Napatan Period, 800–700 B.C., Kurru, grave 51, Harvard University–Boston Museum of Fine Arts Egyptian Expedition, 92-2-97, W: 6.0; L: 9.1; T: 0.8 cm, Faience*

**Plate 13** Sandstone statue, partially restored, probably representing the owner of grave 182, Karanog. Grave 182 had one of the largest pyramids in the cemetery and was for an important personage. The heavy jewelry and flounced robes of the statue show that it represents a peshto, or governor, of Lower Nubia during Meroitic times. The figure itself is a so-called ba-statue, the ba being the mobile aspect of the personality of a deceased individual. The dead man is supplied with wings, probably so that he can fly upward to join the sun-god; the disc on his head represents the solar orb.

*Funerary Statue, Meroitic Period, 100 B.C.–A.D. 300, Karanog, grave 182, Coxe Expedition 1908, E 7005, H: 76.4; W: 53; L: 54 cm, Sandstone*

**Plate 14** Sandstone statue of a lady from the cemetery of Karanog. Her exact tomb is unknown, but she was a member of the elite, to judge from the high quality of her statue. All the ba-statues of Karanog—which stood out in the open, perhaps in a niche in the face of the pyramid crowning each tomb—were originally brightly painted although exposure often caused the loss of such paint. On this statue, traces of the bright red flesh color, and the white of the linen or cotton kilt, survive. A solar disc (now lost) once sat in a metal fitting inserted into the top of the statue's head.

*Funerary Statue, Meroitic Period, 100 B.C.–A.D. 300, Karanog, Coxe Expedition 1908, E 7003, H: 59.0; W: 14.5; L: 35.5 cm, Sandstone*

**Plate 15** Sandstone head. Many of the sandstone statues in the Karanog cemetery had been broken, and the pieces scattered by plunderers and vandals. This head of a ba-statue is carved in a more abstract style than some other, more realistic ones; unusually, the sun disc above its head had been preserved.

*Head of a Funerary Statue, Meroitic Period, 100 B.C.–A.D. 300, Karanog, Coxe Expedition 1908, E 7037, H: 26.5; D: 14.5; T: 12.5 cm, Sandstone*

**Plate 16** Wood and ivory box. Wooden objects were common in Meroitic graves at Karanog, and often included boxes containing toiletry implements, jewelry and other objects. The exteriors of such boxes were embellished with ivory or bone inlay. This box has been heavily restored; most of the wood is modern, but nearly all the inlays are original. Found in a woman's grave (Grave 712), the box illustrates the cosmopolitan nature of Meroitic artistic influences. The partially draped female figures are derived from Roman art, the sphinxes are of ancient Egyptian derivation, and the lion-like faces may evoke Apedemak, a lion-god of Meroitic origin.

*Box, Meroitic Period, 100 B.C.–A.D. 300, Karanog, grave 45, Coxe Expedition 1908, E 7519, H: 28.1; W: 26.9; T: 23.1 cm, Wood, ivory*

type. There were an appreciable number of Nubian sherds also, but these were not generated by contemporary Lower Nubians. Most came from earlier Classic A-Group activity at the site; a few may be from vessels made by Nubians contemporary with the earlier Old Kingdom but living in the Second Cataract zone, not Lower Nubia itself.

Egyptian sources indicate that Upper Nubia, in contrast, had a substantial population. Pharaoh Khasekhem(wy) of the 2nd Dynasty apparently campaigned in Upper Nubia, and Snefru, of the early 4th, certainly did. He brought back 7000 prisoners as well as 200,000 domesticated animals. Later, Sahure (ca. 2458–2446 B.C.) also raided Upper Nubia, depicting captives from there in his funerary temple causeway. His immediate successors had these scenes copied in their temples, but may not themselves have been active in Nubia.

The Egyptians' campaigns were probably not to secure labor for grandiose royal building projects like the pyramids; there was plenty of Egyptian labor available. Rather, they sought booty, and prisoners they could use for specialized purposes. The Nubian prisoners of Snefru and Sahure, for example, may have farmed the lands or herded the animals dedicated to the royal funerary cults and located near the relevant pyramid complexes.

Egyptian relations with Upper Nubia in fact were probably more peaceful than hostile, for Nubia controlled the flow of desirable southern products north to Egypt. A glimpse of the complexity of relations between Nubia and Egypt at this time is provided by a strange grave found at Shellal, just south of Elephantine on the Egyptian-Nubian frontier.

At Shellal George Reisner excavated many A-Group graves, labeled Cemetery 7 and none later than early 1st Dynasty. However, one peripherally located grave dated after the A-Group, to the 3rd or early 4th Dynasty. The burial was clearly that of a Nubian. The grave was small, but its male occupant wealthy and of high status, wearing an elaborate gold necklace and holding two valuable copper objects. On the upper part of each arm was a large V-shaped armlet in ivory, of a type never found in Lower Nubia, but worn by some elite or upper-class Upper Nubians in the Sahure reliefs mentioned above (Fig. 3.1).

As the man was not a prisoner (his gold necklace and other goods make this unlikely), he seems to have been an elite Upper Nubian who died unexpectedly when visiting Egypt, perhaps for trading purposes. Some elite Upper Nubians may have settled permanently in Egypt, for even earlier, in Early Dynastic times, an Upper Nubian—depicted on his grave stone as wearing a V-shaped armlet—was buried in Egyptian style at Helwan, near Memphis.[2]

## The C-Group and Kerma-Group Peoples

Fortunately, the archaeology of C-Group Lower Nubia and Kerma-Group Upper Nubia, after the 5th Dynasty, is relatively well known. Compared with each other, the two cultures share some broad similarities, but for the most part are very different. As in the A-Group, settlements in both regions have rarely been excavated, but the differences are clear in artifact types and mortuary archaeology.

**Fig. 3.1**
*Above, the burial of an Early Bronze Age elite Upper Nubian in
Cemetery 7, Shellal. Below, the ivory armlets; right, an Upper
Nubian ruler (?) depicted on the causeway of the pyramid of
pharaoh Sahure (2458–2446 B.C.)—note the armlet on his left
arm, similar in appearance to the armlets from the tomb at Shellal.*
    *(Right from: L. Borchardt,* Das Grabdenkmal des Königs
S′aȝhu-reᶜ, *Band II:* Die Wandbilder. *Leipzig: J.C. Hinrichs
Buchhandlung (1913), Bl. 5.)*

The most abundant product is pottery. Both the C- and Kerma-Group peoples liked red-polished fabrics, often with blackened mouths or tops, but the repertory of shapes favored by each culture is different. Surface treatment also differed, and the Kerma-Group black-topped ceramic is especially characterized by a distinctive series of out-flaring beakers, mostly of the Classic phase. Other fine-ware bowls, in gray or red fabrics, and with incised and impressed decoration, occur in both groups. However, C-Group designs are complex and cover most of the bowl's outer surface; Kerma-Group designs are simpler, and often restricted to a band around the upper body.

Coarse brown and red wares are common in both groups, but again differ in detail. In the C-Group, the pottery is unburnished, usually in jar form and with loosely organized designs on the upper part of the body. Only in phase IIB do designs become more complex and spread over more of the jar's surface. In the Kerma-Group, especially in its Middle phase, coarse ware vessels are usually bowls, polished and with bold, coarse, and simple incised designs; and jars, with a band of more neatly designed incisions around the shoulder.

Egyptian pottery, and other Egyptian artifacts, occur in both cultures. They reflect trading and other links with Egypt, and help date the Nubian cultural phases in terms of Egyptian chronology. In C-Group IA and B Egyptian pottery and stamp or scarab seals of the late Old Kingdom and First Intermediate Period occur. Egyptian items are thereafter relatively rare, but increase in number in phase III, which can thus be dated to the 15th

Dynasty. Egyptian pottery is rare in Early Kerma, but much occurs in Middle Kerma, which can thus be equated with the 12th and much of the 13th Dynasties. Other pottery, as well as many Egyptian scarab seals, show Classic Kerma was largely coeval with the 15th Dynasty.

Pottery provides one clear set of distinctions between C-Group and Kerma-Group, funerary architecture another (Fig. 3.2). A C-Group tomb, before phase III, consisted usually of a relatively small burial pit, meant for only one body; and a circular superstructure of dry built, rough-cut masonry. Superstructures could be solid stone masonry, or be filled with gravel and sand. Often they are quite small, about 2 meters in diameter, but grow larger over time, to 4 meters or more. The largest are 16 meters in diameter, and about 2 meters high.

Kerma-Group burial pits were also small at first, but expanded in size in Middle and Classic Kerma times, when the main burial (often laid on a bed) was accompanied by several human and animal sacrifices. Later in Classic times pits tended to become small again. Many Kerma-Group tombs had circular superstructures, but not of stone masonry; rather, a relatively low sand-and-gravel mound, reinforced by rings of small stone slabs or heavy pebbles, was typical. The earliest mounds are small (about 1.20 meters in diameter), but elite ones become quite large (8 meters in diameter) before the end of Early Kerma. The Classic Kerma royal tumuli achieve a stupendous diameter of 90 meters.

Our knowledge of the technology and economy of both C-Group and Kerma-Group peoples is impressionistic, for settlement sites have rarely been excavated. Archaeological

**Fig. 3.2**
*Earth and gravel tumulus, reinforced with stone slabs, of
the Early Kerma culture (center left). Also, examples of built
stone masonry tomb superstructures of the C-Group.*

evidence and the social system indicate that for both cereal agriculture, based on flood (and, in Upper Nubia, basin) irrigation, was the subsistence base, and also produced an elite-supporting surplus. Domesticated animals were also economically important: leather items are abundant, while sacrificial animals' heads are placed outside tomb superstructures. In Kerma-

Group contexts, entire animal carcasses often occur as funerary gifts.

The militaristic aspects of both C-Group and Kerma-Group society should be stressed. For the latter, archaeological evidence is directly relevant: archer burials are not uncommon in Early Kerma, a bronze dagger was a standard burial item in Middle Kerma, and Classic Kerma graves are famous for the short bronze swords found with principal and other burials. C-Group graves are less overtly militaristic in archaeology, either for cultural and historical reasons (e.g., the long period during which the C-Group was dominated by Egyptian occupying forces and perhaps forbidden sophisticated weaponry) or because the valuable metal weapons had been plundered.

Other evidence, however, attests to the formidable military capacities of C-Group and Kerma-Group people. For example, in the Old Kingdom and later both Lower and Upper Nubians were impressed or recruited into the Egyptian army and were obviously considered good warriors. When the Egyptians invaded C-Group Lower Nubia soon after 2000 B.C., and built a series of great fortresses to dominate its population centers, they still had to continue subduing the Lower Nubians, "slaughtering the Nubian on his river bank" and plundering or destroying their crops, trees and settlements,[3] suggesting that the Lower Nubians continued to resist. Similarly, in both the early and the mid-12th Dynasty the Egyptians campaigned vigorously in Kerma-Group Upper Nubia but evidently encountered strong resistance.

Most striking of all, the Middle Kingdom Egyptians constructed impressively sophisticated fortresses both to control the C-Group population and to defend the southern frontier of Lower Nubia from attack by Kerma-Group forces. The implications are clear; both Nubian peoples knew how to attack large fortresses by mining, scaling, and frontal assault techniques probably learned from many generations of service in Egyptian armies! The Nubians also fortified their own centers, such as

Kerma in Upper Nubia, which had a heavily fortified town wall.

A final, compelling image conveys well the Egyptians' sense of the Nubians' military strengths. Pharaoh Senwosret III of the 12th Dynasty heavily fortified the frontier with Upper Nubia and set up a stela on which the Upper Nubians are called "cowards and craven hearted," but also seen as capable of overwhelming the Egyptians. To encourage his successors Senwosret also set up a statue of himself "at this border which my majesty has made so that you maintain it and so that you fight for it!"[4]

Thus, at the height of Middle Kingdom Egyptian power, a royal statue on the frontier glowers upriver against the threatening Upper Nubians, while behind it a chain of fortresses stretches all the way back to Elephantine, to ensure control of the evidently also threatening Lower Nubians. However, military prowess was but one aspect of Nubian strength; even more important was their capacity for large-scale political organization.

## *The Earliest Nubian State?*

The earliest known example of what might have been a large-scale political system, in fact a Nubian state, is controversial. In the later Early Bronze Age, corresponding to the 6th Egyptian Dynasty and much of the First Intermediate Period, Nubians are usually thought of by scholars as divided up into small and simply stratified chiefdoms, vulnerable to Egyptian pressure and intimidation. At best, a tendency toward the formation of larger but unstable complex chiefdoms is recognized. However, I have suggested that during this period the Nubian political system became large enough in scale and sufficiently complex to be identified as a state, the earliest known for Nubia.

Our chief evidence for the political map of Early Bronze Age Nubia is the description of the travels of an Egyptian official, Harkhuf, inscribed in his tomb at Elephantine. He and other officials of the 6th Dynasty pharaohs led both trading and military campaigns in different parts of Nubia, regions that they identify by name in inscriptions and graffiti describing these activities. Each Nubian region was organized politically into at least a chiefdom of some sort, because each is identified as governed by a *heka,* or ruler. However, the location of each of these polities is uncertain, and hence so are their sizes and degree of structural complexity.

Harkhuf's expeditions focus on trade with the land of Yam, where he obtained typical southern products such as ivory and ebony. Occasionally more exotic acquisitions hint at a Nubian trading network that was more widespread than we might expect. Once, Harkhuf secured from Yam a pygmy, a correctly proportioned but diminutive person.[5] Harkhuf's pharaoh, a child at the time, wrote him excitedly to post a twenty-four hour guard around the pygmy until he safely reached the royal court at Memphis! Because pygmies today are found only far south of Nubia, in Equatorial Africa, this incident suggests that the Nubians' trading links extended very far indeed, although some were indirect rather than direct.

Like other royal officials, Harkhuf traversed the Nubian lands of Wawat, Irtjet, and Setju in his travels. Because most scholars believe that Harkhuf's donkey caravans (the means by which he traveled) began their land journey at Memphis, the stated time-lengths of his expeditions would require Wawat, Irtjet, and Setju all to be placed in Lower Nubia, and Yam in Upper Nubia. However, I believe Harkhuf's land journeys typically began at Elephantine, far south of Memphis. This permits Yam to be placed south of Upper Nubia; Wawat to be identified as *all* Lower Nubia (as it always was in later times); and Irtjet and Setju to be located in Upper Nubia.

These two different theories about early Nubian geography generate two very different political maps. In the first, Lower Nubia is divided into three polities, each so small in scale it can only have been a simple chiefdom. Harkhuf informs us that Irtjet and Setju, and finally Wawat, all combined together under a single ruler; according to the first theory discussed above, this polity would cover only Lower Nubia, and in scale approximate to a complex chiefdom.

However, the theory I suggest—with Wawat equivalent to all Lower Nubia—would indicate that the polities of Wawat and probably Irtjet and Setju were from the outset large enough in scale to be complex chiefdoms. When they were united, the resulting political system would combine Lower and much of Upper Nubia; this polity would cover so much territory and include so many people (170,000–200,000 at a guess) it could only be identified as a state, albeit a small one as compared to contemporary Egypt. Nevertheless, a Nubian state would be a much more formidable competitor of Egypt than the chiefdoms postulated in the first theory discussed above.

The size and hence status of Yam is quite uncertain. However, its evident power suggests that it was at least a complex chiefdom, or possibly also a state.

How long the complex chiefdom or state combining Wawat, Irtjet, and Setju survived is hard to say. Soon after Harkhuf's time another Egyptian official stated that he attacked the polity of Wawat and Irtjet (with no mention of Setju) and as a result it again split into two separate polities. However, Egypt's power was rapidly waning, and it left Nubia alone through the First Intermediate Period. It is possible, therefore, that the combined polity of Wawat, Irtjet, and Setju, despite occasional setbacks, continued until the Egyptian conquest of Lower Nubia at the beginning of the 12th Dynasty.

There is archaeological evidence on the political organization of Early Bronze Age Nubia, but unfortunately it could fit either of the two theories outlined above. Two issues are involved. First, can we identify archaeologically the presence of rulers in Lower and Upper Nubia; and second, are they rulers of simple chiefdoms, complex chiefdoms, or states?

The known archaeology reveals several Nubian "central places," where unusually large concentrations of population indicate that a political center existed in the Early Bronze Age. In Lower Nubia, these are Dakkeh, Aniba, and perhaps Faras; in northern Upper Nubia, Kerma and the island of Sai. More southerly Upper Nubia is archaeologically unknown for this period.

Settlement archaeology, the best indicator of political central places and their organization, is largely unavailable to us, although the Early Kerma town at Kerma itself

has been partially delineated. However, in the cemetery archaeology of both C-Group Lower Nubia and Kerma-Group Upper Nubia rulers' tombs are probably detectable.

Egyptian sources indicate that rulers existed in Lower Nubia, as we have seen, but scholars have found it difficult to identify rulers' tombs in any of the relevant cemeteries of C-Group Phases IA and B. However, if we postulate that rulers' and elite tombs at this time displayed only subtle and small-scale differences from those of lower-order tombs, the picture becomes clearer.

For example, the great C-Group Cemetery N at Aniba (over 1000 graves) has a central core of Phase IA and B tombs (Fig. 3.3). All were severely plundered, so little artifactual evidence for rulers' or elite tombs survives, and the grave pits are uniform in size, without variations suggestive of differences in status. However, the circular, stone-built grave superstructures *do* vary in size, and provide some index to social complexity and even political leadership. A complicating factor is that in the C-Group as a whole superstructures tend to increase in size over time, but this problem can be avoided if we focus on tombs datable artifactually to the phases of interest here, that is, IA and B.

Thus, at the center of Aniba Cemetery N, the area containing C-Group IA tombs is characterized by small superstructures with average diameters of 1.00–1.90 meters. On the fringes of the Phase IA concentrations, or outside them altogether, are larger superstructures with average diameters of 2.10 meters. These are later (i.e., of Phases IA/B or B). Larger superstructures again (2.40–2.66 meters

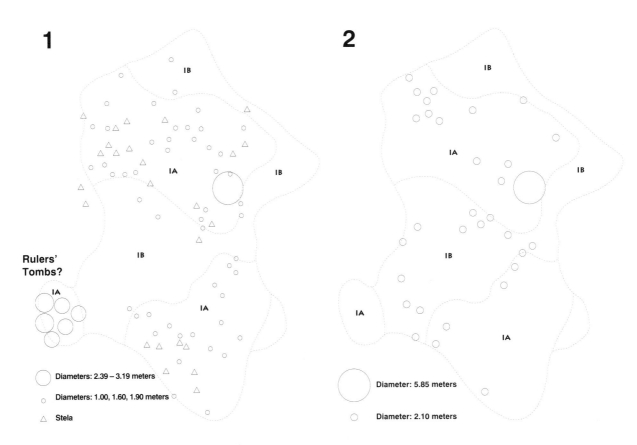

**1**

IB

Rulers'
Tombs?

IA

IB

IA

IB

IB

IA

◯ Diameters: 2.39 – 3.19 meters

◦ Diameters: 1.00, 1.60, 1.90 meters

△ Stela

**2**

IB

IA

IB

IB

IA

IA

◯ Diameter: 5.85 meters

◦ Diameter: 2.10 meters

**Fig. 3.3**

*Aniba, C-Group Cemetery N: the cemeteries of C-Group
phases IA and IB, rendered in schematic form according to
the average diameters of the circular superstructures. The
graves in Panel 1 date mainly to IA, in Panel 2, to
transitional IA – IB; in Panel 3, mostly to IB; the larger
superstructures, of Panel 4, are mainly intrusive ones of
Phase II.*

average diameter) of developed phase IB or later are similarly located; and even larger ones, when found in the IA core area, are artifactually datable to Phases IIA and B, and hence intrusive. Most IIA and B graves are found well beyond the IA and B core areas.

However, although we must not confuse changing superstructure size over time with social and political complexity within each specific phase, such complexity is nevertheless detectable. Among the C-Group IA graves as a whole is a small group that has superstructures larger than normal, with diameters of 2.39, 2.40–2.66, and 2.93–3.19 meters. Moreover, these larger tombs cluster together in an area separate or "set aside" from the others, perhaps to indicate that these tombs were of especially high status. These circumstances indicate that

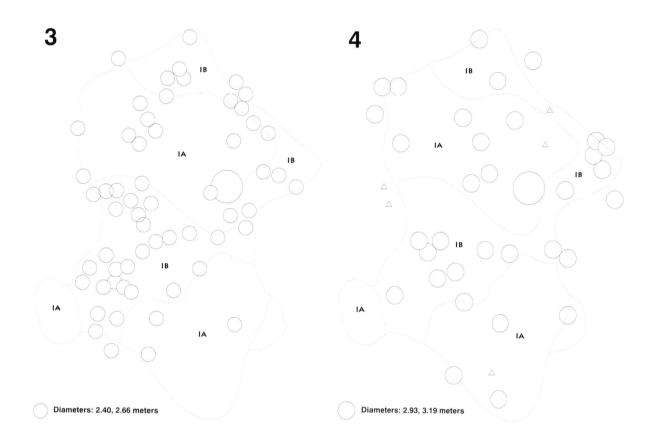

**3**

IB

IA

IB

IB

IA

IA

Diameters: 2.40, 2.66 meters

**4**

IB

IA

IB

IB

IA

IA

Diameters: 2.93, 3.19 meters

they are probably tombs of rulers and their close kin, especially as a socially lower level of elite tombs is indicated elsewhere. Another conspicuous feature of C-Group IA cemeteries is "stelae," carefully dressed slabs of sandstone (sometimes incised with figures of cattle) set upright in the ground. In Aniba Cemetery N these are not associated with the possible rulers' tombs mentioned above, but they are arranged in distinct clusters. This suggests that the tombs closer to them are elite in status, and those farther away (the majority) of a lower order of status.

Unfortunately, it is not possible to detect similar early rulers' and elite tombs at the larger C-Group cemeteries in the Dakkeh and Faras regions. Here, the number of Phases IA and B graves are smaller, plundering severe, and publication less detailed. But it is possible that at Dakkeh and Faras the archaeological and hence political situations were comparable to those found at Aniba Cemetery N.

At the Upper Nubian central places of Sai and Kerma there were large Early Kerma tumuli cemeteries contemporary with C-Group Phases IA and B. Unfortunately, neither has yet been extensively excavated and the Sai graves are also severely eroded, so little data on super-structure size is available. However, Charles Bonnet, who is reinvestigating Kerma's cemetery (originally studied by George Reisner), has identified Early Kerma tombs large enough to be those of rulers, and has also demonstrated that the contemporary town of Kerma was of some significance. It had regularly built mud-brick houses; probably a cult-building of sub-stance; and was defended by a town wall of rammed earth, several meters thick, and rein-forced against sapping with a wooden palisade and a broad, dry moat. All these circumstances suggest a high degree of political centrality and the existence of well-defined rulership.

The existence of rulers in early Nubia is then indicated by archaeology as well as texts; but the exact nature of the political systems involved remains ambiguous and hence debatable.

According to one of the two political maps discussed earlier, the three C-Group central places—Dakkeh, Aniba, Faras—may first have housed rulers of independent polities (Wawat, Irtjet, and Setju), which eventually combine into a single complex chiefdom. One center would then be of the paramount ruler, the other two of his sub-chiefs. As for Upper Nubia, Yam's center would be either at Sai or Kerma, or possibly Kerma housed the paramount chief, and Sai the sub-chief, of Yam.

The other political map, the one I favor, leads to a very different interpretation of the archaeological evidence. Lower Nubia would have been a single complex chiefdom, Wawat, its paramount ruler perhaps living at Aniba, with sub-chiefs at Dakkeh and Faras. Irtjet and Setju, in Upper Nubia, would be complex chiefdoms centered at Sai and Kerma respectively. When Irtjet and Setju combined into a single polity, Kerma was likely its capital; according to Harkhuf, this capital was on the frontier between Irtjet and Setju, and the frontier in question was unlikely, for geographical reasons, to be near Sai. When Wawat (Lower Nubia) was added to the political system, Kerma possibly continued to be the capital, for the sequence of the unification indicates that the initiative for it came from Upper Nubia. Sai and perhaps Aniba would then have become sub-capitals, their rulers being not so much sub-chiefs as incipient bureaucrats, governors serving the state leader residing at Kerma.

Whatever the political arrangements may have been in Early Bronze Age Nubia, it is clear that the Egyptian invasion of Lower Nubia soon after 2000 B.C. must have led to major changes among the Nubians. With Lower Nubia occupied by Egypt (although still inhabited mainly by Nubians) political dynamism was possible only in Upper and perhaps Southern Nubia. As was the case for the Early Bronze Age, the latter remains unknown to us for the next period of Nubian history, the Middle Bronze Age (12th and 13th Dynasties in Egypt); but Upper Nubia became the core of a new

Nubian polity, a powerful competitor to the larger Egyptian state.

## The Kingdom of Kush

It is in fact quite clear that after the Egyptian conquest of Lower Nubia, soon after 2000 B.C., the political map of Nubia changed greatly. Once again, ambiguities in the evidence permit two very different interpretations of the Nubian political system that had developed.

Wawat, or Lower Nubia, was filled with C-Group people (Phase IIA) during the 12th Dynasty occupation, and they were necessarily politically quiescent under Egyptian domination. They were not even permitted to live in the fortified towns that were now the administrative and economic centers of Lower Nubia. As to Irtjet and Setju, wherever they were to be located, they are no longer mentioned in Egyptian sources. Instead, the Egyptians now refer frequently to an important entity called Kush, clearly located in Upper Nubia.

The political system that prevailed in Upper Nubia during the 12th Egyptian Dynasty is open to two different interpretations, because of ambiguities inherent in our chief sources on the geography of Upper Nubia at that time, namely the Execration Texts. These texts are lists of named rulers and regions written on pottery vessels or stone and mud figurines of bound prisoners. The people and places listed, mainly of Nubia and Syria and Palestine, were considered hostile to Egypt; and by breaking or burying the pots or figurines the Egyptians hoped to achieve victory over these enemies magically.

Lists of Nubian rulers and regions occur in Execration Texts that are distributed chronologically through the 12th and early 13th Dynasties. The earliest such list records several polities lying along the river south of Lower Nubia, each with its own *heka*. In the later lists only two riverine regions—Shaat and Kush—are assigned rulers, although in one set of lists other riverine regions continue to be listed by name.

These data can be interpreted in two ways. In one, most scholars conclude that many and perhaps all of the riverine rulers and regions listed were in Upper Nubia. From this it follows that in the early 12th Dynasty Upper Nubia was divided up between several Nubian polities. Later, perhaps only Shaat and Kush continued to have rulers; or possibly the rulers of the other regions still existed but for some reason were not specifically listed. Politically, the implications are that in the earlier 12th Dynasty at least Upper Nubia was politically fragmented into several polities, each of which was small scale in territory and population, hence a simple and relatively weak chiefdom. Theoretically, so far as the evidence of the lists is concerned, this situation might have continued into the early 13th Dynasty.

However, most scholars seem to think that gradually, in the later 12th and 13th Dynasties, a more powerful entity—called Kush—did gradually develop in Upper Nubia. However, the process is seen as a relatively slow one, with Kush achieving only the strength of a complex chiefdom in the Middle Kingdom. In this interpretation, Kush cannot be considered a state in complexity and scale until the Second Intermediate Period, during which, by about

1650 B.C., Kush secured control over the formerly Egyptian held territory of Lower Nubia. Even then, at the height of Kushite power, one authority has suggested that in this "kingdom" of Kush, "Ties of kinship and earlier tribal associations may have remained strong; preventing full development of a class based society."[6] In other words, even at this relatively late date, the Upper Nubian state remained very similar to a complex chiefdom in structure and ideology.

However, the available evidence permits us to reconstruct Upper Nubia's political map in a way different from that outlined above, and this second reconstruction I find more plausible. This second version is based on the real possibility that some and perhaps all of the riverine rulers and regions listed as south of Shaat and Kush may well have not been in Upper Nubia and instead lay farther upstream, in Southern Nubia. Upper Nubia then may have been divided into only two, or perhaps three, polities. Shaat and Kush are definitely Upper Nubian. Archaeological evidence shows that Shaat's central place and political center was on Sai island (its modern name descended from the word Shaat), while Kush's must have been Kerma, the only other central place in northern Upper Nubia. There may have been a third polity in Upper Nubia, centered at Bugdumbush, a large Middle Bronze Age site in southern Upper Nubia.

This second political map, by dividing all Upper Nubia among only Shaat, Kush, and perhaps a polity centered at Bugdumbush, would assign each a territorial scale and probable population appropriate to complex chiefdoms, not the simple chiefdoms suggested by the first theory, discussed above.

However, it is possible to go even further and suggest that from the outset of the Middle Bronze Age (i.e., from the early 12th Dynasty onward), Upper Nubia was organized—in part or in whole—into a state, and not lesser and weaker complex chiefdoms. Several factors support, although they cannot prove, this notion.

First, Kerma always seems to have been much more archaeologically imposing than Sai in the Middle Bronze Age. Therefore, it is possible that even though the Egyptian lists treat the "chiefdoms" of Shaat and Kush as if they were independent of each other, in reality the ruler of Shaat may have been a sub-chief or governor subordinate to the ruler of Kush. Kush and Shaat combined would then have the proportions of a state, not simply a complex chiefdom; and if Bugdumbush represented yet another sub-capital subordinate to Kush, then that state would be all that much larger and stronger. However, Bugdumbush may belong to a complex chiefdom independent, at least initially, of the state formed by a combination of Shaat and Kush.

Second, the Egyptians from the early 12th Dynasty onward—in texts other than the Execration Text lists—in fact refer to Upper Nubia (or, at least, northern Upper Nubia) as if it were a single political entity, called Kush. This too may indicate that Shaat and perhaps the Bugdumbush region were parts of a greater whole, the state of Kush.

Finally, archaeological evidence hints at a state structure in, at least, northern Upper Nubia during the 12th and 13th Dynasties, which correspond to the archaeological phase called Middle Kerma-Group. Among the Middle Kerma graves within the vast and long-lived cemetery at Kerma, Bonnet has identified several unusually large tumuli that, he thinks, must mark the graves of rulers. Tombs of comparable size are not evident in the Middle Kerma cemetery at Sai (although here severe erosion may have destroyed the relevant evidence), suggesting that the rulers of Shaat were of lesser status, and subordinate to the rulers of Kush. The status of the Bugdumbush cemetery in this regard remains unknown.

Middle Kingdom Egypt then faced one of two possible situations in Upper Nubia. Either the Upper Nubians only very gradually consolidated into a state (by 1650 B.C.), which even then was fairly rudimentary in organization. Or, virtually from the outset, Middle Bronze Upper Nubia was always a state, centered at Kerma; and, already strong, grew increasingly powerful and well organized over time. These circumstances obviously influence our interpretation of Egypt's relations with Upper Nubia through this period.

After the conquest of Lower Nubia, pharaoh Senwosret I also campaigned in Upper Nubia, but permanent Egyptian occupation did not follow. Later, Amenemhet II claimed that Kush was a tribute-delivering vassal,[7] but actually this may have referred to more or less equal trading relations. Egyptian imports are fairly common in Middle Kerma Upper Nubia. Finally, Senwosret III (ca. 1878–1841?) campaigned aggressively in Upper Nubia, but again did not retain any of its territory: rather, he fortified the Second Cataract frontier between Upper and Lower Nubia on a scale suggesting that he feared large-scale attack, and even outright invasion, from Kush. All these develop-

ments seem to reflect Kushite strength rather than weakness, and perhaps indicate that the theory of a Kushite state forming early, rather than late, is preferable.

Thereafter, relations between Egypt and Upper Nubia remained apparently amicable for a long time, during which the Lower Nubians' political status changed. For most of the 12th Dynasty, Egypt regularly replaced its garrisons in Lower Nubia with fresh troops, but in the 13th it permitted large permanent populations of officials and soldiers and their families and dependents to live in the fortified towns for generation after generation. These Egyptian communities became more autonomous as the Egyptian state proved increasingly unreliable in supporting and defending them; and their relationship with the C-Group Lower Nubians of Phase IIB became slowly one of collaboration, rather than domination.

The effects on the C-Group were obvious; social complexity and political dynamism, which had survived in suppressed form through C-Group Phase IIA, developed rapidly in the freer circumstances of IIB. Social complexity, the division of society into well-defined levels of wealth and status, became stronger and rulers were again able to express their power and prestige in material terms. Thus, in the great C-Group Cemetery N of Aniba, Phase IIB graves are found all along the edges, but concentrate especially in the northeast corner. Here, about 55 percent of the C-Group superstructures are on average 2.5 meters or less in diameter; 35 percent, 3.00–4.80 meters; and a minority—7.6 percent—5.30–8.00 meters—indicating a three-level hierarchy of status and wealth.

**Fig. 3.4**
*The stela of Sepedhor from Buhen (The University Museum of Archaeology and Anthropology, E 10984). The text describes how Sepedhor renovated the temple of Horus at Buhen, on behalf of his master, "the ruler (heka) of Kush." (From T. Save-Soderbergh, "A Buhen Stela from the Second Intermediate Period [Khartum No. 18]," Journal of Egyptian Archaeology, 35, 1949, fig. 2)*

Moreover, superimposed on this hierarchy was a fourth level, that of rulers and their kin. Far away from the main cluster of IIB graves, in the southwest corner of Cemetery N, was a small, "set-aside" cemetery indicative of special status, which in fact contained tombs so large that some must have been for rulers. No superstructure was smaller than 9.00 meters in diameter, and some were 13.00 or 16.00 meters. Developed social complexity is found elsewhere in C-Group IIB cemeteries; while rulers' tombs are evident at Dakkeh and perhaps elsewhere.

Lower Nubia, in effect, was now being run in collaboration by Egyptians and a series of Nubian chiefdoms.

During the 13th Dynasty, the larger C-Group rulers' tombs abruptly cease; and, in the subsequent C-Group Phase III of the Second Intermediate Period, the lower-order C-Group graves become very Egyptian in form, customs, and grave goods. These circumstances suggest that relations between Egyptians and elite Nubians became so close that the latter moved into the fortress towns, voluntarily adopted much of Egyptian culture, and were buried in Egyptian style in the Egyptian cemeteries that had become typical of the fortresses in the 13th Dynasty. The rest of the C-Group Nubians, following their leaders' example and themselves in closer contact with Egyptians than ever before, also became acculturated—during Phase III—to Egyptian norms in many, but not necessarily all, ways.

By the Second Intermediate Period (ca. 1640–1532 B.C.) political and cultural change was occurring throughout the entire Lower Nile. Egypt became divided between an intrusive Canaanite Dynasty, the "Hyksos" or 15th, controlling Lower and partially Upper Egypt; and a Theban, 17th Dynasty preparing for a war of independence. By about 1650 B.C. Lower Nubia itself passed under the control of the state or kingdom of Kush. Either the Egyptian-Nubian peoples of the Lower Nubian towns found it politic to transfer their loyalty to the Kushite ruler, or Kush imposed its rule over them by force. At some point, some of the fortified towns were sacked, but whether early or late in the process of Lower Nubia's political integration into Kush is uncertain. These Egyptian subordinates to the Kushite ruler set up inscriptions in his name, the earliest such known for an African ruler outside of Egypt (Fig. 3.4).

This was the apogee of Kushite, or Upper Nubian, state power in the Middle Bronze Age. Kush's rulers had a large and well-organized state, with a socially complex population (see chapter 4). They completely controlled southern trade with Egypt, and had diplomatic and commercial contacts with both Thebans and Hyksos. The royal city at Kerma had become very impressive in Middle Kerma times, but now—in the Classic Kerma phase—it displayed an especially monumental brick temple; a large royal palace (only recently discovered); and massive fortifications. In Kerma's cemetery, the Kushite rulers of the Classic phase were buried in a style reflective of their power and prestige. Provided with wealth and surrounded by both elite burials and hundreds of sacrificed harem-women, servants, and guards, these rulers lay under enormous tumuli, some 90 meters in diameter.

Nubian political strength then was such that most of the Lower Nile was now divided up more or less equally among them, the Thebans, and the Hyksos. However, this situation soon changed, as we shall see in chapter 5.

## The Desert Kingdoms and the Land of Punt

The warlike Nubians of the riverlands—the "crocodiles" of Wawat, Shaat, and Kush—were important players in the Middle Bronze Age. So, however, were the "lions," the aggressive eastern desert folk, or Medjayu, as were, more remotely, the people of Punt.

Most information about the Medjayu, and all we have about Punt (which is not yet archaeologically identified), comes from scenes and texts in Egyptian temples and tombs. These at least make clear the Medjayu lived in deserts east of Nubia; their life-style was then necessarily nomadic, for the desert environment prevented sedentary agriculture.

The Puntites are more enigmatic; great traders in incense and other exotica, they must have had other resources not yet known. Punt's geographical relationship to the eastern desert, and Nubia proper, is best documented later. In the fifteenth century B.C. an Egyptian expedition traversed Punt, a coastal land between the modern towns of Tokar and Port Sudan, and moved far inland into savannah lands supporting rhinoceri and giraffes. These inner lands included Irem, which was most likely located in the Berber-Shendi Reach (i.e., Southern Nubia, or the northern Atbara; Irem may actually be a later form of the name of the land of Yam, discussed earlier). Some scholars place Irem in Upper Nubia, but this seems less probable.

Punt therefore lay south of the Medjayu lands, and probably was linked with the more southerly nomads described below and ultimately with Southern Nubia. Punt's southern limit is unknown. Mahal Teglinos, near Kassala, has recently been revealed as the central place (at 11 hectares, or about 27 acres) of the widespread Gash culture of 2300–1700 B.C. Fattovich, the excavator, has suggested that Mahal Teglinos was "an important commercial partner of the early Kerma state (ca. 2500–1500

B.C.)," and "inland gateway to the Land of Punt."[8] However, Punt seems too far north for this to be the case; and Mahal Teglinos' trading partners along the river were most likely in Southern, not central or Upper, Nubia.

To return to the Medjayu, our understanding of their history and culture is much enhanced by knowledge of their nomadic status. The Medjayu were active only east of Lower and Upper Nubia; but modern analogies suggest that farther south were other nomadic populations, spread throughout the Butana, the Southern Atbai and along the Red Sea coast. Little is known of these other nomadic groups until Meroitic times.

As nomads, the Medjayu ranged back and forth between the Red Sea coastal plain (and a few inland centers) and the semi-desert hills and plains where grazing was seasonally available. They were also in contact with the riverine Nubians and the Egyptians. Medjayu origins, like those of most nomads, are obscure. Some scholars argue that nomads were originally hunter-gatherers or agriculturalists who were either trapped in more arid regions by environmental change or forced to move into them. One, Sadr, even suggested that complex and settled societies promoted nomadism so as to have a pool of animals and animal products to draw on; nomadism would thus be "the ranching industry of the early states."[9]

Unlike many nomads, the Medjayu probably included few "agropastoralists" who farmed as well as herded, for the ecological niches necessary mostly lay south of Medjayu land. But, like nomads in general, the Medjayu depended on other, more settled societies for cereals and other foods, and for artifacts like metal weapons and containers that the ever-mobile herdsmen could not produce themselves. Nomads acquire these necessities in several ways, all of which were probably important to the Medjayu at different times in their history. They can trade off animal products or items gained through long-distance trade in which the nomads are intermediaries. They can barter their services as guides, herdsmen, or warriors to more settled peoples. Or nomads can dominate or conquer the latter, and force them to pay tribute or provide arable or grazing lands for the nomads themselves.

Nomads able to dominate or conquer settled folk are sometimes organized into a "nomadic state." This means they have a degree of political and military centralization, and of social complexity, that is unusual among nomads. However, nomadic states centered on arid lands are inherently unstable. Only the conquest of sedentary people provides them with hope of permanence.

Egyptian sources show the Medjayu entering Egyptian service as soldiers and police as early as the Old Kingdom, setting a pattern continuing into the Late Bronze Age. Our best glimpse of the Medjayu's specialized military skills (reflecting their desert origins) comes from a campaign fought in Egypt against the Hyksos by a Theban pharaoh, Kamose (ca. 1555–1550 B.C.). As Kamose's army moved north by river, Medjayu forces in his employ kept pace along the desert edges of the valley so as to intercept any surprise flank attacks by the Hyksos. At night, the Medjayu guarded the camps set up by Kamose's army.[10]

The earliest known Medjayu already have rulers, or *hekaw*, showing them organized at least into simple chiefdoms. Some Medjayu provided support to the Egyptians at these rulers' orders, so the exchange of Medjayu manpower for Egyptian foodstuffs and manufactures was sometimes between institutions, the "governments" of each.

Periodically, hostilities also occurred, especially in the Middle Kingdom when Egypt, occupier of Lower Nubia, expanded eastward to exploit the desert gold mines and met Medjayu resistance or attack. The Medjayu were organized into at least three desert chiefdoms, Aushek and a divided Webetsepet. These polities probably hindered or prevented unfettered Egyptian movement south through the deserts, much as the kingdom of Kush blocked Egyptian expansion upstream of Lower Nubia. Unlike Wawat or Lower Nubia, conquered early and hence dropped from the Execration Texts, Kush, Aushek and Webetsepet continue to appear in the Execration Texts of all periods, indicating that they were considered both independent and hostile.

Nevertheless, despite the periodic hostilities, Egypt's long-term relations with Kush and the Medjayu were those of trade and exchange. Egypt desired Kushite products and Medjayu services, so it is not surprising to find envoys from Aushek visiting the Theban royal court in the 13th Dynasty as honored guests, fed—like visiting bureaucrats and royal kin—from the palace storerooms.

Archaeologically, the Medjayu are unknown until the Second Intermediate Period, when many cemeteries and some settlements with a distinctive material culture, the Pan-Grave, are found in Upper Egypt and

Lower Nubia. In the former, they represent permanent colonies of Medjayu in Egyptian military service; in Lower Nubia, however, the Medjayu seem more akin to invaders. In the Faras-Ashkeit region, for example, the populous C-Group people moved away from the immediate hinterland of intrusive Medjayu settlements, suggesting that the Medjayu were directly taking over parts of the floodplain for herding or farming. Much elsewhere would still have remained in C-Group hands.

If this pattern is true for all Lower Nubia, then a limited form of Medjayu conquest was occurring, suggesting that some of the desert chiefdoms like Aushek and Webetsepet had become expansive nomadic states. Further support for this notion is found in the southern Atbai, where the formerly Gash Group people acculturate (as the Mokram Group) to Pan-Grave or Medjayu norms, as if Medjayu influence and power had expanded in this direction also.

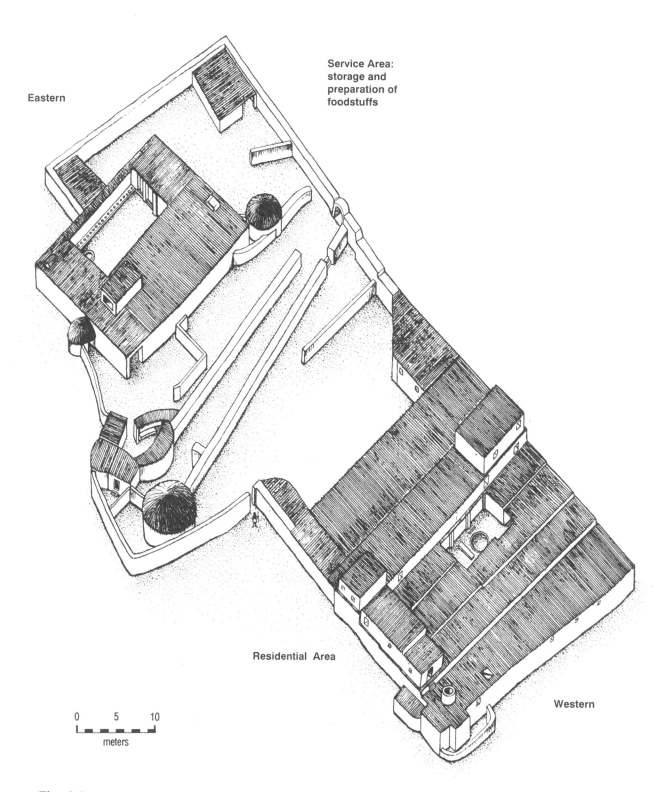

**Eastern**

**Service Area:
storage and
preparation of
foodstuffs**

0    5    10
meters

**Residential Area**

**Western**

**Fig. 4.1**
A reconstruction of the C-Group settlement at Areika, by
Josef Wegner. Drawing by Raymond Rorke.

# Nubian Life in the Middle Bronze Age

*B*efore moving to the next phase of Nubia's story, the Late Bronze Age, we should pause for an impression of Nubian life in the Middle Bronze Age. Here two sites are especially important; illustrative of the C-Group and Kerma-Group respectively, each includes a large settlement that reflects more directly than do cemeteries the life-styles of the Nubians.

Areika, in C-Group Lower Nubia, is comparatively small at 0.28 hectares (almost 3/4 of an acre), but is one of the only two C-Group settlements of any size ever excavated. The other, at Wadi es-Sebua, is not yet published in detail. Other settlements may have been larger, at 1.4 or even 4 hectares (3 and 10 acres respectively).[1]

Kerma, in Upper Nubia, is on a very different scale of magnitude and social complexity, because it was the capital of Kush for much of its history. Its town had a core area of 6 or more hectares, and a total extent of perhaps 25 (over 61 acres). These dimensions are comparable to those of contemporary towns in Egypt, which occupied between 20 to 50 hectares. Nearby, was a vast cemetery, which included the tombs of Kush's rulers. Contact with Egypt was another important and more generalized aspect of Nubian life; and a discussion of contact and its effects will close this chapter.

## Areika: A C-Group Nubian Community

David Randall-MacIver and Leonard C. Woolley excavated Areika, describing it as "a more or less fortified dwelling inhabited permanently by a small number of people" and suggesting that it was the "castle" of a Nubian chief. However, a recent study by Josef Wegner of the University of Pennsylvania leads to different conclusions, and clarified the dates of Areika's occupation—C-Group Phases IIA and IIB, equivalent at Areika to the later 12th and 13th Dynasties (the dates assignable to the Egyptian ceramics recovered).

The plan of Areika differs from that of other C-Group settlements in that the C-Group houses often have curvilinear or irregular plans and are built of rough stone masonry or standing slabs with upper structures of wood and matting. Much of Areika is built of mudbrick, and most structures are rectilinear in plan. Those that are curvilinear are contemporary with the others, as Wegner has shown; some scholars had thought the curvilinear earlier.

The Areika settlement was made up of two principal components, western and eastern (Fig. 4.1). The western, on slightly lower ground, was defined on all four sides by a massive, rough stone masonry wall, apparently defensive in nature. Set off to one side, at the northeast corner, was a large granary. The western component consisted mainly of residential units, representing perhaps a number of households with their rooms grouped around courtyards. Evidence for domestic use—clay divans, storage bins, floor mills for grinding grain—was abundant.

Nevertheless, food was supplied to those living in the western component mostly by the eastern. The latter consisted of a rectilinear building, which included a room with bread ovens opening onto a court with an installation for twenty-four large jars, the whole apparently a combined bakery and brewery of a type often found in Egypt.[2] Hearths were found only in the eastern component, suggesting that other kinds of cooking were also done here. The rectilinear building was flanked east and south by a large courtyard, perhaps used for holding animals and also containing a substantial granary; while on its west was a thick defining wall, with lightly built structures—perhaps animal pens—at either end. The animals would be "food on the hoof," while the granary supplied the cereal needed for bread and beer.

This highly organized community consisted mostly of C-Group people, for the majority of the 540 sherds collected were of this culture. However, no "chief's" residence was indicated, and ten seal-like mud plaques showing a man with a feather in his hair and grasping a kneeling prisoner do not depict a chief, as Randall-MacIver and Woolley thought. Rather, as Wegner suggests, this is more likely the emblem of a C-Group military unit in Egyptian service.

In fact, a substantial minority (30 percent) of the recovered sherds came from Egyptian vessels, often cups and bowls not needed by the Nubians, who produced their own, in Nubian fabrics. These then come from the "table-ware" of Egyptian officers residing at Areika, in charge of its Nubian "garrison" and their families. Areika appears to have been a fortified post built under Egyptian supervision, as part of a system of monitoring and controlling movement along (or into) the Lower Nubian valley. The C-Group people may not have been able to live in the Egyptian fortress towns, but Areika shows that elsewhere they and Egyptians could be in close and sustained contact.

Despite the special circumstances at Areika, it provides invaluable insight into C-Group life, which both correlates with and corrects the impression provided by the abundant C-Group cemetery data found throughout Lower Nubia. For example, in the area of religion, small clay and pottery figurines of animals, and of stylized women, are often found in the C-Group cemeteries. The women are shown usually in a seated position, and without lower arms or lower legs; heads, large and thinly attached, have usually been broken off accidentally. Incisions and impressions on the figurines represent tattooing, actually found on some C-Group bodies. Both animal and female figurines also occur at Areika, showing that they are not restricted to funerary rituals, but also relate to religious and perhaps other activity of the living. Unfortunately, we cannot tell if they were cult figures, originally enshrined; magical figures, disposed of after ritual use; or sometimes even toys.[3]

Fragments of larger pottery figures were also found at Areika, some representing males. Torsos have straps or cords across the chest; feet wear elaborately modeled sandals. Such sandals, made of leather, are commonly found in C-Group graves.

There are many other kinds of debris at Areika, such as beads from jewelry, stone tools and cores from which flint blades had been struck, and spindle whorls used in weaving locally produced linen. However, pottery sherds were the most frequent debris, and Wegner provides a revealing analysis of their relationship to the abundant pottery recovered from C-Group cemeteries.

Fine ware incised bowls and rough brown ware incised jars occur in both cemeteries and settlements; but in the former they are relatively small, and uniform in size, while in the settlement of Areika sizes are much more variable, reflecting the different needs—eating, drinking, storage—these bowls and jars served among the living. Some standard fabrics, such as black-topped, red-polished wares, are abundant in both cemeteries and settlement, but crudely "incised housewares" are rare in the former, common in the latter. At Areika, they represent 15 percent of the total sample; their exteriors were often smoke-blackened because they were used in cooking. The rarity of cooking-pots in C-Group graves suggests that Nubians expected someone else to do the cooking for them in the afterlife!

One important aspect of C-Group pottery, whether from cemeteries or settlements, has not yet been analyzed. Its frequent decoration (and this is also true for the A-Group and Kerma-Group) is usually abstract and geometric rather than naturalistic and representational. Studies of similarly decorated pottery from early Europe suggest that patterns of thought and concepts expressed in the decoration of ceramics can be cross-referenced with similar ones manifest in funerary and domestic architecture, and even in the social and ritual activities associated with these. Moreover, it is argued, ceramic decoration is a dynamic component in this system of interrelationships, for it combines concepts naturally opposed to each other, and helps to resolve contradictions between them.[4]

Similar studies of C-Group and other Nubian ceramics in relationship to their societies and its archaeology as a whole might prove revealing about ancient Nubian social organization and ideology, which in many ways are still quite mysterious.

## Nubia's Earliest City

Today, Kerma is an important archaeological site; but in the Middle Bronze Age it was a living community, which included the highest stratum of Nubian society of the period. Kerma was also Nubia's earliest city, indeed the earliest city in Africa outside of Egypt. At perhaps 25 hectares Kerma might seem small to us, but "city" is the right term. Not only was it a well-built and well-defined urban center with considerable functional and social complexity, but Kerma also headed the settlement hierarchy of Nubia. As Blanton had observed, any "central place" above a certain minimal size is a town or city, depending on its position in the central place hierarchy of the society concerned.[5]

Kerma—explored first by George Reisner and now by Charles Bonnet—provides a richly detailed glimpse of royal and elite life in Bronze Age Nubia. We shall focus on its Classic Kerma Phase (ca. 1700–1550 B.C.) when Kerma housed a ruler controlling all Upper and Lower Nubia. Contemporary Egypt was divided between a Hyksos or Canaanite ruler in the Delta and his restive, ultimately rebellious Theban vassal state in southern Egypt.

Kerma lay on the inner flank of a low rise separating the city from the nearby river. Approached from the south, the city would have looked particularly impressive. Around its central core were extensive settlements, above which rose the massive, fortified walls—10 meters, or 33 feet high—of the city center. Already, the temple and the tall roof of a royal audience hall would be visible above the wall line. Entering the large southern gateway, the visitor found the city center densely packed with houses interspersed with gardens and animal enclosures. Above the flat yellow and brown roofs of the single-storied houses soared the 20-meter (65 feet)-high pylon of the city temple, gleaming white in the bright sun. Northwest of the visitor was the circular royal audience hall, rising 14 meters (46 feet), its conical roof painted with bold, colored designs. Elsewhere was a large royal palace, only recently discovered.

Although impressive, the city center—covering 6–10 hectares, or 15–25 acres—was comparatively small. Bonnet estimates that it housed perhaps 150–200 households, about 2000 people; most of the city's population must have lived outside the defensive walls. The city center did not have the rectilinear outline and orthagonal gridiron layout of some Egyptian towns. Its heavily defended perimeter was irregular, while its layout was shaped by the routes linking its four gateways—one on each side of the walled-in city center. Royal cities in Egypt could display a similar freedom from rigidity, as at Tell el Amarna in the Late Bronze Age, although el Amarna, at

440 hectares, or over 1000 acres, was much larger than Kerma.[6]

The city plan was dominated by the tripartite pattern of temple, audience hall, and palace, which must have shaped ceremonial and ritual movement within the center. On specific occasions, the Kushite ruler and his entourage may have moved from palace to temple or audience hall, and back again, in the presence of the city center's inhabitants, gathered together for the occasion.

The temple, at the center of the inner city, was massively built of mud-brick and had a pylonlike facade. The temple occupied about 1400 square meters, an impressive size by contemporary Egyptian standards; for example, the funerary temple of the pharaoh Senwosret I (set within an architectural complex of 2700 square meters) occupied only 493 square meters. However, unlike Egyptian temples, which emphasized frontal access, the Kerma temple was entered from the side, via a monumental entrance. The interior plan was quite un-Egyptian. A stairway led to a small chamber set high within the otherwise solid mass of the temple. North of the chamber was a long, passagelike corridor, apparently the sanctuary. In the main chamber, animals were frequently tethered; they were probably sacrificed, and laid upon a great circular altar of stone, still approximately in situ today.

Another stairway led up to the temple roof, where small cult structures may have stood. Earlier theories, such as that the temple was the ruler's castle with a palace built on top, or even a very high watchtower, are no longer tenable. On either side of the temple were other cult structures as well as, on the west, priests' residences and manufacturing areas.

The closely packed residences of the city center were built in mud-brick or more perishable materials, and varied considerably in size, reflecting social and economic inequality within the population. Many houses, although large, had only two rooms, fronted by a courtyard; others were more complicated in plan. Houses often had granaries, some quite large; they must have received grain from farms owned by or allotted to the householders, or issued as rations by the ruler. Between the city and the river were vast enclosures in which animals were kept as a further source of food—even the imprints of the animals' hooves have been recovered by archaeologists!

Bonnet has emphasized that Kerma's population was functionally diverse. It included the ruler of Kush, and his family and court; bureaucrats staffing his government; and officers and soldiers who defended the town, and supervised armed forces located elsewhere in the state. Priests, organized hierarchically, serviced the cults. In addition, there were artisans as well as many servants and dependents, while the extramural population, presumably quite large, would be of lower status and little wealth.

Strikingly, a contemporary Egyptian town could be described in almost identical words, a good indication that Egyptian and Nubian society were similar in their complexity.

Almost 3 kilometers east of the city was its vast cemetery (90 hectares, or 200 acres), stretching back in time—like the city itself—into the Early Kerma period. The cemetery's Classic Kerma segment occupies its southernmost part and provides additional insight into

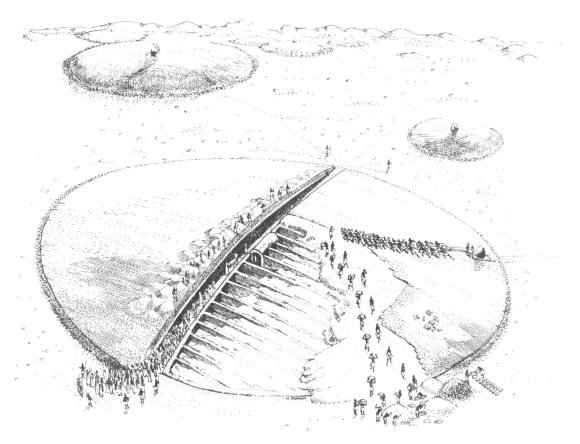

**Fig. 4.2**
*A royal tomb of the Classic Kerma phase at Kerma; the burial is being carried out while laborers complete the building of the tumulus. Drawing by Michael Graham.*

Kerman life-styles, and political and social structures, at this exciting time in Kerma's history.

Furnishings, household, and personal equipment, and dress and adornment are not well preserved in the city, but are well documented in the cemetery. Elite individuals were buried on well-made wooden beds, and often were provided with a box containing items needed for personal care, such as bronze razors and stone vessels for ointment or eye-paint. Many males had a short, beautifully made bronze sword. Egyptian influence, and sometimes origin, was obvious in all these artifacts. Some Kermans wore caps decorated with mica

ornaments, and had fans and other items made of ostrich feathers. Clothing was made of linen and leather. Large amounts of pottery were placed in the graves: some served as tableware, others as storage containers.

The political and social system that the Classic Kerma cemetery represents is fascinating in its complexity. Along the southern edge of the cemetery are four exceptionally large tumuli, certainly royal in status and built in succession—Tumuli XVI, X, IV, and III. The last three are coeval with the 15th Dynasty, while Tumulus XVI is a little earlier (Fig. 4.2).

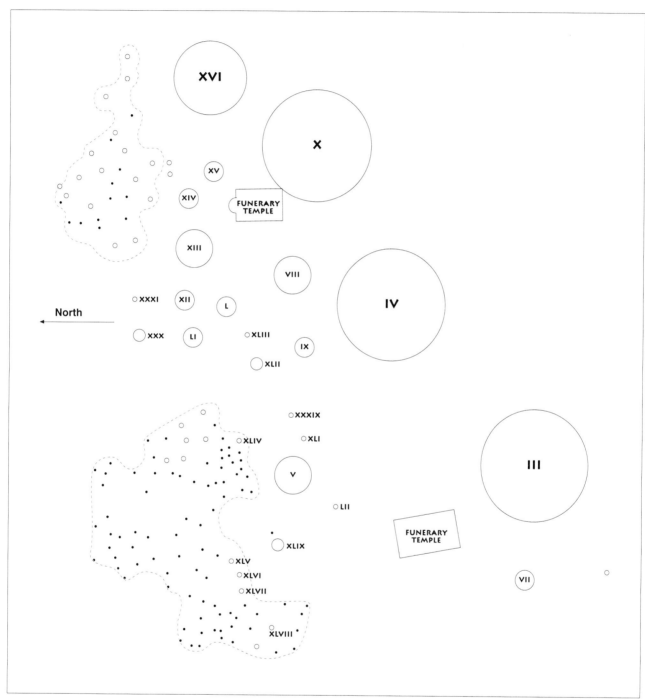

**Fig. 4.3**
  *Schematic representation of the southern zone of the great
  cemetery at Kerma. The grave tumuli are represented
  according to average diameters. Tumuli XVI, X, IV, and III
  are those of the kings of Kush.*

The three later tumuli each had a central corridor, with a side chamber or chambers (central to the tumulus) for the royal burial. These burials were severely plundered, but their special features are evident. The bed that bore the royal corpse, for example, was more luxurious than others; one was of wood partially encased in gold (Tumulus X), another of slate (IV), and a third of blue-glazed quartzite (III). Boat models are found only in royal burial chambers, and were made of wood (X), granite (IV), and blue-glazed faience (III). Finally, the area outside the tomb chamber door was crowded with stone statues and statuettes, of Egyptian pharaohs and officials, which had been plundered from the Egyptian fortress towns and cemeteries of Lower Nubia, now under Kushite control. Some may also have been "traded" from Egypt itself.

The scale of the royal tumuli and of two associated funerary temples built in brick is impressive, even by Egyptian standards. The royal tumuli are low in height (about 3–4 meters, or 10–13 feet), but have an average diameter of 88 meters (288 feet), and occupy 6000–6400 square meters. Egyptian royal pyramids are much higher than the tumuli; but smaller ones of the 12th Dynasty can occupy as little as 6100 square meters (the average is 10,000 square meters), whereas those of the 13th on average occupy only 3300 square meters. The earliest funerary temple (labeled KXI) served Tumulus X; in its final, two-chambered form it occupied 1058 square meters. Temple KII, similar in plan but servicing Tumulus III, occupied 1612 square meters, larger in size than Kerma's large city temple.

The other Classic Kerma graves occupying the southern segment of the great cemetery represent, in my view, a selective group, not a representative cross section of the population. They belong to the elite, and to their servants and those of the rulers (Fig. 4.3).

The archaeological picture is complex. Each royal tumulus (X, IV, and III) contains both "sacrificial" and "subsidiary" burials; and each is associated with a conspicuously large satellite tumulus—Tumuli XIII (attached to X), VIII (for IV), and V (for Tumulus III). Finally, there are many "independent" tumuli graves, grouped into what I call satellite cemeteries. These generally lie northwest or north of the royal tumulus with which they are contemporary. The satellite cemeteries of royal Tumuli X, IV, and III exclude smaller, lower-order graves, which instead are placed together in a "set-aside" cemetery some distance away to the west.

These different kinds of graves—sacrificial, subsidiary, and satellite elite (and lower order)—represent different elements of Kerma's complex society, elements I think we can at least tentatively identify.

The sacrificial burials, disposed along the central corridors of the royal tumuli and sometimes numbering in the hundreds, were of people of relatively low status, according to the associated archaeological features. Sacrificed to meet the ruler's immediate needs—for sexual partners, servants, and guards—these individuals included many women. Their proximity to the royal burial chamber was to facilitate the ruler's access to them, and was not a mark of prestige.

The subsidiary graves cut into the royal tumulus are socially differentiated (according to their floor sizes) into several levels of elite graves as well as smaller graves for servants and dependents. The largest, therefore highest-status, graves are few (about 3.4 percent of the subsidiary graves in each royal tumulus); the next two levels of size are—in descending order—increasingly frequent (10–17 percent; then 28 percent). Overall, I suggest that the subsidiary graves represent the royal court or household; court officials and servants lived in close proximity to the living ruler, and hence were buried in comparable proximity to the deceased ruler.

The especially large satellite tumulus associated with each royal tumulus is certainly intended for a high-ranking relative of the ruler. Their royal status is indicated by the great size of the tumulus; their exceptionally big burial pits (23.8–109 square meters); the large quartzite cones crowning at least two of them— a feature found otherwise only with the rulers' tumuli; and the supporting brick framework of Tumulus VIII, a feature also of the rulers' Tumuli IV and III. A good probability is that these large satellite tumuli were for queen mothers, or the chief queen of the ruler.

The satellite cemeteries, containing relatively large tumuli, represent ranked groups of individuals. In the satellite cemetery generated by the royal Tumuli X and IV about 46 percent of the tumuli were quite large, with an average diameter of 29.50 meters. There is another distinct grade of size below these, as well as even smaller tombs. The satellite cemetery of ruler's Tumulus III, the latest royal tomb, was less complex: two tumuli were rela-

tively large (average diameter 23 meters), but others did not exceed 15 meters in average diameter.

The satellite cemeteries represent, I would suggest, the Kushite government, the upper levels of the bureaucracy, army, and priesthoods—buried separately from the ruler, just as they lived farther from him than the court. We may even be able to detect changes over time in the governmental structure. The greater variety in tumuli size in the satellite cemetery contemporary with royal Tumuli X and IV might correspond to a functionally variegated government, with its chief officials arranged in a clearly articulated hierarchy of authority and responsibility. The lesser differentiation in the satellite cemetery of Tumulus III hints at further sophistication, a government divided into specialized departments, with the "head" of each more or less equal in rank to the "heads" of others, but with two higher-ranking officials set over the whole system.

In general, the social complexity and the advanced degree of political centralization evoked in the city and cemetery of Kerma would seem to be those of a state, not a complex chiefdom, and to indicate that a long process of state formation preceded these developments in Upper Nubia.

## Egyptians and Nubians

One very important aspect of Nubian life in the Early and Middle Bronze Ages is the contact Nubians had with Egyptians, and the effects of this on Nubian society and culture. Some scholars believe that cultural and political developments in Nubia were stimulated mainly by contact with Egypt, largely in an imitative way; but it is much more likely that dynamic forces inherent in Nubian society and not external stimuli were basically responsible for these developments.

"Acculturation," the adoption by one society of some or all of the culture of another, was an important phenomenon in Nubian history. However, Nubian selection of Egyptian cultural traits was always voluntary and partial. Ancient states were imperialistic but not proselytizing, so even when Nubians were dominated by Egyptians—as some were, at some periods—they were not pressured or forced to acculturate. Indeed, the greatest assimilation by Nubians of aspects of Egyptian culture occurred when Nubians dominated Egypt, during the 25th Dynasty (chapter 6).

Nubians were highly selective as to which Egyptian traits they chose to adopt. Some traits were found functionally useful, like writing; others, like Egyptian art styles in Napatan and Meroitic times, provided a vocabulary for expressing Nubian ideas about religion and kingship. Even when the cultural transfer was more fundamental (e.g., when Egyptian gods were venerated by Nubians, or Egyptian notions melded into Nubian kingship), the borrowed traits or ideas tended to be reinterpreted and hence altered by the Nubians.

In other words, acculturation by the Nubians was part of a larger process dependent primarily on dynamic forces inherent in Nubian society. The core culture remained Nubian, but was also one continuously being transformed over time—characteristic of a vital society that seeks change so as to avoid falling into decline or entropy, the loss of social and cultural energy.

In the Early and Middle Bronze Ages, there is little trace of Nubian acculturation to Egyptian norms, except in two special cases, Nubians settled permanently in Egypt and the C-Group in Phase III, during the 15th Egyptian Dynasty. Naturally, small communities isolated from Nubia in Egypt did completely acculturate over time. For example, Nubian bowmen settled at Gebelein during the First Intermediate Period married Egyptian women, were buried in Egyptian style, and soon are no longer distinguishable from Egyptians. Similarly, the Pan-Grave or Medjayu peoples settled in Egypt in the Second Intermediate Period increasingly became more and finally fully Egyptian in material culture and burial customs. The special circumstances affecting the Egyptianization of the C-Group people have already been discussed; earlier, the C-Group showed little trace of Egyptian influence, despite a long period of contact with Egypt.

Otherwise, in Nubia before the Late Bronze Age, Egyptian influence is seen only in very limited ways, indicating that Nubians were resistant or indifferent to Egyptian culture as a whole. So far as textual evidence is concerned, several Egyptian Execration Texts of the later Old Kingdom (equivalent to C-Group IA-IB, and Early Kerma-Group) do refer to partially acculturated Nubians (they have Egyptian names). However, they represent only 6.7 percent of the hundreds of Nubian enemies named, indicating that acculturation was not only partial, but also involved few Nubians. Another set of data consists of graffiti throughout Lower Nubia recording several pharaohs with Egyptian names but unknown to Egyptian history. Some scholars suggest that they were Nubian rulers imitating pharaonic kingship, but more probably they were local Egyptian power-holders of the late Middle Kingdom, asserting their independence of the weak government in Egypt itself.

Egyptian textual evidence shows that there were many ways in which Nubians learnt about Egyptian culture. At all times, there was probably a steady flow of Nubians into and out of Egypt, serving as police or soldiers for a while and then returning to Nubia. Some Nubians, like the C-Group in the Middle Kingdom, lived around centers that were Egyptian in culture and ideology, and eventually entered into a symbiotic relationship with those centers' Egyptian inhabitants. And Egyptians were employed by independent Nubian rulers. The early Execration Texts mentioned above identify a good many Egyptians (about 25 percent of all individuals, foreign and Egyptian, named) who might have been serving Nubian rulers; another set of Execration Texts (early Middle Kingdom) hints that Nubians might have employed Egyptian and even Asiatic mercenaries. Finally, Egyptian officials and bureaucrats in Lower Nubia served the "ruler of Kush" in the Second Intermediate Period, and it is evident that other Egyptians were employed for various purposes at the city of Kerma itself.

However, Kerma in Classic Kerma-Group times is an excellent example of how limited Egyptian influence was, even when Egyptians were serving Kushite rulers. For example, the two funerary temples in the royal cemetery derive from Egyptian prototypes, and were possibly built under Egyptian supervision, but there is little evidence for an Egyptian-style ritual being practiced in them. And while the great city temple (described above) has a vaguely Egyptian appearance because of its "pylon" and general proportions, its internal plan, and the rituals the plan implies, are quite un-Egyptian.

The Kushite royal graves display a similarly restrictive use of Egyptian traits. An Egyptian winged sun-disc was painted on a burial chamber wall in Tumulus III, and the royal owner of Tumulus X was buried in a coffin, an Egyptianized custom. But overall the burial rites and funerary architecture are markedly non-Egyptian, and use Egyptian artifacts in novel ways. Thus, placing large numbers of "captured" images of Egyptian pharaohs and officials outside each royal burial chamber was a peculiarly Nubian custom, unparalleled in Egypt.

The Nubian life-ways described above were soon to change in drastic ways, for the end of the Middle Bronze Age was marked by an outright war of expansion launched against Nubia by an Egypt freed of the Hyksos interloper and militarily more aggressive and efficient than ever before.

# CHAPTER FIVE
# Colonialism and a Reborn State in Nubia

*B*ronze Age Nubia was probably not tribal in structure, but instead was home to a long process of state formation. Lower and Upper Nubia may have combined into a state toward the end of the Early Bronze Age, and later Upper Nubia may have formed a state from the outset of Middle Bronze times. It certainly was one by 1650 B.C. when it took over control of Lower Nubia from Egypt.

In the Late Bronze Age (ca. 1550–1070 B.C.) the momentum of state formation halted, or perhaps took on a new, more subtle form, in Lower and Upper Nubia. Egypt controlled both, militarily and politically, through this period. For their Nubian populations—always in a majority—this was a colonial experience, because many Egyptians emigrated into Nubia and settled there permanently. Southern Nubia, however, remained independent; and may itself have included a state form of organization.

The Nubian capacity for state formation was not destroyed by the colonial experience. Soon after 1070 B.C. Egypt withdrew from Nubia; subsequent hostilities with Egypt compelled most Lower Nubians to retreat into Upper Nubia. Within two centuries (by ca. 850 B.C.) the latter was ruled by a Nubian dynasty buried near Napata (a town near the Fourth Cataract), and in scale was again clearly a state.

The Napatan state was very dynamic, with an unprecedented capacity for expansion. By

750 B.C. the Napatan rulers dominated southern Egypt, and in 715 B.C. they conquered the Egyptian Delta. The resulting state combined Egypt; and Lower, and Upper—and perhaps even part of Southern—Nubia; if this last is true, the Egyptian-Nubian state was the largest ever found along the Nile in ancient and medieval times.

Egypt's internal fragmentation by 750 B.C. facilitated Nubia's expansion, but does not explain how Nubia became so powerful. Directly, Nubian power was based on the military and political organization of the Napatan state; but these in turn were rooted, at least in part, in the earlier Nubian experience of colonial government under the Egyptians. Scholars disagree, however, as to how these factors were interrelated.

Some suggest that after Egypt retreated from Nubia, the Nubians of Upper Nubia "returned to an essentially tribal way of life."[1] In this hypothesis, the Napatan royal line—starting in about 860 B.C.—would either have been a "lineage or local tribal group," possibly of southern Nubian origin,[2] or "locally influential chiefs" who gradually won control of Upper Nubia because they were supported by a small Egyptian or Egyptianized elite (mainly priests), which had provided some semblance of centralized rule after Egypt withdrew.[3]

Other scholars, such as Robert Morkot, emphasize that Nubians were leading players in the administration of Egyptian-held Nubia; and that this factor relates to the "emergence of a powerful independent Kushite state."[4] Building on this insight, I would suggest that Upper Nubia was likely to have survived as a state after Egypt's withdrawal; and that it was

this state that generated the Napatan rulers, or was taken over by them, should they have come from southern Nubia.

The continuity of a state-level organization in Upper Nubia after Egypt's withdrawal depended on Nubia's strange political status under the Egyptians, and on the likelihood that much of its administration was run by Nubians, and possibly Egyptian-Nubians, the product of intermarriage.

Egypt treated Nubia, on the one hand, as an extension of the provincial system of governance typical of Egypt itself. Its administrative entities were organized to produce revenue for pharaoh and the gods' temples, yet its own productivity and prosperity—the sources of revenue—were also fostered. Indeed, much revenue stayed in Nubia, to support its administrators, army, and local temples. On the other hand, Egyptian Nubia's overall government was structured as if it were a vassal state systemically independent of Egypt. The pharaohs were directly acknowledged in official and temple inscriptions throughout Nubia; and occasionally actually appeared there, either to lead a military campaign or for other purposes. In reality, however, Nubia was governed by the "Viceroy of Kush," who reported directly to pharaoh (not to the southern Egyptian vizier); and the viceroy himself functioned as "pharaoh"—or better, as pharaoh's "emanation"—in Nubia, served by two "viceregal deputies" of Lower and Upper Nubia respectively, somewhat as pharaoh was served by the two viziers, of Lower and Upper Egypt. A "troop commander of Kush" oversaw Nubia's military forces, and collaborated with, rather than served, the viceroy.

This system served pharaoh well for much of the New Kingdom, but the viceroy was displaying great power and potential for autonomy even before Egypt's withdrawal; and it is likely that the system he headed (if not the office itself) survived to provide centrality in a still prosperous Upper Nubia, and fostered the rise of the Napatans.

## The Conquest and Governance of Nubia

At the opening of the Late Bronze Age, Egypt systematically undertook the conquest of Nubia, finding it necessary before it felt secure enough to begin a similar program in Western Asia. Lower Nubia fell quickly, but Upper Nubia—the core of Kush—fought long and hard against the Egyptians. Kush was sufficiently threatening that Egypt's expansion into Asia could not be seriously undertaken until Nubia had been subdued.

For eighty-eight years Egypt fought a Nubian campaign every thirteen years (on average) as compared to one every twenty-seven years in Asia. Egypt's problems were twofold; Kush was strong and resistant, and it might receive military support from other Nubian polities, farther upstream in Southern Nubia. An early attempt to forestall the latter (pharaoh Kamose's army appeared in Miu in the Shendi Reach, probably via a flanking movement) was succeeded by a steady hammering of Kush itself.

Pharaohs Amenhotep I and Tuthmosis I conquered Sai, Kush's former subcapital, and the latter traversed all Upper Nubia, claiming to have divided it up among three vassal Nubian rulers (of Sai, Kerma, and Bugdumbush?). Under Tuthmosis II, Kush counterattacked, possibly led by these three erstwhile "vassals," and Tuthmosis' successor Hatshepsut had to fight at least four campaigns in Upper Nubia.

The site of Kerma itself may directly reflect these events. Bonnet notes that its defenses became particularly strong at this period, as if in anticipation of Egyptian attack; and that the town may have been sacked by Tuthmosis I, but regained independence and prosperity for a time.

After 1460 B.C. Egypt enjoyed full control of Lower and Upper Nubia until 1070 B.C., and organized the two regions as a combination of provinces and "vassal state" as discussed above. The viceroy, and the troop commander of Kush, visited Nubia often, but resided (and were buried) at Thebes, so as to maintain close contact with pharaonic government. The viceregal deputies, however, lived, with their families and staffs, permanently in Nubia; the capital of Wawat, or Lower Nubia, was usually Aniba (once, at least, replaced by Faras), and that of Kush, or Upper Nubia, was first Soleb and later Amara.

The farmlands and grazing areas of Egyptian Nubia were divided up in a most interesting way. In the 18th Dynasty, at least, Egyptian towns (probably largely Egyptian in population) were developed throughout Wawat and Kush; each was governed by a commander or mayor, and would have had a substantial agricultural hinterland, to ensure its subsistence and generate revenue for the state. These Egyptian centers, however, were set within a spatially larger administrative and economic matrix, namely, several Nubian "princedoms," which seem to have been quite large in territory and population. Lower Nubia was covered by perhaps three, centered respectively at Kubban, Toshka, and Debeira, and Upper Nubia by as many as six—perhaps the former "territories" of Sai, Kerma, and Bugdumbush, now subdivided. The prince, or petty king, of each of these was regarded simultaneously as ruler of his people and as an official of the Egyptian government, responsible for maintaining order, generating revenue, and carrying out the instructions of pharaoh's government.

This mode of Nubian governance may have changed over time. In Lower Nubia, at least, the Nubian rulers lived in large towns or "capitals" filled with Egyptianized Nubians but set aside from Egyptian centers. Later, in the 19th and 20th Dynasties, the Nubian elite and, increasingly, the Nubian population as a whole, moved to the Egyptian centers. Moreover, the title "(Nubian) ruler," or *wer,* is much rarer, so the administrative system may have become more homogenized, with Nubians and Egyptians increasingly combined in its structure and operation.

Throughout the New Kingdom, Nubia was not just revenue producing, but was also highly accessible to Egyptian institutions and officials in addition to those actually resident in Nubia. Large estates were established in Nubia for the benefit of remote temples in Egypt like Amun's of Karnak and that of Seti I at Abydos. And officials of the central government came and went frequently, exercising the same authority as they held in Egypt, and—as in Egypt—quarreling with other officials over jurisdiction. But in all these regards, Nubia's experience was the same as the provinces of Egypt itself.

## Nubians in Colonial Nubia

Some scholars believe that the Nubians were thoroughly demoralized by the colonial experience. It is suggested that in Wawat, or Lower Nubia, many were reduced to peonage, and others fled to Upper Nubia, or Kush, where "the Egyptian grip was not so strong" and a "tribal way of life" still possible.[5] However, others—with whom I agree—see the Nubian experience as more positive, one providing the Nubians with the means to survive as a state even after Egypt withdrew from the region.

The provincial mode of governance, operative in both Egypt and Nubia, was pervasive and sometimes arbitrary, but—as the Nubians would have found—not unduly oppressive. Egyptian governmental aims in both Egypt and Nubia were simple: to maintain the frontiers, enough internal order and responsiveness to guarantee a good revenue flow, and adequate supplies of manpower for regular labor and military levies. Within this context, the populations of both Egypt and Egyptian Nubia likely enjoyed substantial local autonomy and even individual freedom, restricted only by the limited governmental demands noted above, and by community customs and mores, which were probably quite strong. Egypt's state economy was redistributive, taking in income (much from land owned directly by temples and other government institutions) and re-allotting it for various purposes; but it was not monopolistic. Private entrepreneurship and land ownership was substantial, even among government employees, most of whom were employed part-time.

Of course, if the Nubians—as distinct from Egyptians settled in Nubia—had been specifically singled out for exploitation, taxed excessively, stripped of their lands, and treated virtually as slaves, the Nubian experience would have been much more negative. However, this does not appear to be the case. As we shall see below, Nubian rulers enjoyed high status and may eventually have merged with the Egyptian administrative elite as a whole. Moreover, Nubian society—at least in Wawat in the 18th Dynasty—was not an undifferentiated mass of economically depressed people, but instead complex and stratified, with some members obviously wealthy, and many comfortably off.

Economically, the "Annals" of the pharaoh Tuthmosis III (1479–1424 B.C.) do not indicate that Egypt was unduly exploitive of Nubia. The "tribute," or more accurately revenue, of Wawat and Kush included an annual harvest tax, comparable to that levied in Egypt; and "ships" laden with Nubian products, especially exotic items imported from independent southern Nubia (the latter trade was probably managed by the government, and not something required of Nubian individuals and groups). Gold was another important Nubian product, but was presumably recovered by state-sponsored panning or mining, especially in the inhospitable Eastern Desert, where the richest gold mines lay.

Cattle were a regular part of the Nubian "tribute," but they were not demanded in excessive amounts. The annual average from Upper Nubia in the "Annals" was about 300, from a region that—according to the Middle Bronze Age evidence—was very rich in herds. "Slaves" (*hemu*) and others intended for permanent service in Egypt were also regularly included, but their numbers are small—for example, one year Wawat and Kush combined sent only about fifty "slaves"—and many, if not all, probably came from independent southern Nubia, not Egyptian Nubia.

Nubians, like Western Asiatics, participated in a spectacular, perhaps annual, ceremony, the presentation of tribute to pharaoh at one of his palaces in Egypt (Fig. 5.1). Such ceremonies were intended to emphasize pharaoh's status as "world ruler," and so in a sense they set the Nubians apart from Egyptians. In these ceremonies, Nubians and Western Asiatics represented the "other," the alien foreign world over which Egypt's gods had given pharaoh dominion. Yet in reality these tribute ceremonies (which are depicted in the tombs of many Egyptian officials) reflect the dualistic nature of Egyptian Nubia, simultaneously alien in a symbolic sense, yet increasingly closely integrated with Egypt in a real sense.

First, tribute ceremonies were *not* restricted to foreigners. In such ceremonies, Nubian rulers prostrate themselves before pharaoh, and other Nubians carry or accompany typical Nubian products and animals to be presented to pharaoh. This is a largely symbolic event; most of the Nubian revenue was processed directly by state agencies and was not seen personally by pharaoh. However, any official—Egyptian or Nubian—prostrated himself in pharaoh's presence, and the personalized and symbolic delivery of state income involved

TOMB OF HUY.   WEST WALL: SOUTH SIDE (4).

*Scale ¼*

**Fig. 5.1**

*The presentation of Nubian tribute to pharaoh Tutankhamun
(1333–1323 B.C.), as represented in the tomb of the Viceroy of
Kush, Huy. In the upper register, from the right: the three
princes or rulers of Lower Nubia, including Hekanefer; a
Nubian princess, and four princes, intended to live at
pharaoh's court; Nubians bearing gold, and a Nubian princess
in her ox-pulled chariot. Below, from the right: three rulers or
princes of Upper Nubia; Nubians bearing gold; and a giraffe.*
 *(From: N. de G. Davies,* The Theban Tomb Series, *vol.
4:* The Tomb of Huy. *London: Egyptian Exploration Society
[1926], pl. XXVII.)*

Egyptians also. The annual taxes levied upon
the towns and the town hinterlands of Egypt
itself were personally brought to the royal court
by the mayors and other local officials responsible for revenue collection. As depicted in
vizier Rekhmire's tomb, they carry gold in bas-

kets, hold other products, and lead cattle, very
much as Nubians and Asiatics do in the
"tribute" scenes.[6]

The most detailed of the Nubian
tribute scenes (in the tomb of the viceroy Huy;
Fig. 5.1) reveal just how complex the relations

between Nubians and Egypt were. The prostrating rulers are apparently foreign vassals, but in reality members of an Egyptian administrative system, as we know from the titles they carried. Nubian princesses are being sent to join pharaoh's harem, and princelings to be raised at pharaoh's court, and then returned to Nubia educated in loyalty to him. Certainly, these practices were applied also to Western Asiatic princesses and princelings, but high-ranking Egyptians also sought for their daughters to enter pharaoh's family, and for their sons to achieve the rare privilege of education and service at the royal court; so once again the division between Nubians and Egyptians tends to dissolve in reality.

Finally, we see in such scenes handsome Nubian males who are being sent to serve pharaoh permanently, as well as cruelly bound prisoners evidently intended for servitude in Egypt—both categories are referred to in Tuthmosis' "Annals" and elsewhere. But this does not mean that Egyptian Nubia had become a slave pool for Egypt—indeed, since Egyptian Nubia was now an "administered zone" and not a "zone for incursion," the Nubians were political subjects "no longer alien (and thus vulnerable to capture), but subject and thus vulnerable to exploitation."[7] As we have seen, however, the Nubians were not unduly exploited (after all, the generation of revenue depended in large part upon the Nubians' well-being); and the "slaves" seen in the scenes probably all came from independent Southern Nubia.

In Wawat our best direct evidence on the Nubians comes from the Nubian princedom of Tekhet, which included the Faras-Ashkeit region thoroughly investigated by a Scandinavian team. The pattern seen there is probably typical for all Lower Nubia. In the 18th Dynasty, Tekhet was ruled first by the Nubian Ruiu (whose brother may have served in the Egyptian administration at Elephantine), and then in succession by his two sons, Djehutyhotep and Amenemhet. Elsewhere, we know of the ruler of another princedom, Miam (modern Aniba), a Nubian called Hekanefer whose father may have been another Ruiu, a Nubian official of the Egyptian administration of Aniba. The official status of the Nubian rulers as Egyptian officials, and the appearance of their relatives in the "Egyptian" bureaucracy, reveals an already high degree of integration.

The rulers of Tekhet lived in a large town south of the important Egyptian administrative center of Faras, together with a large Nubian population, which was C-Group in origin but largely Egyptianized in culture. The town itself was not located by archaeologists, but the cemetery of this community shows that it prospered over time, with a wealthy elite increasingly prominent. However, in its later phase—in the later 18th Dynasty—the cemetery is mostly lower class in composition, and it does not continue into Ramesside times. The Scandinavian team therefore suggested that here and throughout Lower Nubia the Nubians were in decline, and eventually died out; others suggest that they emigrated into Upper Nubia.

However, an alternative model seems likelier, namely, that first the rulers, then the elite, and finally the rest of such Nubian communities chose to reside at or near the Egyptian centers, which lay not far away. Here they were buried, alongside Egyptians and

Egyptian-Nubians, in the town cemeteries, where multiple internments (many people buried, over time, in a single burial chamber) were common. This has created the false impression that population levels fall in Nubia during the 19th and 20th Dynasties. Overall, the pattern just described suggests that the bureaucracy of Egyptian Nubia was increasingly dominated by Nubians, who—by the end of the New Kingdom—would have formed an elite experienced in running a relatively complex and sophisticated system of centralized government. This in turn would contribute to the continuity of state-level organizations after Egypt withdrew, even if the Lower Nubians withdrew into Upper Nubia, as seems to have been the case.

We know much less about the situation in Upper Nubia. Some scholars suggest that Egypt closely controlled only the northern part of this region, while the southern—equivalent to the Letti Basin—was largely autonomous, and even periodically in rebellion against Egypt. For various reasons, this latter notion seems unlikely. On the present evidence, slight as it is, we may hypothesize that Upper Nubians underwent the same experience as the Lower Nubians, and came to dominate the administrative system. This is a reasonable hypothesis, even if it is possible that some of these Nubians did not become as Egyptianized in culture as the Lower Nubians. However, archaeologically the status of the former Kerma-Group people, for most of the New Kingdom, remains unknown; and much excavation is required to test the notions outlined above, and perhaps to generate new ones.

## The Independent Rulers of Southern Nubia

As in the Middle Bronze Age, the Egyptians continued to interact with the nomads, or Medjayu, of the deserts east of Nubia, and continued to trade with the people of Punt, on the Red Sea coast. The former Medjayu chiefdoms, perhaps the ultimately "nomadic states" of Aushek and Webetsepet disappear from the record, and new polities, like the chiefdom of Akuyta, appear. Over these Egypt seems to have maintained an uneasy dominion, with the Medjayu functioning more as allies than subjects. As for the Medjayu who had settled in Lower Nubia, they maintained their distinctive material culture, in some cases well into the New Kingdom, but do not seem to have played an important part in Nubian affairs.

However, of greatest interest, outside of Egyptian Nubia, are the polities that may have existed in Southern Nubia. No Bronze Age archaeology has yet been recovered for this region, so some scholars argue that it was uninhabited, or used only by nomads who left few archaeological remains. But the historical record suggests otherwise, and further indicates that Southern Nubia was not only of great interest to the Egyptians, but may ultimately have produced the family from which the Nubian rulers of post-New Kingdom times came.

Egyptian New Kingdom texts refer to periodic conflicts (as well as other kinds of contact) with a constellation of Nubian regions, named Irem, Gawerses, Tiurek, Weresh or Weretj, and perhaps Tirawa. Because they usually occur together in Egyptian lists of "southern" enemies, it is likely that they were also physically contiguous to one another, running along a stretch of the Nile Valley, and including or extending into desert or semidesert regions on either side. Some, and perhaps all, had a separate ruler, and hence each was a polity of some kind—a simple or complex chiefdom, or even a state.

Some scholars suggest that some or all of these five polities were relatively small-scale ones, located in Upper Nubia and filling the periodically rebellious Letti Basin area in particular. However, the historical circumstances discussed above indicate that they lay farther upstream, in Southern Nubia; and this likelihood is reinforced by the record of the expedition sent to Punt by Pharaoh Hatshepsut (1473–1458 B.C.) in the 18th Dynasty. This indicates that Irem was accessible from Punt, and therefore likely in Southern, not the more remote Upper, Nubia. Moreover, Irem included semi-arid or savannah environments supporting rhinoceri and giraffes, which were unlikely to have been found in Upper Nubia or its environs by this time. The same record indicates that the people of Irem were darker-skinned than the Puntites, wore different kinds of clothes, and probably had a different culture.

Certainly, environmental conditions suggest that Southern Nubia would have had a substantial population in the New Kingdom; and its people were well placed to be middlemen in the trade in exotic products between more southerly regions and Egypt. In this regard, the Egyptians may even have had contractual relationships or treaties with the polities of Southern Nubia. However, there were also hostilities: Egypt sometimes sent armies into this region, and on occasion Southern Nubia polities, especially Irem (as the northern-most, or the most powerful?), threatened or attacked Egyptian-held Upper Nubia.

On the one hand, the Egyptians may have sought to intimidate Southern Nubia and so protect Upper Nubia, and gain advantages in the flow of trade; Egyptian campaigns could also have secured the Nubian "slaves" discussed above. On the other, the Southern Nubians were probably determined to protect their political independence and control over trade routes; they may also have been tempted to raid and plunder the wealthy Upper Nubian province.

These circumstances suggest that some of the Southern Nubian polities, like Irem, were militarily powerful, centrally organized, and wealthy—and became increasingly so over time as interaction with Egypt continued and expanded. The degree to which any of them were complex chiefdoms, or even large and complicated enough to be called states, can only be established through archaeological survey and excavation; but certainly the delineation of Bronze Age Southern Nubia remains one of the most exciting challenges facing archaeologists in Nubia.

## The Mysterious Tombs of Kurru

This excitement is intensified by the fact that Upper Nubia, for the period between the New Kingdom and the 25th Dynasty, is archaeologically almost as mysterious as Southern Nubia; and by the possibility that the histories of both regions became closely interrelated at this time.

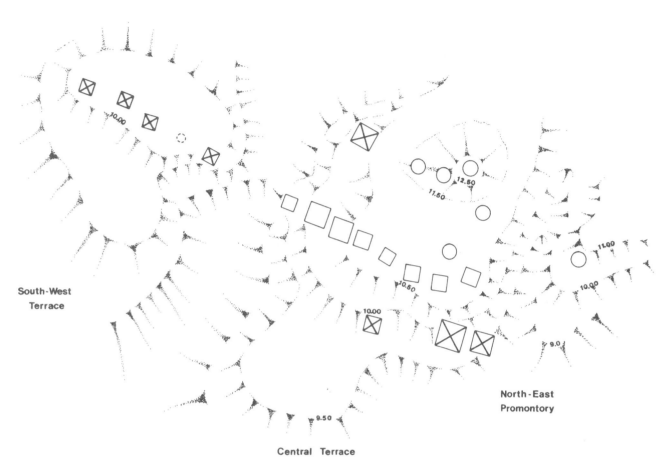

South-West
Terrace

North-East
Promontory

Central Terrace

*Fig. 5.2*
*Diagrammatic representation of the tombs at Kurru.*
*Circles represent circular superstructures; squares are*
*"mastabas;" and squares with crossed diagonals are*
*pyramids. Drawing by Nicole deLisle Warshaw.*

After 1000 B.C. neither politically nor culturally significant archaeological remains are known in Upper Nubia prior to the rulers' tombs of Kurru, near Napata, which begin in about 860 B.C. Yet, on the Egyptian side, we do catch glimpses of continuing relations with Nubia, before 860 B.C. In 925 B.C. Shoshenq I, then pharaoh of Egypt, invaded Judah and Israel, and had Nubians ("Kushites") in his army. Later, his son Osorkon I sent against

Judah another army, headed by a general called Zerah the Kushite. In both cases, Nubians who had been settled in Egypt for generations might have been involved, but it is equally possible that the Nubians in question were recruited in Upper Nubia (the nearest inhabited part of Nubia at that time), or even dispatched from thence by some Nubian "ally" of the Egyptians.

Moreover, in about 840 B.C.—soon after the sequence of royal tombs at Kurru began—Takeloth II, another Egyptian pharaoh, sent as "tribute" to the contemporary ruler of Assyria a rhinoceros, elephants, and monkeys, which could only have been obtained from Nubia. Since no hostilities with Nubia are recorded, the mechanism involved was trade, or even "diplomatic gifts," from the Nubians—the logistical challenge of capturing and forwarding a rhinoceros and elephants being particularly striking. So far as we know, live elephants had never before been forwarded to Egypt.

These references suggest that a centralized power may well have continued to exist in Upper Nubia (with significant connections with Southern Nubia, from whence the rhinoceros and elephants mentioned above would have come), a power finally finding archaeological expression at Kurru. Here, from 860 B.C. onward, an imposing cemetery (Fig. 5.2) developed over two sets of natural terraces, separated by a narrow valley; and, beyond a second valley, on a promontory to the northeast. Efforts to date the earliest Kurru tombs to the period just after the New Kingdom have been made, but are unpersuasive.

A low knoll on the central terrace represented the highest and hence perhaps most prestigious ground; here, four tombs with relatively high, circular superstructures were built, followed by two lower-lying ones, one on the northeast corner of the central terrace, the other "in balance" on the northeastern promontory. The superstructures were of sand and gravel, with a rough stone masonry skin. Later tombs were rectilinear "mastabas," built of well-cut stone masonry and running off to the southwest, along the upper part of the central terrace. Finally, on the terrace's lower

slopes (the only ground left available if the earlier tombs were to be left undisturbed) three stone-built pyramids were erected, with a fourth on the southwest corner of the terrace. These are inscriptionally dated to pharaohs Piye, Shebitku, Shabako, and Tanwetamani of the 25th Dynasty (ca. 747–656 B.C.).

Because the Kurru cemetery ended up as a royal one, it is reasonable to assume that the tombs dated before Piye were also for kings (and queens), particularly as no tombs of comparable scale and elaboration are known elsewhere in Upper Nubia for this period. Indeed, Mastaba VIII is plausibly identified as King Kashta's (Piye's father), and XXIII may belong to Alara, a known royal predecessor of Kashta. Mastabas VII and XXI may have been for their queens. Later, the queens of Piye and his successors were buried in cemeteries separate from the king's tombs, to the northeast and southwest. The remaining mastabas and the earlier graves with circular superstructures[8] total eleven graves, distributed over less than a century. Four of five may be for the rulers of Upper Nubia at this time; the rest were probably for their queens.

The origins of this royal line are uncertain. They may have been generated by the Upper Nubian elite, which, I suggest, maintained centrality after Egypt withdrew. Or they may have been an intrusive group who took over the Upper Nubian state and combined it with their home polity, which would most likely have been in Southern Nubia. This second possibility needs to be taken seriously, given the connections between Upper and Southern Nubia, as indicated by Takeloth's tribute, and the fact that Southern Nubia may have been included—at least in part—in the realm of the 25th Dynasty.

The rulers buried at Kurru, and hence the people they governed, were evidently familiar with Egyptian culture, but they were not themselves "Egyptianized" in any fundamental way. The evolution from circular superstructure to mastaba, for example, seems to be a purely Nubian process, and not a result of Egyptian influence or the presence of Egyptian architects.

The mastabas are essentially a monumentalized form of the circular superstructures, involving techniques and materials easily accessible to the Nubians. The circular superstructure, defined by a rough stone skin, is transformed into a stone-built mastaba, similar in size and proportions to the circular superstructures; the latter had a diameter, on average, of 7.00 meters, while the diagonal of the average mastaba was 9.50 meters. A further indication of the gradual transition from circular superstructure to mastaba is that one mastaba incorporated a circular superstructure within it, whereas another mastaba was earlier than the latest circular superstructure.

Further continuity is seen in the horseshoe-shaped enclosures (already built in dressed stone masonry) of the later circular superstructures, which become—corresponding to the change to greater regularity—the rectilinear enclosures of the mastabas. A single-cell chapel was attached to the latest tumuli, and continues to be used for all the mastabas. Finally, the burial-pit type of the mastabas is

clearly derived from those associated with the circular superstructures.

The introduction of the pyramid, under Piye, is surely Egyptian-inspired, probably by the sight of the great pyramids in the Memphite region, which Piye captured.[9] But the change is still sensitive to the indigenous Nubian tradition of royal tombs, for the Kurru pyramids, like the mastabas (and unlike their Egyptian prototypes), are quite small—the average diameter is 13.50 meters. The pyramids have rectilinear enclosures and single-cell chapels, derived from the mastabas and not the Egyptian pyramids.

This architectural evolution, and the conceptual world it reflects, hints then at a fundamentally Nubian culture developing along its own lines, but assimilating Egyptian influence when the latter seems desirable to the Nubians. The artifacts associated with the Napatan tombs are, with a few exceptions, more Egyptian in character, and indicate a knowledge of Egyptian funerary customs and beliefs. Nevertheless, the milieu in which these objects and notions occur remains a distinctively Nubian one.

The archaeological evidence just reviewed cannot conclusively show whether the rulers buried at Kurru were Upper or Southern Nubian in origin. Certainly, Southern Nubians were probably little Egyptianized in culture, and we might expect the Upper Nubians to be more Egyptianized than is the case with the Kurru tombs; but we know so little of Upper Nubian indigenous culture in the New Kingdom that a definite conclusion cannot be reached.

# The Great Kingdom: Napata and Meroe

*The Challenge of Napata and Meroe*

W e have seen that in the Bronze Age Nubian political systems were of debatable status. Scholars disagree about whether specific polities were simple or complex chiefdoms, or even sometimes states. All agree, however, that in Napatan-Meroitic times the whole of Nubia was bound together in a single great kingdom, recognized as such by the other powers of the day. To these powers Nubia was "Kush" or "Ethiopia," the latter being the term used in Greek and Latin. Its center was first Napata (in Upper Nubia) and later, after 250 B.C., Meroe (in Southern Nubia), hence the term used here— Napatan-Meroitic.

The great kingdom of Napata and Meroe is of considerable importance for the history and cultural development of Africa as a whole, but it provides enormous challenges to the historian and archaeologist. While we know much about it, much more is unknown. Napatan-Meroitic Nubia is filled with known but unexcavated sites, and with others remaining to be discovered. Many questions need answering: what was the nature of the political system of the kingdom, what degree of social complexity did it reach, will we ever fully translate its written language, Meroitic, and hence learn more of its history?

We know, at least, that Napatan and Meroitic history is closely intertwined with that of contemporary Egypt, especially in the Napatan period. The latter begins about 860 B.C., with the earliest tombs of Kurru (see chapter 5); all its rulers were buried near Napata (hence the term "Napatan") until, in about 250 B.C., the royal cemetery was transferred to Meroe.

Egypt, contemporary with Napatan times, underwent many vicissitudes. After 1000 B.C. it gradually fragmented into some eleven small states, and then experienced the period of rule from Napata, about 750–660 B.C. When this ended, Egypt reunited under an indigenous Egyptian dynasty, the 26th, only to become part of the Persian Empire from 525 to 404 B.C. Briefly independent again, Egypt was recaptured by Persia in 343 B.C.

The Napatan state, ruled in succession by some forty kings, combined together Southern[1] and Upper Nubia, and much of Lower Nubia. As we have seen, from pharaohs Kashta to Tanwetamani, Nubia also controlled first much, then all, of Egypt, thus creating the largest state ever found along the Lower Nile in ancient and medieval times.

Egypt's Napatan rulers vigorously resisted Assyrian efforts to invade first the Southern Levant (a traditionally Egyptian sphere of influence), and then Egypt itself. Securely in control of Egypt, the Napatans did not try to restore full Egyptian unity, for an Egypt politically reintegrated might well turn against its Nubian conquerors. Finally, however, in part because of Assyrian pressure, the Nubians relinquished Egypt.

Once this happened, the status of Lower Nubia becomes uncertain. Although now very thinly settled, its key centers nevertheless remained populated, but by whom? Some suggest that places like Ibrim (in the center of Lower Nubia) were held continuously by Napata into the first century B.C.; but others argue that all Lower Nubia was dominated first by the 26th Dynasty, and then Persian-held Egypt, until 500 B.C.[2] By 400 B.C. at least,

Napatan forces seem to have ranged freely in Lower Nubia, but soon, a little before the end of Napatan times, the Egyptian situation changed yet again.

Alexander the Great ended the Persian occupation of Egypt in 332 B.C., and it soon became ruled by a Greek-speaking, Macedonian Dynasty (the Ptolemaic, 304–30 B.C.) founded by one of Alexander's generals. Some scholars think that by 270 B.C. Ptolemy II controlled northern Lower Nubia, from Aswan to Maharraqa, a region named the *Dodeka-schoenos*, or "Twelve Schoeni," by Ptolemy's Greek-speaking officials. That the Ptolemies held all Lower Nubia, as some believe, is unlikely.[3]

The Meroitic period, following the Napatan, was very long, some 600 years (250 B.C.–A.D. 350); for this period, we know of some fifty-seven kings, as well as a few reigning queens. Their annals were kept in Meroitic, a native language for the writing of which an alphabet was invented by 100 B.C. (earlier, the Napatans used Egyptian, and Egyptian hieroglyphs, at least for their monumental inscriptions). Meroitic as yet is only partly decipherable; the longest and most important inscriptions remain untranslated.

Contemporary Egypt was first Ptolemaic, then Roman. It became a Roman province in 30 B.C. as a result of Rome's imperial expansion; after A.D. 330 (after the Roman Empire had become divided in two) Egypt was ruled from Constantinople, capital of the Eastern Roman Empire.

The Meroitic kingdom was perhaps even larger than the Napatan. It included Southern and Upper Nubia, and *may* also have annexed the "Gezira" ("Island"), that is, the Blue and White Niles and the territory between them. Sites partly or largely Meroitic in culture extend along the Blue Nile as far south as Sennar, about 300 kilometers upstream of Nubia, and the same might be true of the White Nile, although this remains to be proved. Certainly, the people of the Gezira were at least strongly influenced by Meroe, and probably dominated by it, even if the Gezira was not formally integrated into the kingdom.

In northern Nubia, as before, the situation was complicated. The Meroites generally had good relations with Ptolemaic Egypt, although they may have intermittently occupied the Dodekaschoenos, normally held by Egypt, but relations with Rome were initially hostile. Rome claimed all Lower Nubia as a client-state, provoking a Meroitic attack on Aswan in Egypt, in turn followed by a Roman counterattack that reached as far south as Napata. After further hostilities, peace was made in 21/20 B.C., and was sustained over a very long period.

The Dodekaschoenos continued to belong to Roman Egypt, while the rest of Lower Nubia became increasingly important to the Meroites. By the first century B.C. it was ruled by a governor (*peshto*) based at Faras; later, the regional capital shifted to Karanog (Meroitic Nalote; see chapter 7). By A.D. 200 settlement in both Roman and Meroitic Lower Nubia had become dense. Most of the Dodekaschoenos' inhabitants were in fact probably Nubian (and Roman and Meroitic officials collaborated in their governance), but they adopted a Romano-Egyptian culture very different from that of Meroitic Lower Nubia.

So far as outstanding issues in Napatan-Meroitic studies are concerned, all scholars agree that a much more representative range of sites needs to be excavated if we are to have a full picture of Nubian society, and the changes it experienced over time. Even the two chief centers, Napata and Meroe, are only partially excavated. With regard to mortuary remains, the royal cemeteries near Napata and Meroe, and to some extent the elite cemeteries of the latter, are relatively well known; Lower Nubian cemeteries provide a good sample of its population, but elsewhere few cemeteries of the period have been excavated. Although excellent studies of the extant material are being produced, they increasingly point up the excavational deficiencies I have just listed.

Other major issues are much more contentious. For example, some scholars argue that the Meroitic state at least was poorly integrated politically, despite its formal recognition of a single ruler. Thus William Adams suggests that we may "have to envisage a semi-autonomous feudal principality comprising both the Napatan [Upper Nubian] and Lower Nubian provinces of the Meroitic empire."[4] Others, however, think that centralization was more of a reality, an opinion with which I agree; as Trigger suggests, provincial officials perhaps "enjoyed a normal relationship to their superiors."[5]

The nature of the "fall" of Meroe, the collapse of both state and civilization, also stimulates divergent opinions. In the most dramatic versions, an already decaying kingdom was dealt a deathblow by an invasion (ca. A.D. 350) led by King Aezanas of Axum, a neighboring state located in what was to become

Abyssinia (today called Ethiopia). But one scholar has suggested that the inscriptions describing Aezanas' campaigns may refer to "purely local border raids within Ethiopia,"[6] and had no effect on Meroe. Today, as we learn more about the several successor kingdoms into which the great kingdom fragmented after A.D. 350, it is becoming clearer that Meroitic civilization did not "die," but rather underwent a transformation in which strong continuities from Meroitic times existed. Nevertheless, the causes of this transformation remain obscure, and require investigation.

Perhaps most contentious of all is the significance of "Egyptianization," of acculturation to some important aspects of Egyptian culture on the part of Napatans and Meroites. Was Napatan-Meroitic civilization dependent upon periodic stimuli from Egypt, or was it an internally stimulated phenomenon, albeit one incorporating some powerful Egyptian influences? We will return to this issue later.

## The Land and Its People

However elaborate its superstructure of government, the basic resource of any state is its land and people. Napatan and Meroitic society was essentially a riverine one, extending from central Lower Nubia to modern Khartoum, and perhaps along the Blue and White Niles upstream of the latter. However, Napatan and Meroitic sites are not found east or west of the Nile, except in the western Butana (the Butana being the region between the Nile and Atbara rivers). Although future discoveries may alter this perception, it seems that the semidesert

and savannah lands, as well as the whole Atbara River region, lay outside the frontiers of the kingdom.

Even so, the Napatan-Meroitic kingdom evidently encompassed very different environments, and hence peoples of different subsistence and surplus producing economies, and of different life-styles. In the south, the Gezira had a higher rainfall than the north, permitting "seasonal shifting agriculture throughout the whole region," a mix of cultivation and intensive herding along the White Nile, and "extensive agriculture" and "widespread animal husbandry" along the Blue Nile.[7]

The Nubian Nile proper, from the Sixth Cataract to central Lower Nubia, was primarily agricultural in economy. Simple irrigation methods linked to the annual Nile flood kept the numerous "basins" (low-lying depressions away from the river, but still subject to flooding) agriculturally productive, although animal raising was also quite important. Lower Nubia, as we have seen, was something of a special case. Its Meroitic southern two-thirds became densely settled only in the second and third centuries B.C. Throughout Lower Nubia extensive use was made of the animal-powered water-wheel (*saquia*), which enhanced agricultural productivity. Whether *saquias* were used elsewhere in Nubia is uncertain, but they may not have been as necessary as they were in Lower Nubia.

This sketch, based on modern analogies as well as (a very incomplete) archaeology, leads to an important conclusion: as in Egypt, the Napatan-Meroitic kingdom's prosperity depended on agriculture, supplemented by animal herding.[8] This economy must have produced a substantial surplus, for society was complex in itself, and supported an elite class as well as a state organization with a full panoply of kingship, bureaucracy, priesthood, and military. Trading, and warfare for purposes of plunder (and perhaps slaving, although this is doubtful), increased the wealth of the state and its elite. But much of the government's activity must have involved the collection and redistribution of revenue in cereals, other foods, and livestock; ownership or use of land could have been the elite's most significant asset, in terms of both income and status.

Napatan-Meroitic society was probably not homogeneous, but neither was contemporary Egypt's, with its growing Greek minority and Roman garrisons. We have little clear-cut information on ethnicity in the Napatan-Meroitic kingdom, but on the linguistic side we know that even in Napatan times the elite probably spoke Meroitic, a language not written down until the second century B.C. Yet, by Christian times (chapter 8) Nubian, a language different from Meroitic, was spoken throughout Nubia, and its existence has been detected as early as the Late Bronze Age. Did Meroitic and Nubian speakers share the Nubian Nile? And what was the ethnic and linguistic status of the Gezira, which interacted with the great kingdom, and may have belonged to it?

On the other hand, Napatan-Meroitic society was homogeneous in that it probably did not include nomads among its subjects. Nomads are notoriously difficult for a state based on sedentary agriculture to control, and those flanking Nubia were in any case possibly too powerful and well organized to be easily subjugated. According to modern analogies, Kordofan on the west and the Butana on the east were likely traversed by nomads, but we have not yet found Napatan-Meroitic sites occurring in either region.

One ecological niche, however—the western Butana, adjoining the region of Meroe—was not used by nomadic herdsmen because it lay outside the Butana's clay plains and their seasonally rich grass cover. This niche was exploited by the Meroites (and perhaps Napatans). They grazed animals and grew crops on the fertile soils of its shallow valleys (wadis). Along these wadis (which all opened up onto the Meroe region) a number of settlements, as well as sometimes imposing temples, developed, their water needs met in part by large artificial pools (*hafirs*). The whole pattern suggests a government-organized exploitation of the western Butana, as does the archaeology of its southern and southwestern edges. Stretching along these is a line of Meroitic settlements and *hafirs* that may mark and defend the frontier between the nomads and the western Butana, which in effect could also act as a buffer for Meroe itself. Indeed, just south of this apparent frontier a rock inscription at Gebel Qeili celebrates the victory of King Shorkaror (A.D. 20–30) over unnamed enemies who—given the geographical context—were probably nomads.[9]

Finally, we can even suggest how this diverse society was organized in terms of governance, at least in Meroitic times. Government was a centralized hierarchy structured according to the geographical regions described above. The pharaoh resided at Meroe, governing Southern Nubia directly or through an appointed representative. Lower and Upper Nubia were separate provinces, both overseen by the *peker* (a titular, rather than actual "crown prince"), an official based at Napata who reported to the pharaoh at Meroe. The *peker* may have directly controlled Upper Nubia, but Lower Nubia was administered by his representative, the *peshto,* or governor. If the Gezira was also part of the kingdom, it too probably had its own governor (or governors, one for the White Nile, the other for the Blue), appointed or at least confirmed in office by the Meroitic pharaoh.

The infrastructure of each province perhaps consisted of towns and their districts, each headed by a mayor or equivalent official. This is the model suggested by the relatively well-known administration of Lower Nubia, but some scholars find this assumption unwarranted.

## The Kingship

Most of our information about Napatan-Meroitic kingship comes from scenes and texts on temple walls (Fig. 6.1, 6.3), and triumphal stelae set up near temples to record the benefits king and god reciprocally present each other. These sources present the king as political leader, warlord, and chief ritualist of the kingdom; but how real was this apparently total power?

In some African and other states royal power was substantially limited by a "Council of Nobles," which could intervene decisively in the royal succession and condemn the ruler to commit suicide "on all sorts of pretexts." Even the divinization of the king could "complete his isolation from temporal matters

by locking him in an illusory omnipotence."[10] However, rulers could seek greater independence, by building their own bureaucracy and establishing an army loyal to them, not any other institution, although the good will of the military toward the king might then become an important factor.

In Napatan times the latter situation seems the case (as if dependence on a "council" had existed, but had been ended). Whether this was also true in Meroitic times remains unknown, since the possibly relevant texts are untranslatable.

The Napatan succession was a relatively stable process, in that a rule of succession existed. Not matrilineal, as often thought, but rather patrilineal, it decreed that the heir normally had to be a son of a paternal brother of the deceased king.[11] However, this created not just one candidate, but rather a "pool" of candidates, from whom the "army" (i.e., army leaders?) chose the next king. Their choice had to be ratified in some way by the state god Amun, a process over which the priests might have had some influence. Sometimes, circumstances required exceptions to or deviations from the norm, as when the "best" or most powerful choice did not belong to the pool.[12]

Once in place, the Napatan or Meroitic king seems to have enjoyed considerable power, insofar as we can tell from the limited sources. The gods, and hence their priesthoods, were dependent on the king for the building of temples, the supply of cult items, and the allotment of lands and personnel to provide subsistence and income to the temple establishments. The bureaucracy, both central and provincial, was at least formally

**Fig. 6.1**
*A Meroitic royal personage, depicted on the pylon of his
funerary chapel, near Meroe. From C. R. Lepsius,*
Denkmaler aus Aegypten und Aethiopien, *vol. x.
Berlin: Nicolaische Buchandlung [1849–1856] bl. 49.)*

responsive to the royal will, although scholars
argue as to how effective this really was. And
warfare, an important feature of the Napatan-
Meroitic state, was very much under royal control; the ruler sometimes led his forces into war,
or at other times issued their orders. Military
power would then have reinforced royal
authority in other spheres of government.

These at times large-scale military
campaigns could sometimes involve Egypt. Most
spectacular was Piye's campaign, upon which
Napatan control of Egypt was based, and which
revealed the Nubian forces to be both highly
aggressive and highly skilled, as did the
Napatans' later conflicts with the Assyrians
prior to the relinquishment of Egypt. Later,

Aswan in southernmost Egypt was twice attacked, first because rebellious officials of a Napatan ruler took refuge there, and later because it was the Roman base for military operations against the Meroites.

The Napatans, and presumably Meroites, also clashed periodically with nomadic peoples, the Blemmyes (Meded), east of Lower and Upper Nubia, and the Adadas (Rehrehs), east of Southern Nubia. The former on occasion raided riverine towns, plundering their temples, and also interfered with an important desert trade route linking Southern Nubia to Egypt. The Adadas were even more aggressive, periodically invading Southern Nubia—possibly seeking land upon which to settle, or power over tribute-paying peasants—and having to be driven off by Napatan armies. The Meroitic expansion into the western Butana, described above, may have been intended to buffer Southern Nubia against such pressure.

The most spectacular Napatan campaigns, however, are also the most enigmatic, for the locations of the regions involved remain uncertain. As recorded under the pharaoh Nastasen (335–315 B.C.), these "foreign lands" were to some degree centrally organized, for each had a *wer,* or ruler, and the plunder from them typically included women (over 2000 in one case); gold, sometimes in large amounts; and enormous numbers of cattle and other domesticated animals, a grand total of almost two million. The nomadic regions east and west of Southern Nubia were unlikely to support so many animals, yet the regions involved must have been reasonably accessible for so many animals to be driven into Nubian territory. It is

likely, then, that these are chiefdoms or even proto-states located within the Gezira, which must have been accumulating wealth through trading in cattle and perhaps other products (ivory, ebony, etc.?). Afterward, the Meroites were likely to have continued raiding (as well as trading with) such a productive area or even, as we have seen, incorporated it within the kingdom.

Art and archaeology inform us about the life-styles of Napatan and Meroitic royalty. The kings wore distinctive clothing and regalia (Figures 6.1, 6.3), at first—in the Napatan period—closely following the traditional Egyptian model, but later a more original ensemble. The king wore a close-fitting white robe with—in the earlier Meroitic period—a cloak worn over it. Often a fringed shawl in red material was worn over the right shoulder, and had two or more tassels on long bands. The origins of these items were complex, and aspects of Ptolemaic royal dress were incorporated within it for a period. When the pharaoh is shown in a more active role, such as overthrowing enemies, he wears usually a knee-length kilt and, once, body armor probably made of leather, although metal would also be possible.

There were a variety of crowns, some modeled after those of the Egyptian pharaoh, but a distinctive favorite was a caplike head covering with two uraei (sacred cobras) decorating it. Napatan-Meroitic rulers also displayed a rich array of heavily modeled jewelry, including earrings, neck ornaments bearing ram's heads (emblematic of the god Amun), and armlets. When armed, the pharaoh carried bow and arrows, a sword slung in a scabbard hanging across his back, and a spear.

**Fig. 6.2**
*A Royal Cemetery near Meroe.*
*(From: C.R. Lepsius,* Denkmaler aus Aegypten und
Aethiopien, *vol. X. Berlin: Nicolaische Buchandlung
[1849–1856], bl. 138.)*

Neither the town of Napata, nor the city of Meroe (occupying about 1 square mile, or almost 259 hectares), has been fully excavated. However, it is clear that at both there were not only large temples, but clusters of palaces, usually in the vicinity of some of the temples. These palaces were often square in plan, somewhat like the smaller palaces of the *peshtos* at Karanog in Lower Nubia (see chapter 7), but the details of their internal layout is as yet poorly known.

Best known of the royal monuments are the kings' tombs, grouped first near Napata and later Meroe (Fig. 6.2). The superstructure was always pyramidal (with, however, a flat rather than pointed top), built either of stone masonry or, after A.D. 50, red brick or rubble covered with white plaster. Queens, princes, nobles, and even commoners were also buried under pyramids, with an attached chapel like that found with royal tombs. However, only the royal chapels had pylon gateways. Even the royal tombs were relatively small compared to Egyptian royal pyramids (which are all much earlier in date) and more steeply angled. The largest royal pyramid occupied less than 850 square meters, the smallest about 50 square meters.

In chambers below the pyramid the royal body and a rich array of equipment and gifts were placed. Unfortunately, none survived intact, although some important surviving artifacts from both Napatan and Meroitic royal tombs have been recovered.

## Gods and Goddesses of Nubia

However important the king was in the social hierarchy of Napatan-Meroitic Nubia, the global picture or world view of the Nubians was dominated by a pantheon of gods and goddesses. Certainly, the king had a unique relationship to these powerful beings, and is the only human ever shown, in temples at least, as performing the cult for them. However, in contrast to Egyptian ideas about kingship, it seems that "the Meroitic ruler held his office by virtue of what he was rather than what he did for the gods."[13]

The Nubians' deities must have been seen as responsible for the birth and maintenance of the cosmos, as well as for specialized and individualized roles within that cosmos. The pantheon itself will probably increase in number as new evidence is uncovered, but it is clear by now that four deities dominated Nubian religion. In the funerary realm, Osiris and Isis; and in the temple cult, Isis, Aman, and Apedemak. All except the last are of Egyptian origin, yet they probably took on a distinctively Nubian character.

The principal cult centers of Isis, Aman (i.e., Amun, in Egyptian terms), and Apedemak in effect defined the geographical extent of the kingdom. Isis temples occurred throughout Nubia, but her chief shrine was on Philae Island, near Aswan in Egyptian territory. Philae was a tremendously popular place of pilgrimage for Nubians as much as Egyptians, and Meroites were in fact deeply involved both in its cult and in the administration of its temple estates.

Aman had many forms. A popular one was Amanape, but many Nubian towns had their own particular Aman. His cult, therefore, was quite widespread, and at Meroe itself was honored by a massive temple as large as that of Gebel Barkal, near Napata, his other chief cult center. However, historically Aman was strongly associated with central, or Upper, Nubia, where his cult had first been implanted by the Egyptians during the colonial period (see chapter 5).

Isis and Aman are usually shown as fully human in form, but Apedemak often has a lion's head (Fig. 6.3). His cult occurred throughout Nubia, but so far as present evidence goes, all his important temples were in Southern Nubia, at places like Meroe, Naqa, and Musawaret el Sufra.

Other important deities are known. They include some who were Egyptian in origin, like Horus and Mut, but others are Nubian, like the god Mash, whose cult in fact is so far found at only one place, Karanog (see chapter 7). Two particularly important gods, if of "second rank," were "hunter-gods and deities of the desert,"[14] Arensnuphis and Sebiumeker. They are usually represented together, as guardian statues in front of temples. Arensnuphis may be Egyptian, Sebiumeker Nubian in origin.

**Fig. 6.3**
*A representation of the Nubian god Apedemak (far left) on a temple wall at Naga. Facing him are members of the Meroitic royal family, with the king in front.*
*(From: C.R. Lepsius,* Denkmaler aus Aegypten und Aethiopien, *vol. X. Berlin: Nicolaische Buchandlung [1849–1856], bl. 62.)*

Temples were frequently being built and rebuilt throughout Nubia; some were at or near the great cities, but temples may also have been found in relatively small villages, like that of Meinarti in Lower Nubia.[15]

The larger temples are the better known, and are usually of two types. One is "Egyptian" in form: rectangular in plan, it has a pylon, forecourt, columned offering hall, and a sanctuary at the rear, surrounded by small chambers. The other is peculiar to Nubia: its basic form is of a single, square chamber with a

pylon entrance. This "Nubian"-style temple was probably built for many gods, but it associates strongly with Apedemak, the lion god, and resonates faintly with Nubia's remote past.

At Middle Bronze Age Kerma (see chapters 3 and 4) one of the funerary temples in the royal cemetery had large blue faience lions (reminiscent of Apedemak's status as a lion god) inlaid in its facade[16]; and *all* the "temples" of Kerma (K XI, II, and I) had stairways to their roofs, which may have served as open-air, sunlit cult venues. Apedemak temples apparently also permitted more sunlight to enter than did the "Egyptian" temple type. These slight indications suggest that Apedemak was not only Nubian in origin but may have deep roots in the Nubian past.

It has been suggested that, prior to the colonial period and the appearance of Egyptian gods in Nubia, the Bronze Age Nubians themselves had no specific gods of their own. This seems a priori unlikely; and in fact, as we have seen, Kerma had a substantial temple, indicative of a god's cult, from the Early Bronze Age onward. If more Bronze Age settlements are excavated, they too will likely have temples of some kind, and provide for Napatan-Meroitic gods a kind of "prehistory."

Their gods were probably quite important to the Napatans and Meroites in general, not just to their kings and priests. So far, no evidence for domestic cult places has been found, but many pious graffiti were scratched on temple walls and pylons, or at "sacred places" out in the countryside, by visitors evidently of low status; moreover, a number of personal names invoke the presence of a specific deity, or of an anonymous "god" likely to be the town or village god of the person in question.

## Egypt and Nubia
### in Napatan-Meroitic Times

A subject only referred to indirectly so far is of great importance for Napatan-Meroitic Nubia, namely, its apparently strong acculturation to Egyptian norms. We have already seen that many of Nubia's gods were Egyptian in origin, and its art—the scenes on temple and funerary chapel walls, for example—is evidently Egyptian in some of its stylistic aspects. It follows closely the conventions of Egyptian art, and the dress and regalia worn by gods, kings, and others is often modeled on Egyptian prototypes.

Moreover, periodic "waves" of influence from Egypt can be detected throughout Napatan-Meroitic times, and some scholars have correlated these with major new initiatives evident in Nubia culture. The products of such influence might have distinctive Nubian attributes, it is suggested, but they nevertheless required stimuli from Egypt to come about. Without such stimuli, Napatan-Meroitic culture tended to stagnate and degenerate, for Nubians could not find such stimuli within their own society and ideology.

These scholarly notions of stagnation, degeneration, and stimuli are evidently laden with values and preconceptions that are not really appropriate. Nubian culture, whether in Napatan-Meroitic times or earlier in the Bronze Age, often takes on forms unfamiliar to scholars conversant with ancient Egyptian culture. However, as I emphasized when discussing the Bronze Age, this unfamiliarity may encourage us to underestimate what was happening in terms of political, ideological, and other developments among the Nubians. Nubian achievement must be estimated in its own terms, via the evidence supplied by Nubian archaeology and, increasingly in Napatan-Meroitic times, texts, not by reference to a misleading standard of comparison with some other, better-known culture.

This is not to deny that Napatan-Meroitic culture did absorb much from Egypt, in a variety of ways, the full complexity of which

# THE MEROITIC ALPHABET

| Hieroglyph | Cursive Letter | Phonetic Value | Hieroglyph | Cursive Letter | Phonetic Value |
|---|---|---|---|---|---|
| 🖼 | ꟼ2 | a | 🖼 | 4 | l |
| ꟼ or 🖼 | ꟼ or / | e | 🖼 | ᐸ | kh |
| 🖼 | 4 | i | 🖼 | 3 | kh |
| 𐤖𐤖 | /// | y | ♯ | ⫽ | s |
| 🖼 | ∂ | w | 🖼 | 3 | sh |
| 🖼 | ᐯ | b | 🖼 | 3 | k |
| ⊞ | ⋜ | p | △ | /Ɔ | q |
| 🖼 | 3 | m | 🖼 | ȶ | t(i) |
| ≋ | ᴙ | n | 🖼 | /ȶ | te |
| 🖼 | ⋏ | ñ(i) | 🖼 | ᴗ | te |
| ⊟ | ⱳ | r | 🖼 | ⱬ | z |

**Fig. 6.4**
*The Meroitic alphabet (Adapted from F. Ll. Griffith, Karanog.*
The Meroitic Inscriptions of Shablul and Karanog.
*Philadelphia: The University Museum [1911] p. 11.)*

will not be realized for a long time. But we must place this interaction within a context that at least contributes to an understanding of its effects upon the Nubians, and also reminds us that these effects were, in the final analysis, quite limited.

First, in Napatan-Meroitic times intercommunication up and down the Lower Nile, between Egypt and Nubia, was developed to a degree unequaled in their mutual histories. That Napatans and Meroites were sensitive to developments in Egypt at many levels—religious and political ideology, art styles, and artifact types—is therefore not surprising. The interaction between Egypt and Nubia was particularly strong for historical reasons, but it was also part of a broader phenomenon. The contemporary Hellenistic and Roman periods were a time in which aspects of Egypt were often much admired throughout the eastern Mediterranean, and symbiosis between Egyptian and other cultures manifested itself in a number of ways. The Greeks resident in Egypt, including the Ptolemaic rulers themselves, became Egyptianized to a significant degree while yet maintaining a distinctively "Greek" culture, and in Roman times—among other things—the cult of Isis became widespread in Italy and elsewhere.

Second, the important ways in which Nubia manifested its cultural independence of Egypt should not be overlooked. These are manifold, if sometimes subtle. For example, the royal pyramids of Napata and Meroe descend from, I have suggested above, an almost purely indigenous Nubian line of tomb development. The Egyptian connotation of the pyramid of course was a reality, but in fact Egyptian pharaohs had not been buried under pyramids for centuries at the time the pyramid emerged as the chosen type of Nubian royal tomb; hence, in effect the process attests to a selective and indeed original attitude toward Egyptian culture.

Many other examples could be cited. Nubian religion was not monopolized by Egyptian deities, as we have seen, and even its Egyptian deities could be said to have been "Nubianized," to have gained histories, regional associations, and roles peculiar to Nubia and not their Egyptian homeland. In art, basic conventions may have been Egyptian, but in style and content it became distinctively Nubian, especially in Meroitic times. Perhaps most importantly, the Nubians retained their own language, rather than adopting Egyptian (although many Nubians must have been bilingual in Egyptian and their own tongue); eventually, they invented an alphabet (based on Egyptian hieroglyphs!) so that a Nubian language could be fully employed in all aspects of life—religion, ideology, administration, and business. Imbedded in the Nubian language or languages, of course, was a very particular and specifically Nubian world view, a whole range of important ideas about the supernatural, social organization, and the natural world that were very different from those of the Egyptians.

As I suggested earlier, it might be a useful idea to consider the Nubians' selective adaptation of certain Egyptian gods and ideas, of artistic conventions and artifact styles, of even—for a time—the Egyptian language and writing system (in Napatan times) as the discovery of a vocabulary through which the Nubians could express their world view in a way that had not been possible or desired throughout much of the Bronze Age. This process would have begun in the period of close contact, the colonial period of the Late Bronze Age, and been sustained and intensified by such experiences as the Nubian occupation of Egypt in the 25th Dynasty, and the close and often friendly relations between Egypt and Napatan-Meroitic Nubia.

The adoption of this vocabulary was not a simple process, and involved a degree of emulation on the Nubians' part. Yet over time it became transformed, as a medium of expression, into an increasingly Nubian phenomenon, most obviously by the invention of written Meroitic, but also in many other ways. This in itself testifies to the dominant role of internal Nubian dynamics, social and other, that ultimately shaped Nubian society and culture throughout their long history, and were to continue to do so in the future.

## CHAPTER SEVEN

# The People of Karanog

**W**ithin the Meroitic kingdom one community is exceptionally well documented, providing a uniquely detailed glimpse of Meroitic life not possible from any other source yet known. In this chapter, we focus on this community, the people of Karanog, the modern name for the Meroitic town of Nalote in Lower Nubia. Other locations have been suggested for Nalote, but this one seems to fit the available evidence best.

## Lower Nubia in Meroitic Times

As we have already seen, Egypt—first under the Ptolemies, and then the Romans—competed for a long time with the Meroitic state for the control of Lower Nubia. By about the time of the birth of Christ, this situation stabilized, with Lower Nubia divided between the two powers. The *Triakontaschoenos*, the land of the "Thirty Schoeni" (*schoenus* was a measure of length equaling about 8.7 English miles), as Lower Nubia was called in the bureaucratic Greek of contemporary Egypt, was occupied in the north by a Roman province, the *Dodekaschoenos,* or the "Twelve Schoeni," with a southern frontier at modern Maharraqa; the rest was a province of the Meroitic kingdom. However, even in the Roman province the population was substantially Meroitic, for Meroitic settlements had been developing throughout Lower Nubia—hitherto largely empty since 1000 B.C.—since the second century B.C. In Meroitic Lower Nubia, settlement became increasingly dense in the second century A.D., with the process already well underway in the first.

Meroitic Lower Nubia flourished through the second and third centuries A.D., but in the fourth its political and social organization underwent large-scale change, and the distinctive Meroitic culture faded away. Its replacement, equally distinctive but very different, was the culture common (with some variations) to the kingdoms of the Blemmyes and the Nobatai, which respectively dominated the northern and southern parts of Lower Nubia. These are discussed in chapter 8. That the Meroitic culture of the region should end is not surprising, for it was an integral part of the Meroitic kingdom as a whole, which, by about A.D. 370, had also, for different reasons, "collapsed."

The status of Meroitic Lower Nubia is still a matter of debate among scholars. For example, here I shall identify the province's name as Akin, but there is not general agreement on this. More importantly, some scholars see Akin, or Meroitic Lower Nubia, as a region that enjoyed great political and economic autonomy within the Meroitic kingdom; in this view, royal control over the province from faraway Meroe was loose and weak. However, there are good reasons for thinking that Meroitic royal government was a fairly highly integrated and strongly centralized system, of which Akin, under royal control, was very much a part.

One reason for this notion is evidence from Akin itself indicating that its governance was part of a well-developed bureaucratic hierarchy that ultimately peaked in the royal capital. Since at least the first century B.C. Akin was ruled by a *peshto*, or governor. The *peshto*

reported to a superior official, the *peker*, whose headquarters lay at Napata, in Upper Nubia. In this perspective, then, Lower and Upper Nubia formed a single administrative entity, the *peker* directly administering the latter (unless there was also a *peshto* for Upper Nubia!) while his deputy, the *peshto*, managed Lower Nubia. However, in his turn the *peker* reported to the Meroitic pharaoh residing in Meroe, probably as did similar governors of the other provinces making up the Meroitic state. The titles involved themselves reflect the royal control of the system. *Peker* literally means "crown prince," and although in reality the actual heir to the throne may rarely have held this office, its title underlines its dependency on and service to the pharaoh; and *peshto* is derived from the Late Bronze Age title for the Egyptian viceroy of Nubia, the "king's son," again emphasizing the link to the king, in this case the Meroitic ruler. Even the provincial officials within Akin expressed in some of their titles and epithets their status as representatives of royal government.

A second indication of the efficiency of royal government within the Meroitic kingdom is the very complexity of the provincial government of Akin. The *peshto* exercised authority over both civil institutions and the temples, and he was assisted by a staff of officials; others ran the administration of the provincial temples and their probably substantial land-holdings, while each temple had its own priesthood, so closely linked to the rest of the bureaucracy that the temples too were part of the government. Finally, at the local level, individual towns and their districts each had their own mayor or headman with his own staff.

Given the complexity of structure, it is reasonable to suppose that comparable complexity would be found in the other regions of the kingdom and would characterize the upper as well as the lower levels of the administrative hierarchy of the state, even if we lack as yet the evidence to prove this.

The history of the Meroitic state also attests to the existence of an efficient royal government: without it, the kingdom could not have managed a large-scale society, collected substantial revenues, undertaken major building projects, and pursued an active, and when needed aggressive, foreign policy—all of which it seems to have done. There were cultural differences between Akin and the south, but this was probably common throughout the large and expansionistic Meroitic state; and such differences do not necessarily imply a weak form of royal government. It is also true that much of the bureaucracy of Akin was dominated by interrelated families whose claim upon offices may have been to some degree hereditary, and that these families profited from entrepreneurial activity, such as producing agricultural surplus from lands they owned or rented and engaging in trade with Roman Egypt as well as, perhaps, other parts of the Meroitic kingdom. However, very similar circumstances were found in Late Bronze Age Egypt, where they coexisted with a relatively efficient and centralized form of royal government;[1] and the same may have been the case in Meroitic Nubia.

Finally, the military situation in Akin also indicates how closely it was integrated with and dependent on royal government as a whole. Akin was Meroe's front line of defense against Roman Egypt, should the latter become hostile as it had been in the past; and, in addition, both Akin and the *Dodekaschoenos* were threatened by a powerful nomadic kingdom, that of the Blemmyes, located in the deserts to the east. One might then expect Akin to have bristled with fortified places and troop garrisons. In reality, military officials are rarely referred to in the otherwise well-documented bureaucracy, and most of Akin's towns and villages were not defended by fortifications, except for a few, strategically key positions. Evidently, Akin's security from attack depended upon the kingdom as a whole. A Meroitic intelligence service or early warning system extended up into Roman Nubia and throughout the eastern desert, and the Meroitic state was very capable of rapidly moving troops on a large scale to a threatened area. In 23 B.C., it should be remembered, a large Meroitic army, coming from south of Lower Nubia and reputedly 30,000 strong, took the Roman occupiers of the region (and within southernmost Egypt itself) completely by surprise. Up to that point, Rome had planned on Lower Nubia being ruled by a vassal king, and the Meroitic state becoming a Roman client-kingdom; she retaliated vigorously for the Meroitic attack, but also gave up these ideas and recognized Meroitic independence, which was based on Meroitic administrative capability and military strength.

Indeed, Meroitic strength was such that throughout the third century A.D., and probably earlier, Rome shared the administration and defense of Roman Nubia, the *Dodekaschoenos*, between Romano-Egyptian officials and troops, on the one hand, and a powerful cadre of Meroitic officials on the other. The latter had important military as well as administrative roles (unsurprisingly, since Roman Nubia and its gold-mining operations in the eastern desert had to be continuously defended against the Blemmyes), but they also represented the Meroitic king, for whom they must have been an important source of information on Roman Egypt and its intentions. In addition, the Meroitic ruler himself periodically sent envoys and missions to Roman Egypt, carrying out diplomacy at a higher level of negotiation.

Why was Akin important to the kingdom of Meroe? Several factors can account for this. By filling Lower Nubia with farmers, and providing it with an efficient government, the Meroites ensured that no empty or poorly organized zone existed into which Roman Nubia might be tempted to expand. Moreover, Akin's arable lands, combined with the larger holdings in Upper Nubia, probably produced an agricultural surplus, especially as a newly introduced irrigation device—the animal-powered water wheel—made intensive and repeated cropping possible. Such a surplus could provide important revenue to a state that, unlike Ptolemaic or Roman Egypt, had a moneyless economy; in Meroe, as earlier in Bronze Age Egypt, grain would have been a basic "currency," used to pay wages and supply rations to the employees and dependents of the state.

Akin's position in the general trading network, both internal and external, of the Meroitic state was probably also important. Akin certainly imported substantially from Roman Egypt, securing luxury items, such as glass and bronze vessels, but also wines and oils in bulk; in return, it may have exported part of its own surplus of grain and dates. But Akin was also in the classic position of the middleman: it could pass imports on to Upper Nubia and Meroe itself, and in turn transfer southern products—for example, woods, ivory, agricultural produce, animal products, and, perhaps in bulk, cotton—on to Roman Egypt. Cotton was a major product of Meroe and cotton clothing was not unusual in Meroitic Lower Nubia, although not necessarily grown there; Roman Egypt, however, seems to have been still largely dependent on linen and wool, cotton not being grown extensively in Egypt until later. Such a trading system no doubt provided opportunities for private trading, but the domination of Akin by government officials indicates that the state—always needing to maintain and expand revenue—was also heavily involved; again, analogous situations can be found in Late Bronze Age Egypt.

It is true that the desert routes lying east of Nubia and directly linking Meroe city itself, and the Sudanese heartland, to Roman Egypt were also very active at this time. The introduction of the camel had much expanded their capacity as import and export routes as well as diplomatic and military links. However, desert routes also had problems: their aridity meant that transporting bulky materials would always be difficult, and the attacks by the Blemmyes and other nomads were a recurrent problem. Akin's very prosperity ensured that it would also be part of the trading system, and the riverine route it possessed was more secure, and more attractive for the movement of trade in bulk, despite the interruptions to continuous travel presented by a series of cataracts between Akin and Meroe. Through canalization, portage, and the use of short routes overland, these barriers to movement had been efficiently circumvented since the Middle Bronze Age, centuries before Meroe came into being.

## The Pattern of Settlement and the Region of Nalote

The archaeology of Meroitic Lower Nubia, although never fully recovered, is richly documented and reveals a pattern of settlement that fits the picture sketched above of a province closely integrated into the national system of government.

Lower Nubia consists of three agriculturally productive zones, separated from one another by long, agriculturally poor, and usually thinly settled stretches of the river valley. The northernmost zone was the core of Roman Nubia; the southernmost contained, at Faras (Meroitic Pachoras), the earlier capital of Akin. However, this capital was later transferred to the centrally located fertile zone, and was established at the site called Karanog today and identified in this book as Meroitic Nalote. The officials who resided here, including the *peshto* of Akin, were buried in a cemetery some 4.5 km upstream. Its surprising distance from Nalote has prompted some to suggest that the capital was not at Karanog but at modern Aniba, a site occupied in the Bronze Age and closer to the cemetery. However, Karanog or Nalote was a substantial Meroitic town, which must have generated a cemetery somewhere, yet none is to be found in its immediate vicinity, or between it

and the cemetery in question. In contrast, no trace of Meroitic occupation has ever been found at Aniba itself. Moreover, the uniquely designed palaces of the *peshtos are* identifiable at Karanog town, as we shall see below, a further indication that the cemetery they were buried in serviced this town specifically. Nalote or Karanog appears to have served as capital throughout much of the second and third centuries A.D.

The settlement pattern within the Nalote region and its environs must be reconstructed by reference mainly to its cemeteries, more often located and excavated than the towns they serviced. If we conclude that each major cemetery reflects the nearby presence of a large town and its satellite agricultural villages, then we begin to see how settlement was organized so as to meet both local and national needs.

The central fertile zone, or Nalote region, was separated from Roman Nubia by an agriculturally poor stretch, but archaeology reveals a surprisingly high number of Meroitic settlements distributed along this stretch, some of them (judging by their cemeteries) rather large, and run by resident officials. The inference is that their food supplies were provided by the state, via the administration of Akin, and that they served significant functions for the kingdom. These towns linking Akin and the frontier could certainly have facilitated the economically and diplomatically important river traffic between the Meroitic state and Egypt, but they could also have served to monitor conditions in Roman Nubia and act as early-warning stations should the latter become hostile. In all of these roles, the towns were aided greatly by the Meroitic cadre present in Roman Nubia itself, and were probably linked to that cadre. The latter was dominated by a large family, the Wayikeyes, some of whom at least chose to be buried just south of the frontier, near one of the Meroitic towns in question.

Within the fertile zone, the Nalote region itself, we find (according largely to the cemeteries) only four major clusters of settlement along its roughly 22-km-long stretch. The spacing between these clusters was fairly evenly spaced, on the average about 3.5 km, in reality sometimes between 4.5 and 5.1 km. This distinctive patterning may reflect two factors: first, the Meroites of Akin were urbanized, and liked to live in or near to substantial towns; and second, these towns were carefully spaced out so that each would have the appropriately sized agricultural hinterland it needed to feed and supply its population, and provide rations, estates, and farms for the resident officials, priests, and other state dependents.

Nalote was located at about the center of this zone, as one might expect from its role as administrative center of its region as well as of Akin as a whole. Another major area of settlement was at the upstream end of the zone, around and facing (on the opposite bank) the site of Qasr Ibrim, Meroitic Pedeme. This site's importance was both religious and military. Since Napatan times its high hilltop had supported temples, which grew in number and importance. It had also been fortified—the Romans had to take it in 23 B.C. when they retaliated against Meroe's attack on them. The strategic significance of Pedeme was varied. It could be rapidly reinforced by military contingents from farther south, and troops from Pedeme could move north to defend Akin and even invade Roman Nubia or strike out eastward into the desert should the Blemmyes or others threaten the desert trade routes or attempt to raid Akin itself. Certainly, any force invading Meroe from the north would be halted by the need to besiege and capture Ibrim, giving the Meroitic ruler the chance to mobilize and dispatch additional forces to the north. In these circumstances, we might guess that the large population living opposite Ibrim (itself a rather small town in area) included many troops and their officers; the priests, administrators, and personnel of Pedeme's temples; and the large agricultural population they needed to feed. The relevant west bank cemetery contained hundreds of graves (it was never fully excavated), but unfortunately it was severely plundered, and no inscriptional material identifying the officials and priests buried there survived.

Upstream of Pedeme arable land shrank again (although a significant population existed in the regions of modern Masmas and Toshka) until the southern fertile zone was reached. Here, the general pattern of settlement was similar to that of the Nalote region, with a major central place at Faras or Pachoras, the former capital. There was even another major hilltop site, Gebel Adda—Meroitic Ado—which was a sacred place and, somewhat later than Qasr Ibrim, was also fortified, probably to guard Akin against Blemmye attacks from the east. Members of the Wayikeye family of Roman Nubia were settled here, perhaps because their military expertise was needed for the new fort.

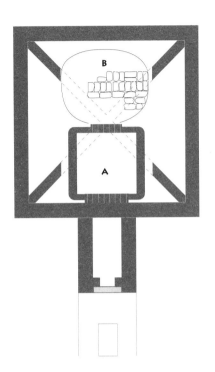
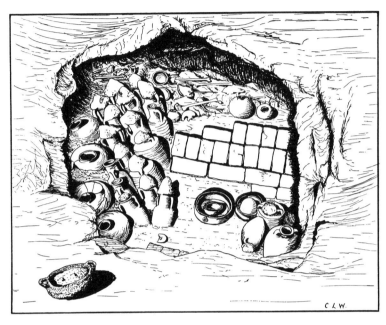

**Fig. 7.1**
*The plan of a tomb at Karanog (G 187), as recorded by Leonard Woolley.*
*(From: C.L. Woolley and D. Randall-MacIver,* Karanog: The Romano-Nubian Cemetery, *Text. Philadelphia: University Museum of the University of Pennsylvania [1910], fig. D.)*

## Karanog/Nalote: The Town and Its Cemetery

Between 1907 and 1910, David Randall-MacIver and Leonard Woolley completely excavated the cemetery of Karanog (Fig. 7.1) and selected parts of the town on behalf of The University Museum, University of Pennsylvania, which now has in its collection the bulk of the Karanog material; the remainder is in the Egyptian Museum, Cairo. Their observations show that Nalote town was an impressive one by Lower Nubian standards. Three of its four sides were located, defining an area of about 4 hectares (about 11 acres); the remainder had been cut away by a change in the river's course, so originally the town might have occupied 6 or 8 hectares (15.0–19.5 acres; Fig. 7.2). Unfortunately, comparisons with other towns are difficult, because they have rarely been fully defined in Nubia. However, Buhen—a much earlier Egyptian fortified town near the Second Cataract—occupied 6.3 hectares (15.5 acres), which were never fully occupied. Upper Nubia had more arable land and supported larger populations and towns; Kawa, occupied in

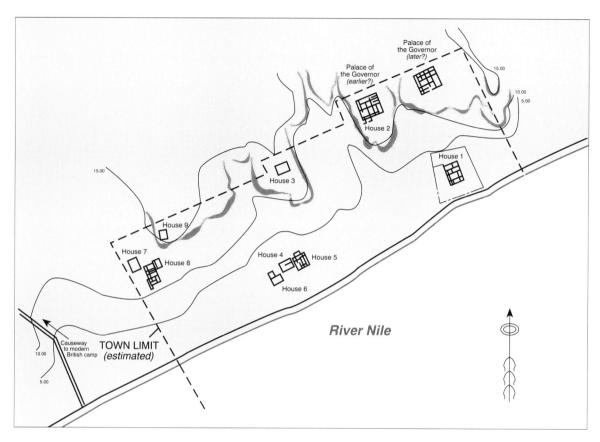

**Fig. 7.2**
*Map of Karanog town, insofar as excavated by Randall-MacIver and Woolley.*

Meroitic times as well as earlier, covered about 17 hectares (42 acres) and hence was 2 or 4 times larger than Nalote. The royal city of Meroe itself, farther south, was much larger, at perhaps 260 hectares (1 square mile), but it was probably a special case: in ancient states the royal capital was often much larger than any other town.

The buildings within Nalote were probably numerous and often densely concentrated. On the basis of their selective excavations, and of surface remains, the excavators suggested that the "town was one of narrow and irregular streets . . . that turned and twisted between houses two or three stories high which, though oriented regularly, were dotted here and there at random, having no uniform frontage." The town continued to be occupied, and was partially rebuilt, in post-Meroitic times, which further complicates the interpretive picture. There were probably many smaller, less solidly built structures filling the spaces between the larger ones, but surface traces of these would be much less obvious. All houses were of mud-brick, with a limited use of stone masonry.

**Fig. 7.3A**
*The distribution of chronologically significant artifacts in
Karanog cemetery; metal seal rings.*

Overlooking the town, on separate low bluffs, were two very substantial buildings, one of which remained remarkably well preserved into modern times. We shall return to them later.

The cemetery of Nalote, since it was completely excavated, provides a more comprehensive overview of the town's population over some two or three hundred years, but by no means all the actual bodies survived, for most tombs had been plundered, sometimes severely, and some bodies had largely or completely dis-appeared. From the 783 graves, 1124 skeletons were recovered, but the original number of bodies cannot be easily calculated. Of the 982 bodies that could be assigned an age or sex 35 percent were male and 44 percent female, which might have roughly reflected the real male-female ratio. Twenty-one percent were children, an unrealistically low figure; infant and child mortality must have been very high, so very young children may have been buried elsewhere or otherwise disposed of.

*Fig. 7.3B*
   *The distribution of chronologically significant artifacts in*
   *Karanog cemetery; ivy vine motifs, jars with stripes and ivy*
   *vines on body or shoulder, and early and later vine motifs.*

Like many ancient cemeteries, that of Karanog displayed distinctive patterns in terms of the spatial distribution and of the association between different types of graves, burial customs, funerary art and inscriptions, and artifacts. However, the interpretation of these patterns is a complicated matter. To some degree, they reflect the social and economic complexity—the division into upper, lower, and middle classes—of the community, but much of the patterning reflects specific funerary beliefs and customs that make it difficult, for example, to identify the occupations or professions of tomb owners, unless inscriptional data survive— and this occurs only in a minority of cases. Moreover, the patterns are also in part due to change over time, with some types of tombs and artifacts losing popularity and gradually disappearing as new types became more popular, then dominant.

Change over time is certainly a factor in the Karanog cemetery, in which two major, successive time phases are detectable, although detailed analysis would provide a

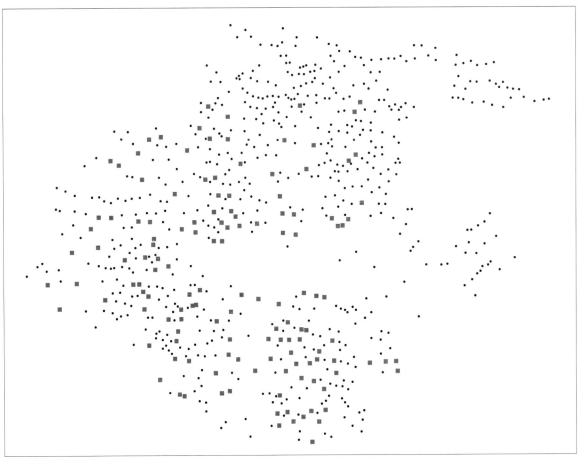

***Fig. 7.3B***
*The distribution of chronologically significant artifacts in
Karanog cemetery; type i jars.*

more finely gradated chronological picture. The northern and southern halves of the cemetery have similar numbers of graves, and have been equally affected by plundering, so that certain striking differences between the two halves probably accurately reflect a difference in the time periods they occupy. Thus, in the north half many graves contain metal seal rings, and the abundant decorated pottery exhibits preferences for ivy-vine motifs and for decorating most of the body of a jar, rather than just the upper part. These traits are much rarer in the southern half. In contrast, a specific and rel-

atively common type of jar, large in size with a marked shoulder (form i, representing about 18.5 percent of the total recorded vessels), is about 2.6 times more common in the southern half than it is in the northern (Fig. 7.3; these distribution patterns, and the percentages quoted later, are based on the work of Stacie Olson, of the University of Pennsylvania.)

The statistical variability is too great to suggest that these differences merely reflect different customs and preferences among contemporary segments of the population; and in fact a number of imported items found in the

**Fig. 7.4**
*The social structure of the Karanog cemetery. Drawing by
Raymond Rorke.*

cemetery and approximately datable in absolute terms indicate that the northern half is in large part earlier than the southern. Of thirteen such items in the southern half, 77 percent date later than the majority (80 percent) of the imported items in the northern.[2] Indeed, it is possible to suggest that the cemetery began in the northeast, grew over time toward the southwest, and later swung off toward the southeast.

### The People of Karanog/Nalote

Although we cannot learn as much as we would like, the cemetery and the town of Karanog, or Nalote, do give us an extraordinary amount of information about its people. Our single most important source is the inscriptions, on funerary stelae and offering tables, that were especially common in the southern half of the cemetery. These are in Meroitic, but are partially translatable. The content of these inscriptions shows that for much of its history the bureaucracy and the priesthoods resident at Nalote were dominated by several large, interrelated families; the spatial distribution of the objects, and the tombs associated with them, reveals that each of these families concentrated its burials within specific but contiguous zones within the cemetery (Fig. 7.4).[3]

Thus, distributed throughout the western half of the cemetery were graves probably (only a few inscriptions survived) of a large family of officials related to the *pekers* of Upper Nubia and the *peshtos* of Lower Nubia. Farther to the southeast were the tombs of another family, whose members were priests of the god Mash, a deity found only at Nalote and in its

region. The location of the graves of these two families in the cemetery suggests that their earlier generations might represent the elite of Nalote before it became the provincial capital and residence of the *peshto* of Akin, although their later generations overlapped with this change in the town's status.

When Nalote became the provincial capital, new institutions, and new levels of the bureaucratic and priestly hierarchy, became established there; they are represented by the families buried in the southeast quadrant of the cemetery. This is dominated physically by six tombs with conspicuously large superstructures. Three of these tombs can be allotted, through their associated inscriptions, to the *peshtos* of Akin Khawitrer (Tomb 183), Meleton (187), and Natewitrer (203), and one of the remaining three would have belonged to the *peshto* Baroteye, active in the period A.D. 253–261; the other two surely also belonged to *peshtos*. In fact, a funerary inscription from Faras lists eleven *peshtos* of Akin, perhaps in chronological order; the four known *peshtos* from Karanog occupy the third, fifth, sixth, and eighth places in the list; and other *peshtos* placed close to them in the list were probably buried at Karanog also, even though their inscriptions have not survived.

Further inscriptions show that the tombs of the *peshtos* at Karanog were surrounded by those of relatives, who were often also officials or priests, and of perhaps other officials and dependents. Immediately northeast was the burial ground of another family, its members priests, and officials, of a lower rank than those associated with the *peshto*, and hence representing a lower level in the hierarchy.

**Plate 17** Kohl tube. One of the most elaborately decorated of the kohl tubes recovered from Karanog cemetery, it was in box E 7519 (Pl. 16). The people of Karanog painted their eyelids with a dark powder (called kohl in Arabic), mixed with adhesive liquid. The powder was kept in wooden tubes, often much larger than necessary for the purpose, and hence reflective of the wealth and prestige of the owner.

*Kohl Tube, Meroitic Period, 100 B.C.–A.D. 300, Karanog, graves 45, Coxe Expedition 1908, E 7514, H: 17.8; D: 4.3 cm, Wood, ivory*

**Plate 18** Bronze oil lamp and stand. Definitely an import from Roman Egypt, it was found in a large grave that belonged to one of the wealthy peshtos, or governors, of Lower Nubia in Meroitic times. Acanthus leaves decorate the top of the stand, and some thread, or a wick, is visible in the lamp's spout.

*Lamp, Meroitic Period, A.D. 225–275, Karanog, grave 187, Coxe Expedition 1908, E 7147, H: 35.0; W: 10.4; D: 9.5 cm, Bronze*

**Plate 19** Faience cup. Faience containers were rare at Karanog. This cup recalls the shape of the ceramic cups often found in burials but is made of blue and purple faience. The decoration also recalls that of the ceramic cups; the large purple elements may be stylized grape-bunches; cable bands in relief are seen above and below.

*Cup, Meroitic Period, 100 B.C.–A.D. 300, Karanog, grave 139, Coxe Expedition 1908, E 7366, H: 8.5; D: 8.5 cm, Faience*

**Plate 20** Painted jar. This striking vessel has a schematized vine-leaf pattern running around the shoulder; the body has a frieze of three upreared cobras, their wings projecting forward so they spit forth a stream of ankhs, the Egyptian (and Meroitic) hieroglyph for "life." Such cobras are associated with the sun-god, and the sun-god's delegate on earth, the king; the cobras protected both god and king from evil, and punished their enemies.

*Jar, Meroitic Period, 100 B.C.–A.D. 300, Karanog, grave 301, Coxe Expedition 1908, E 8168, H: 33.6; D: 17.2 cm, Ceramic*

**Plate 21** Ceramic jar. Depictions of giraffes on pottery were not uncommon in Karanog cemetery; apart from this vessel perhaps as many as six others were so decorated. This scene is particularly striking: five superbly drawn giraffes range around the jar (which has had its neck broken off, probably accidentally), interspersed with two trees, and a squat human figure (not visible in the photograph). The meaning of the scene is unknown, and giraffes had probably not existed in the environs of Lower Nubia for many centuries. They were, however, still to be seen in or near Southern Nubia, and the artist evidently has a clear idea of their appearance.

*Jar, Meroitic Period, A.D. 75–125, Karanog, grave 162, Coxe Expedition 1908, E 8293, H: 37.0; D: 19.5 cm, Ceramic*

**Plate 22** Ceramic jar. It comes from the earlier part of the cemetery and may antedate the realistically rendered giraffes seen in E 8293 (Pl. 21). Here, the giraffes are drawn almost as if caricatures, but probably the painter was simply much less skillful than some others. A great range in artistic proficiency is typical of Lower Nubian painted pottery.

*Jar, Meroitic Period, A.D. 75–125, Karanog, grave 528, Coxe Expedition 1908, E 8154, H: 38.7; D: 22.0 cm, Ceramic*

**Plate 23** Ceramic jar. The elaborate scene on this vessel is very freely painted but complex in subject matter. Altars are surrounded by flying insects and geese; actual examples of the distinctive horned altar depicted here have been found in Meroitic cult-places.

*Jar, Meroitic Period, 100–1 B.C., Karanog, grave 712, Coxe Expedition 1908, E 8157, H: 28.9; D: 28.1 cm, Ceramic*

**Plate 24** Ceramic jar. Cattle appeared in only about five pottery vessels from Karanog Cemetery: this pot shows three cattle in a row with a snake above. Cattle must have been common in Lower Nubia, and the rarity of depictions suggests that those actually pictured may be in some way sacred, or intended for a sacred or special purpose. Cattle also appear on two exceptionally large and finely worked bronze bowls from Grave 187, which belonged to a peshto, or governor; on one bowl an offering of milk to an elite woman is depicted, suggestive again of a special value assigned to at least some cattle.

*Jar, Meroitic Period, A.D. 75–125, Karanog, grave 129, Coxe Expedition 1908, E 8192, H: 31.0; D: 26.7 cm, Ceramic*

**Plate 25** Ceramic jar. Although its decoration is relatively simple, this pot is of interest because the pattern of crescents and balls running around the upper part may correspond to the ball-beads, and the crescent-decorated robes worn by some Meroitic royalty. Perhaps this is an indirect reference to the latter. Above is a simplified vine-leaf pattern.

*Jar, Meroitic Period, 100 B.C.–A.D. 300, Karanog, grave 221, Coxe Expedition 1908, E 8284, H: 23.5; D: 20.0 cm, Ceramic*

**Plate 26** Three ceramic vessels. Painted in a very free style, these are of interest because they are stylistically so similar that they may have been produced by the same painter, or at least workshop. All are from Karanog Cemetery. The faces are all shown as mouthless and with accentuated ears; on E 8275 each face has a crescent on the forehead, apparently scarification, which is seen on a number of ba-statues as well. In the Sudan today, this patterned scarification refers to tribal, ethnic and other affiliations, and presumably did so in Meroitic times as well.

*Cup, Meroitic Period, A.D. 1–50, Karanog, grave 655, Coxe Expedition 1908, E 8724, H: 8.3; D: 9.1 cm, Ceramic*

*Jar, Meroitic Period, A.D. 1–50, Karanog, grave 530, Coxe Expedition 1908, E 8275, H: 20.5; D: 18.2 cm, Ceramic*

*Bowl, Meroitic Period, 100 B.C.–A.D. 300, Karanog, grave 304, Coxe Expedition 1908, E 8478, H: 2.4; D: 9.5 cm, Ceramic*

**Plate 27** Ceramic cup. Cups were frequently found in Meroitic graves, accompanying the large water, wine, or beer jars also placed with the dead. On this cup a herdsman and his dog (wearing a sturdy collar) drive along two cattle. Grave 189 was a modest one, but the scene on the cup is very unusual, and curiously is best parallelled on the two fine bronze bowls from the peshto's (governor's) grave (187), to which Grave 189 is quite close. Perhaps the owner of 189 was related to, or a dependent of, the governor buried in Grave 187.

*Cup, Meroitic Period, 100 B.C.–A.D. 300, Karanog, grave 189, Coxe Expedition 1908, E 8451, H: 7.8; D: 9.7 cm, Ceramic*

**Plate 28** Large ceramic jar. Two human figures are separated from each other by schematic trees. Each holds a stick, and one holds an amazingly truncated dog by a leash, so perhaps they represent herdsmen. No cattle are shown. The stiff, highly schematic style indicates an artist much less talented than others who decorated the Karanog pottery.

*Jar, Meroitic Period, 100 B.C.–A.D. 300, Karanog, grave 535, Coxe Expedition 1908, E 8193, H: 36.5; D: 19.9 cm, Ceramic*

**Plate 29** Ceramic cup. The carefully executed design on this cup is typical of a so-called academic style that has been identified among Meroitic potters. The design represents branches ending in pomegranates.

*Cup, Meroitic Period, 100 B.C.–A.D. 300, Karanog, grave 325, Coxe Expedition 1908, E 8469, H: 8.0; D: 9.8 cm, Ceramic*

**Plate 30** Ceramic cup. Painted in free-flowing style, it depicts a series of cobras, each topped by a sun-disc, indicating that they represent the cobras or uraei who protect the sun-god and punish his enemies.

*Cup, Meroitic Period, 100 B.C.–A.D. 300, Karanog, grave 377, Coxe Expedition 1908, E 8472, H: 8.2; D: 8.8 cm, Ceramic*

**Plate 31** Ceramic cup from Shablul, another Meroitic site excavated by Randall-MacIver and Woolley for The University Museum. It depicts birds pecking at the ground, presumably for food; but the presence of ankhs, the hieroglyph for "life," suggests that the scene also may have religious meaning.

*Cup, Meroitic Period, 100 B.C.–A.D. 300, Shablul, Coxe Expedition 1907, E 5271, H: 8.5; D: 8.7 cm, Ceramic*

**Plate 32** Box lid. This is the lid of a pottery box (the box itself was not recovered) with a lively crocodile painted upon it. Crocodiles occur on other Karanog vessels and would have been found in reality throughout Nubia.

*Box Lid, Meroitic Period, A.D. 1–50, Karanog, grave 735, Coxe Expedition 1908, E 8737, H: 3.9; W: 9.7; L: 17.0 cm, Ceramic*

**Plate 33** Two ceramic jars. In the Meroitic cemetery of Karanog, a small amount of exotic-looking pottery was discovered. It is handmade (Lower Nubian Meroitic pottery is usually wheel-made) and occurs in burnished red or black wares, sometimes with incised or impressed decoration of relatively simple style. These two jars are examples of these handmade jars; both were found associated with typically Meroitic objects. This style of pottery was apparently a product of Southern and Upper Nubia, and its occurrences at Karanog reflect the exchange system that existed within the large and culturally diverse Meroitic state.

*Jar, Meroitic Period, 100 B.C.–A.D. 300, Karanog, grave 118, Coxe Expedition 1908, E 8565, H: 26.5; D: 26.1 cm, Ceramic*

*Jar, Meroitic Period, 100 B.C.–A.D. 300, Karanog, grave 741, Coxe Expedition 1908, E 8550, H: 20.0; D: 21.5 cm, Ceramic*

**Plate 34** Two ceramic cups, belonging to the X-Group, or Ballana, culture of Lower Nubia. X-Group pottery replaced the rich variety in form and decoration of Meroitic pottery with a few, repetitive shapes and a very restrained form of decoration, of which these two cups are typical.

*Bowl, X-Group Period, A.D. 320–550, Toshka West, Yale-Pennsylvania Expedition 1961–1962, 66-11-60, H: 11.0; D: 9.3 cm, Ceramic*

*Cup, X-Group Period, A.D. 320–550, Toshka West, Yale-Pennsylvania Expedition 1961–1962, 66-11-55, H: 7.4; D: 10.1 cm, Ceramic*

Finally, on the extreme northeast, were the tombs of yet another family, whose members were priests of Amanape, a Meroitic god whose cult was widespread.

Within the framework of these families and their functions we can see how, in the cemetery, the social and economic complexity of the community at Karanog was given material expression. Evidently, this community was gradated, or structured into a hierarchy in terms of higher and lower status and greater or lesser wealth; a particularly telling way of expressing these differences, even in death, was to vary the size of the tomb superstructure accordingly. The substructures of most Karanog graves consisted of either a pit containing a vaulted or roofed chamber, the rest of the pit being filled with soil after the burial had taken place, or of a cavelike chamber, cut entirely in the earth and accessible through an open corridor, also filled in once the body and its gifts were placed in the tomb. Many tombs had no superstructures, but a large number did, built in mud-brick, and sometimes with stone masonry foundations. Only the lower part of each superstructure survived, but there is good evidence to suggest that most if not all can be reconstructed as small pyramids, with steeply sloping sides and a flat, rather than pointed, top.

The variable sizes of these pyramids were an important marker of wealth and status. Those of the *peshtos*, as we might expect, were the largest in the cemetery, whereas those of their relatives and dependents, and of the lower-ranking family to the northeast, were all markedly smaller as well as internally "graded" in size among themselves. The tombs of the priests of Amanape, farther northeast, include three high-status pyramids as well as smaller ones, reflective of their internal hierarchy; and similar, if less-marked variability occurs among the tombs of the priests of Mash, southwest of the *peshtos*' burial ground. Moving back in space, and perhaps in time, through the western half of the cemetery, we can see again considerable variation in pyramid size, from "large" through "medium" to "small," reflecting substantial differences in wealth and status stretching back into the earlier history of the community of Nalote.

Given these material expressions of socioeconomic complexity in the cemetery, it is not surprising to find the same phenomenon indicated for the town, but much less clearly because the town was only very partially excavated (Figure 7.2). However, insofar as these excavations go, we see that elite structures and residences (the latter typified by a large house occupying 351 square meters, set within a large enclosure) lie on the northeast side of the town, while the southwest part of the town was occupied by markedly smaller residences averaging (in the first phase of the town's history) only about 139 square meters in area and packed closely together. These data indicate that the town had elite and nonelite zones, with the former deliberately placed on the north, so that the prevailing north wind would blow the odors and dust of the town in general away from the elite residences.

Nalote must have included some public buildings of large size, but—with two exceptions—these were not located and excavated, and perhaps some had been swept away by the river. For example, the presence of priests of Mash and of Amanape in the Karanog cemetery indicates that the town had at least two temples. Amanape also had a temple at Qasr Ibrim, upstream from Nalote; but a cult of this important state god was likely to have been practiced at Karanog itself. The god Aman, and the goddesses Isis and Mit, are also associated with Karanog; whether they had their own temples, or chapels within the other temples, is not clear. Such temples were likely found at all Meroitic Lower Nubian centers. Even the small agricultural village of Meinarti, near the Second Cataract and occupying only about one-quarter of a hectare (a little over half an acre), apparently had its own temple.[4] At Meinarti, the temple was associated with magazines, which were probably a feature of most temples and used to store the produce from the temple estates that supported the cults and their personnel. Such granaries probably occurred in Karanog also.

Fortunately, two public buildings of great interest did survive at Karanog. Set close to each other, on separate bluffs overlooking the town, they have been identified respectively as a "castle" and a "house." In reality, both are very similar in plan, and hence in function, and can probably be identified as the palaces of the *peshtos* who governed Akin from Nalote, where they lived. Each palace must have served several generations of *peshtos*, one eventually being abandoned, or put to other uses, when the other was built. Which of the two was earlier is unknown: one was exceptionally well preserved, the other severely denuded, but these circumstances may have no connection with their relative ages.

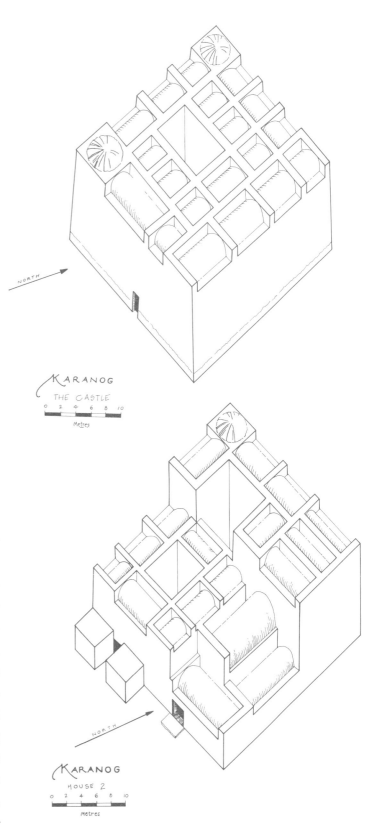

**Fig. 7.5**
*The two palaces of the governors (peshto) at Karanog, reconstru[cted] by David O'Connor. Above, Karanog, "the Castle;" belo[w], Karanog, "House 2." Drawings by Nicole deLisle Warsh[...]*

# The People of Karanog

The palaces provide a unique glimpse into the settings designed for the public and private lives of the *peshtos* (Fig. 7.5). Each palace was quite large and similar in size (the ground areas were 624.5 and 650.25 square meters). A detailed study of the architecture, the chief surviving evidence for function, reveals that one palace—called "House 2" by the excavators—had, on the ground floor, a series of conspicuously large halls filling its eastern quadrant. In these, the *peshto* and his staff carried out the business and ceremonies of government, one of the halls, with a centrally placed doorway, probably being the *peshto's* "throne room" or audience hall. Its roofline may have been higher than those of the adjacent halls, so as to admit enough light. The northwest third of the palace contained the ground floor of the residence of the *peshto* and his family: it rose perhaps three stories high, and may have included an airwell. The southern quadrant was occupied by a domestic or service unit; built around an airwell, it included a kitchen, food preparation areas, and magazines as well as servants' rooms on its second floor. This unit supplied the residence with its meals, supplies, and required services. The other palace (the "castle" of the excavators) was laid out and functioned basically in a similar way, with some variations: in this case the entire building, built around an airwell, rose three stories high.

Socioeconomic complexity, the hierarchy of status and wealth, is thus well documented for the people of Karanog, but it is much more difficult to establish the various occupations they practiced. We know of some officials and priests—the more important

ones—through the inscriptions, and we can reasonably suppose that the community would have included the lower levels of the bureaucratic and priestly hierarchies; a large service segment—people who worked directly for the elite, for government offices, and for the temples; artisans, producing items such as pottery and basketry; builders, masons, and stonecutters; and probably many agriculturists, living in Nalote or its satellite villages and working the fields and farms that filled the town's rural hinterland. To some degree, these various groups might have been recognizable archaeologically in the town, had it been fully excavated; but they cannot be identified in the cemetery, for all the graves appear to have shared a common culture of funerary goods that excluded items representative of an individual's actual occupation. The basic elements supplied to the dead were clothing, jewelry, and sandals; items needed for personal care and pleasure, such as kits of toilet objects (tweezers, cosmetic spoons, and other objects) and containers and applicators for kohl (eye paint); or luxury items such as glass and bronze vessels. In addition pottery containers, sometimes in large numbers, were placed in tombs, but these reflected domestic needs rather than occupational interests. A large water or beer jar, and an accompanying cup, were typical; other large jars may have been, in actuality or symbolically, grain containers.

Naturally, the burial goods, like the tomb superstructures, did reflect the relative wealth or status of the deceased; some graves were quite poorly furnished, others very richly, and many fell at various points between these two extremes. As Stacie Olson's analyses demonstrate, this variability was reinforced by the presence or absence of expensive imported items: attractive but cheap glass beads, largely produced in Roman Egypt, were found in many graves, but imported glass vessels occurred in only about 7 percent of the graves, and distinctive vessels containing (or symbolizing) imported wines and oils only in about 5 percent.

The occasional reflections of occupational specialization that do occur in the cemetery turn out, on analysis, to be quite complicated in meaning. A single agricultural tool (which must have been common within the living community) was found, but in the fill of a pyramid, where it might have been lost by accident during the building operations. In another tomb, a substantial chisel was not accompanied by any other appropriate tools, such as hammers, mallets, or adzes; rather, it was associated with both toilet implements and an archer's equipment. Somewhat more frequently found items reflective of occupational interests were implements used for weaving cloth and ferociously barbed arrowheads, usually made of iron, and other items connected with archery; even these, however, occurred in only about 2 percent and 2.7 percent of the graves respectively, and do not necessarily indicate the burials of "weavers" and "soldiers" or "hunters."

For example, although it is possible that weaving implements were usually associated with females (plundering and disturbance makes it hard to be sure), some of these women were buried in relatively poor tombs, and others were associated with relatively large superstructures and rich burial equipment.

Perhaps weaving at Karanog was simply a typically "female" occupation at all levels of society, which does not preclude the possibility that some households wove on a factorylike scale, for the market or on behalf of a government establishment. Arrowheads and related equipment also seem subject to multiple interpretations. In a few cases they were associated with female or child burials (one arrowhead lay on a child's chest); here perhaps they might be "magical," protectors against supernatural danger. The burials of at least two of the *peshtos* contained archery equipment, so perhaps the possession of this was generally typical of the elite. At first glance another relatively high-status tomb appears definitely to be that of a "warrior." The burial was male, and the funerary gifts included forty-one arrowheads and a spearhead, the only one found in the cemetery, but they also included a musical instrument, hardly a warrior's trademark—so perhaps this was simply another member of the elite. Finally, some of the relevant burials were not of warriors but of their victims: Tomb 371 contained a man with an arrowhead imbedded in his thigh, and in Tomb 628 was a man who had been shot in the back with an arrow!

## The World of the Mind in Nalote

To attempt to enter the mind of ancient peoples, to find out their ideas about themselves and their world, and about the cosmos to which they belonged, is a fascinating exercise. It is also a presumptuous and difficult one, especially in the case of the people of Nalote, who left few written documents behind them, and those in a largely unknown language. Yet through a variety of sources, especially the partially translatable inscriptions, the funerary art, and the decorated pottery from the cemetery, we can find out some important things about the Nalotian world view, and ask some other important questions, even if we cannot answer them.

The inscriptions make it clear that for the elite of Nalote prestige was derived from the offices (sometimes, over time, several) in which one served the state, and from family and other relationships with distinguished men at Nalote and elsewhere. It is by no means certain that office, civil or priestly, in Nalote was purely hereditary, and complete acceptance of such a principle is usually resisted by centralized states like the Meroitic kingdom. However, it is clear that certain families were strongly associated with specific institutions, and probably did their best to ensure that appointments within these went, if possible, to relatives. Office and priesthood seem male prerogatives; women mention them only to reflect the prestige they derive from male relatives who serve in these capacities. Both men and women also stress their relationships—sometimes perhaps familial, at other times ones of patronage—to high-ranking people, such as the *peker* or governor in Napata, the *peshto* of Akin, the "envoy to Rome" (Meroitic ambassadors to Roman Egypt), and even priests and officials in faraway Meroe.

The socioeconomic complexity and hierarchy reflected in the archaeology of the cemetery and discussed above show clearly enough that the established social order was imagined to continue among the dead. But the inscriptions also give more specific information about beliefs concerning the afterlife, for they often refer to the funerary deities Osiris, Isis, and Anubis. Derived originally from Egypt these deities had long been firmly integrated into the Meroitic belief system, but their presence implies that Egyptian ideas about the nightly regeneration of the dead in the grave, and their daily rebirth into the world of the living, in association with the rising sun, were held by the Meroites also.

However, it was the tomb itself, as a total assemblage, that gave clearest expression to Nalotian ideas about the dead, most explicitly in the larger and more elaborate elite tombs. Below ground, in the burial chamber or cave, the dead were supplied with items suggesting that in the afterlife they would regenerate and need for their enjoyment the same equipment used by the living—clothing, jewelry, luxury objects, food, drink, oil, cosmetics, and even beds and musical instruments. Perhaps, too, the dead were also imagined to need magical aids to avert supernatural danger or secure supernatural power in the afterlife, but if so, no obvious devices for these purposes were supplied, whereas in Roman Egypt they were, especially in the form of richly decorated, magically powerful coffins.

Yet the dead of Nalote were certainly supernaturally transformed beings, as the sometimes elaborately developed superstructures made clear. The superstructure and its ancillary features both established and illustrated the relationships between the dead and the world of the living. In front of some tombs was a stone offering table, sometimes supported by a brick plinth: the offering table's inscriptions celebrated the tomb owner's status, but it was also where relatives and funerary priests placed the

*Fig. 7.6*
*Design on a bronze bowl from Karanog, Tomb G 187.*
*(From: C. L. Woolley and D. Randall-MacIver,*
Karanog: The Romano-Nubian Cemetery, *Text.*
*Philadelphia: University Museum of the University of*
*Pennsylvania [1910], pl. 27.)*

food and poured the libations the dead needed. Beyond the offering table was a small brick chapel, built against the face of the pyramidal superstructure. This chapel could also contain offerings, or perhaps bowls with burning incense, on ritual occasions, but at its rear was set up a funerary stela that often recorded the deceased's name, titles, and distinguished relatives and patrons, and sometimes depicted him or her. The stela was, then, a focus for the offering cult and a means of linking the benefits of the cult to the deceased.

Finally, above the chapel rose the steep-sided pyramid, sometimes towering to an impressive height and originally painted white, so it would have seemed to radiate light in the bright sun. In many tombs, we can guess that a niche was built into the pyramid face, and in this was placed a statue, in sandstone, of the deceased; none was actually found in situ. These statues varied greatly in quality but were originally brightly painted to represent dark- or light-red skin and white clothing. In their totality, pyramid and statue were complex in

meaning. In Egypt, and surely also for the Meroites, the pyramid was a solar symbol, associating the dead with the concepts of the creation of the cosmos (wherein the pyramid can be visualized as the mound on which creation takes place) and the continuous regeneration of that cosmos by the daily rising of the sun, with the pyramid representing sunlight shining down. The deceased, in the form of a statue, is then seen emerging from this mound, and from this stream of "light;" in these ways he or she reenters the world of the living and becomes accessible to it. In a unique way, these Meroitic statues combine two concepts derived from Egypt. The fully human form of the statue represents the *ka*, or life-force, of the deceased, standing impassively to display its status and receive offerings. However, behind each human form a magnificent pair of wings sweeps down its back, showing that the statue represents also the *ba*, that form of the deceased that makes him or her mobile and permits one to fly out into the world and soar upward to join the sun in its triumphal progress across the sky. Finally,

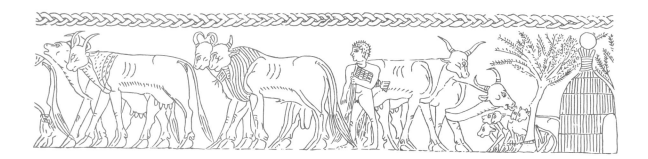

a sun disc rising from the statue's head represents the divine solar force that makes these events possible and transforms the dead person into a solar deity.

These statues, and the images painted on funerary stelae, also provide some direct information about the living Nalotians, but we must allow for the distorting effect of funerary beliefs and customs. Some faces, for example, bear deliberately inflicted scarification, still marks of social and ethnic significance in modern Sudan and surely once exhibited by living Nalotians. We also have several statues of *peshtos*, in which each wears an elaborate robe or kilt and a large necklace, chest amulet, and armlets—probably all of gold in real life; these probably do illustrate the ceremonial dress of these high officials. However, many other people are shown wearing only kilts, or are even (rarely) completely naked, but these depictions must refer to some idealized condition in the afterlife. In Nubia, winters can be quite cold, and Nalotians must often have worn more and fuller clothes than what we see in the funerary art.

Further access to the ideas and attitudes of the people of Nalote is provided by the richly decorated pottery found in many of the tombs, alongside plainer and more mundane wares. This decorated pottery occurs in graves of all socioeconomic grades, and was also much used in the settlements and villages. Divided up into types, such pottery can be most valuable for chronological purposes, and it also represents an important industry, and even an art. The designs and images on the pottery were clearly intended to be aesthetically pleasing, and scholars have even identified the products of specific artists or workshops, such as "the vine-leaf school," the "academic school," and the "antelope painter." However, this pottery cannot have been purely decorative: its designs and images must have had meaning to the Meroites, and even roles to play in their lives. Here we shall hazard a few observations about these possible meanings.

Despite its great variety, the motifs of the decorated pottery of Nalote (and elsewhere in Lower Nubia; these styles are rarer in the south, but this may reflect accidents of discovery as much as real cultural differences) can be grouped into three broad areas: the use of abstract designs, such as lines and rectangles; the use of highly formalized motifs whose naturalistic origins remain obvious, such as ivy-vines, lotuses, and motifs derived from Egyptian hieroglyphs for "life," "protection," and so forth; and the use of more specifically naturalistic subjects—birds, animals, reptiles, and, rarely, humans. As in so much of Meroitic art, we find woven together indigenous motifs and other themes drawn from ancient Egyptian traditions (passed on through Graeco-Roman Egyptian as well as Meroitic art) and from the art of the Greek and Roman worlds, but the results are very coherent in terms of design, and likely to be coherent in terms of the meanings they had for the Nalotians.

For example, the frequent use of magically potent hieroglyphs, like "life" and "protection," may have been thought to have enhanced the life-force of the pottery's users, or their contents, or protected them from evil; Meroitic clothing was also decorated with such hieroglyphs. Figures of deities, however, do not occur, except for lower-order ones such as the protective demigod Bes; such representations of deities were appropriate for temple walls, or on tomb door-jambs, but decorum inhibited their representation on pottery. However, in more restrained and subtle ways the presence of deities is evoked; the hieroglyph "protection" was associated with Isis, and the lotus with the sun-god; images of a lion-face amulet replicated on a pot's surface (not from Karanog) may refer to Apedemak, the important Meroitic lion-god.

Royalty is not represented in an explicit way on this pottery, also for reasons of decorum; and yet the royal presence that suffused the Meroitic world is evoked. The magnificent vulture, grasping two swords, is certainly an icon of royalty; cobras, some winged, as the punitive agent of the sun-god recall the Meroitic pharaoh's responsibility to overthrow disorder in the world—Meroitic kings, like Egyptian ones, wore a uraeus or cobra on their headdress. Sometimes the royal imagery becomes very subtle. An apparently meaningless combination of ball beads and crescents found on some pots actually recalls the regalia and robe decoration of some Meroitic royalty.

Even the more naturalistic subjects of the decorated pottery are not straightforward "scenes of daily life" or "of the natural world," as we might first have thought. For example, giraffes are represented on a number of pots, sometimes realistically, sometimes as almost comical caricatures. Yet the giraffe did not occur in Lower Nubia; it was an animal typical of the heartland near Meroe. But if the purpose was to evoke this heartland for the viewer in Lower Nubia, why not depict the elephant also? This was another typical animal of the farther south, and elephant iconography occurs even in religious contexts. Was the elephant *too* sacred to depict on pottery?

Representations of herdsmen with their dogs, sometimes driving cattle, and of lines of cattle, some wearing decorative collars, seem more likely to represent "daily life," yet this too may be a false impression. Certainly animal herding occurred in Akin, but so— much more often—did plowing, harvesting, and other agricultural pursuits, but these are never depicted. If we turn to two beautifully decorated bronze bowls, associated with the tomb of the *peshto* Meleton, we may find a clue as to the meaning of this decoration (Fig. 7.6). On these bowls cattle are prominent; some are being driven, some wear decorative collars. In addition, milk is being offered to an elite couple, before a primitive-looking hut set in an open landscape with trees. These images can hardly represent the urbanized and sophisticated elite of Akin. Rather, a mythological context is indicated; perhaps these are the mythical ancestors of one of the great families of Akin, imagined in some remote, otherworldly past or place. If so, the herdsmen and cattle on the pottery may be further references to the same theme.

In all, then, the material from Meroitic Karanog or Nalote provides a richly detailed view of a provincial nobility and population; other excavated Meroitic sites from Lower Nubia are comparable in general terms, but do not have some of the attributes that made Karanog so special and intriguing. As elsewhere throughout the Meroitic kingdom, however, the distinctive culture of Karanog was soon to come to an end.

# After Meroe: The Great Divide

*Nubia and Christianity*

A Meroite carried back in time to 1300 B.C. would find himself in a conceptual world that was still recognizable. The temples built in Late Bronze Age Nubia by Egyptians were similar in plan to many Meroitic temples, and decorated according to artistic conventions later used in Meroe as well. On the temple walls, a Meroite would be able to identify the pharaoh as well as familiar gods like Amun and Isis, gods who had created the cosmos and now protected it.

That same Meroite, set a thousand years into Nubia's future, would be in a fundamentally alien world. Landscapes and life-styles would be similar to those of his own day, but everywhere temples were replaced by cathedrals and churches (Figure 8.1). In the great cathedral of Faras, for example, our Meroite would stare in bewilderment at brightly painted walls depicting not the ancient and familiar gods but instead Christ as judge on the Last Day; the Madonna and Child; and Shadrach, Meshach, and Abednego in the fiery furnace, with the archangel Michael spreading his peacock wings protectively over them. The Christianization of the Nubians created for them a new conceptual world, and separated them from their rich but pagan past.

Nubia's neighbors, the states of Egypt and Axum (in modern Ethiopia), began to Christianize fairly early, but Nubia's conversion took place later, between A.D. 543 and 580. Nubia remained Christian for a long time, but after A.D. 1500, Islam gradually became the dominant, and finally the only, religion practiced by Nubians. Nubia's Christian and Islamic civilizations are important historically, but are not covered in this

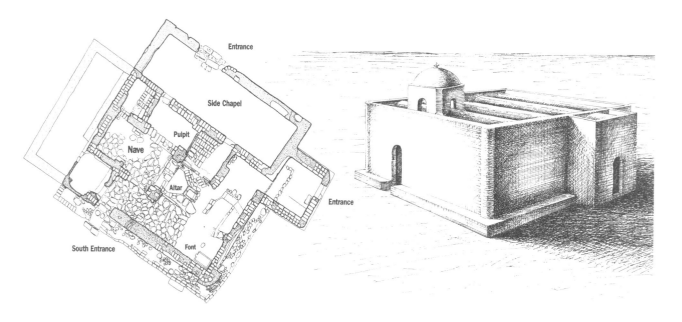

**Fig. 8.1**
*Church excavated at Arminna by the Pennsylvania-Yale
Expedition to Nubia, directed by W.K. Simpson. Drawing by
Raymond Rorke.*

book. However, we do need to ask how the Meroitic kingdom and its distinctive civilization became transformed into the very different world of Christian Nubia.

### Meroe's Successor Kingdoms

The answer to this question is not yet clear, for it lies in the still largely mysterious 250-year period between the last known Meroitic pharaoh—Yesbokheamani (A.D. 283–300)—and the arrival of Christian missionaries (A.D. 543). The latter found in Nubia political and social systems so highly integrated that once their leaders accepted Christianity the new religion spread rapidly throughout Nubian society. But where did these systems come from?

An answer can only be very tentatively sketched here, for "post-Meroitic" Nubia has only recently become the focus of renewed scholarly and archaeological attention, and over the next decades our knowledge of it will surely expand and change.

By A.D. 543 (and presumably for some time before this as well) Nubia was divided into three independent kingdoms, each on the scale of a state. Nobatia ran from Aswan to the Third Cataract; Makouria from thence to Meroe city (by that time largely in ruins); and Alodia, or Alwa, from Meroe far up the Blue and perhaps White Niles. Were these states essentially new entities that had arisen on the ashes of a completely collapsed Meroitic kingdom and civilization; or were they in some way a transformation of the Meroitic world, and still linked to it by important continuities?

The second alternative is the one increasingly favored by scholars, and fits well with recent theories about the "collapse" of states. Foreign attack or detrimental environmental change can trigger collapse, but most often factors internal to the society involved are the cause. The collapse of states, and the ending of civilization or cultural traditions, is not the same thing. States disintegrate periodically, but civilizations tend to continue; they are maintained, and partly transformed, by the social groups that replace a collapsed state, groups that may ultimately form a new state. Finally, a state's collapse is not automatically followed by a descent into political and social chaos. Rather, "smaller politically autonomous units" survive while the "severe social troubles" that might preclude the reformation of a state often do not occur.[1]

The archaeological evidence suggests strongly that the circumstances just described apply to post-Meroitic Nubia. In this period, there are major changes in material culture, but also a continuation of important Meroitic traits. Moreover, political institutions—on a smaller scale—survive and prosper, and seem to be shaped in part by ideologies of Meroitic origin.

Post-Meroitic Nubia consists of two or perhaps three cultural regions, most clearly differentiated by variations in ceramic typology. The Ballana or X-Group culture (Aswan to the Third Cataract) is typified by wheel-made pottery, with a small range of shapes and decoration. In contrast, the Tanqasi culture of Upper Nubia produced only handmade pottery, as did Southern Nubia.

Post-Meroitic Nubia seems definitely less strongly urbanized than before, but there is not a complete break; most people continued to be sedentary agriculturalists living in villages, and some settlements, such as Ibrim in Lower Nubia, are large and well built enough to qualify as towns. Temples are no longer conspicuous in the archaeological landscape, yet cult practices surely continued, and the ongoing existence of some Meroitic gods is indicated in other kinds of evidence. Royalty and the elite are no longer buried under pyramids typical of Meroitic times; instead, earthen tumuli are the universal form of tomb superstructure. However, tumuli, as well as pyramids, had probably been used for many Meroitic graves also.

Highly developed art forms, such as wall scenes in carved or painted form, and inscriptions and written documents, seem virtually absent. However, these apparent changes are in large part due to the fact that temples were no longer being built, or inscribed funerary objects produced. These were the usual sources for Meroitic art and inscriptions. Writing *was* in use in post-Meroitic Nubia, as we know from a few inscriptions and surviving documents, although Greek appears to have been the preferred form of written communication, at least in northern Nubia. The dominant spoken language was probably Nubian, for this was the language of Christian Nubia.

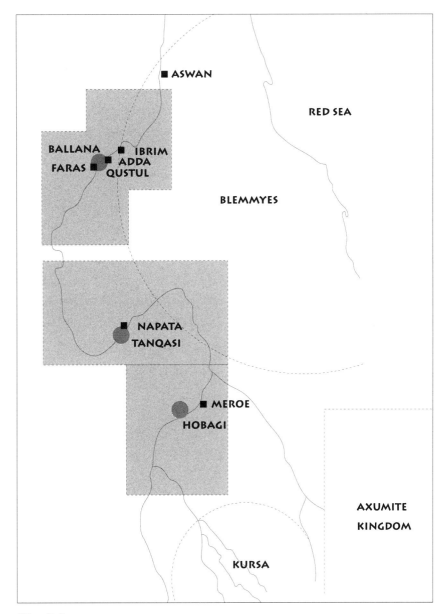

***Fig. 8.2***
*Map of post-Meroitic Nubia.*

## The Kings of Post-Meroitic Nubia

In the political realm, archaeology indicates three "central places" existed in Lower, Upper, and Southern Nubia, respectively. Each central place implies the existence of a polity large enough to be a complex chiefdom or small state; and each polity was probably the core of what became the three kingdoms of Christian Nubia (Fig. 8.2).

Each central place is currently documented by its associated cemetery, rather than the settlement, or settlement cluster, itself. In Lower Nubia the relevant cemetery is divided between the sites of Ballana and Qustul. The tumuli here are much larger than elsewhere in Lower Nubia; one, for example, has a 78 meter diameter, and is 12 meters high. Below the tumuli were chambers containing richly equipped burials, some of them certainly kings and other royalty, supplied with silver crowns inlaid with semiprecious stones. These crowns are inspired by Meroitic prototypes. These royal and elite tombs contained many exotic items, mostly from Byzantine Egypt; many come from trading and diplomatic contacts, some were plunder from Nubian raids on southern Egypt.

A comparable central place cemetery has not yet been decisively identified in Upper Nubia, although a group of conspicuously large tumuli at Tanqasi may prove to be the place. In Southern Nubia, however, an apparently royal cemetery comparable in general terms to that of Ballana and Qustul does exist.

Here, at Hobagi, grave tumuli can be as large as 40 meters in diameter; some stand within stone-walled, elliptical-shaped enclosures. They date to roughly A.D. 340–440, and recent excavations reveal that the associated burials were supplied with very high status objects decorated in Meroitic style, and even inscribed with Meroitic hieroglyphs. Moreover, the funerary rites and probably the mortuary regalia seem to derive from those used earlier for Meroitic royalty. Hobagi cemetery, therefore, seems that of yet another successor state

or complex chiefdom of Meroitic traditions; and in fact nearby is an unexcavated, walled site (about 1 hectare in area) tentatively identified as a "military camp" and "imperial residence."

Historical evidence also provides increased understanding of northern Nubia in post-Meroitic times. In A.D. 298 the emperor Diocletian abandoned the *Dodekaschoenos*, and the "Nobatai" (i.e., the inhabitants of Meroitic Lower Nubia) were invited to defend it from the Blemmyes, the aggressive nomads of the eastern desert. The latter however were probably now organized as a "nomadic state,"[2] and secured control over the *Dodekaschoenos* for a period. Eventually, they were driven out by a Nobatian king called Silko, who was probably among the rulers buried at Ballana and Qustul.

The Nobatai and the Blemmyes had a complicated relationship with each other and with Byzantine Egypt. Nobatai and Blemmyes fought each other, but also joined in raids on Egypt; yet they also appear sometimes as allies of the Byzantines. In A.D. 524, for example, the emperor Justinian felt able to propose sending a joint force of Nobatai and Blemmyes to help the king of Axum (in modern Ethiopia) in his conflict with enemies from southwestern Arabia! Clearly, some post-Meroitic Nubians at least were not isolated from the greater world around them. Future research is likely to provide exciting new discoveries about these successors to the great kingdom of Napata and Meroe and, ultimately, to the early Nubian states of the Bronze Age.

# *Endnotes*

## *Introduction*

1. H. W. Fowler and F. G. Fowler (eds.), *The Concise Oxford Dictionary of Current English*, Oxford: Clarendon Press, 1964, p. 218.

2. The Nile cuts its way through limestone (Egypt) or sandstone (southern Egypt and the Sudan). Occasionally, it encounters an area of harder rock, which breaks the riverbed into several narrow channels, difficult if not impossible to navigate. Each of these complicated stretches is a cataract.

3. S. Wenig, "Nubien," in W. Helck and W. Westendorf (eds.), *Lexikon der Ägyptologie*, Band 4, Wiesbaden: Otto Harrassowitz, 1980, p. 527.

4. On the question of Nubian origins, see W. Adams, *Nubia Corridor to Africa*, London: Allen Lane, Penguin Books, 1977, chap. 13; W. Adams, "Geography and Population of the Nile Valley," in S. Hochfield and E. Riefstahl (eds.), *Africa in Antiquity I. The Arts of Ancient Nubia and the Sudan; The Essays*, Brooklyn, NY: The Brooklyn Museum, 1978, pp. 16–25; B. Trigger, "Nubian, Negro, Black, Nilotic?" in ibid., pp. 26–35.

## *Chapter 1*

1. W. Adams, *Nubia Corridor to Africa*, London: Allen Lane, Penguin Books, 1977, p. 669.

2. F. M. Snowden, Jr., *Before Color Prejudice. The Ancient View of Blacks*, Cambridge: Harvard University Press, 1991, p. 51.

3. M. Bernal, *Black Athena: the Afrocentric Roots of Classical Civilization, The Fabrication of Ancient Greece, 1785–1985*, vol. 1, New Brunswick, NJ: Rutgers University Press, 1987.

4. P. Hazard, *The European Mind 1680–1715*, transl. by J. L. May, Harmondsworth: Penguin Books, 1964, pp. 27–45.

5. D. N. Edwards, *Archaeology and Settlement in Upper Nubia in the 1st Millennium A.D.*, Cambridge Monographs in African Archaeology 36, BAR International Series 537, 1989, p. 22.

6. K. Sadr, *The Development of Nomadism in Ancient Northeast Africa*, Philadelphia: University of Pennsylvania Press, 1991, p. 83.

## *Chapter 2*

1. J. Reinold, "Néolithique Soudanais: les coutumes funeraire," in W. V. Davies (ed.), *Egypt and Africa, Nubia from Prehistory to Islam*, London: British Museum Press, 1991, pp. 27–28.

2. A-Group graves sometimes combined several bodies; thus 277 has 66 graves, but 88 actual burials.

3. B. Williams, *The University of Chicago Oriental Institute Nubian Expedition Vol. III, Part 1: The A-Group Royal Cemetery at Qustul: Cemetery L*, Chicago: University of Chicago Press, 1986, pp. 14–18.

4. W. Adams, *Nubia, Corridor to Africa*, London: Allen Lane, Penguin Books, 1977, p. 130; see also B. Trigger, *Nubia Under the Pharaohs*, London: Thames and Hudson, 1976, pp. 42–43.

5. B. Williams, *The University of Chicago Oriental Institute Nubian Expedition Vol. III, Part 1: The A-Group Royal Cemetery at Qustul: Cemetery L*, Chicago: University of Chicago Press, 1986, chap. 5.

6. Tomb "U-j" at Abydos; see W. Kaiser, "Zur Enstehung des gesamtagyptischen Staates," in *Mitteilungen des deutschen archäologischen Instituts, Abteilung Kairo* 46 (1990):287–99.

7. C. M. Firth, *The Archaeological Survey of Nubia. Report for 1901–1911*, Cairo: Government Press, 1927, pp. 204–207.

## Chapter 3

1. See M. Lichtheim, *Ancient Egyptian Literature Volume 1. The Old and Middle Kingdoms*, Berkeley, Los Angeles, London: University of California Press, 1975, p. 137.

2. G. Reisner, *The Archaeological Survey of Nubia. Report for 1907–1908, Volume I: Archaeological Report*, Cairo, 1910, pp. 50–51 (Grave 7:190); H. Fischer, "Varia Aegyptiaca. 5, A Nubian (or Puntite) of the Archaic Period," *Journal of the American Research Center in Egypt* 2 (1963):34–39.

3. Z. Zaba, *The Rock Inscriptions of Lower Nubia*, Prague, 1974, pp. 98–109 (Inscription No. 73).

4. See M. Lichtheim, *Ancient Egyptian Literature Volume 1. The Old and Middle Kingdoms*, University of California Press, 1975, p. 118–20.

5. D. Silverman, "Pygmies and Dwarves in Old Kingdom Egypt," in *Serapis: A Student Forum on the Ancient World*, Vol. 1, Chicago, 1969, pp. 53–55.

6. B. Trigger, *Nubia Under the Pharaohs*, London: Thames and Hudson, 1976, p. 94.

7. S. Farag, "Une inscription memphite de la XIIe dynastie," *Revue d'égyptologie* 32 (1980) p. 76, line 11+x.

8. R. Fattovich, "At the Periphery of the Empire: the Gash Delta (Eastern Sudan)," in W. V. Davies (ed.), *Egypt and Africa. Nubia from Prehistory to Islam*, London: British Museum Press, 1991, p. 46.

9. K. Sadr, *The Development of Nomadism in Ancient Northeast Africa*, Philadelphia: University of Pennsylvania Press, 1991, p. 1.

10. Following the translation in H.S. Smith and A. Smith, "A Reconstruction of the Kamose Texts," in *Zeitschrift für Ägyptische Sprache und Altertumskunde* 103, 1976, 59–60, 62 note e.

## Chapter 4

1. The smaller of these two C-group settlements (both marked in outline, but not excavated) is recorded in W. B. Emery and L. Kirwan, *The Excavations and Survey Between Wadi es-Sebua and Adindan 1929–1931*, Cairo, 1935, Plate 61 (the "C-Group settlement" is near Nag' `Abdalla). The larger settlement (and the map may be misleading about its actual size) is found in B. Williams, *The University of Chicago Oriental Institute Nubian Expedition, Volume 5: C-Group, Pan-Grave and Kerma Remains at Adindan Cemeteries T, K, U and J*, Chicago: University of Chicago Press, 1983, Plate 1: "C-Group set," near cemeteries T and J.

2. B. Kemp, *Ancient Egypt. Anatomy of a Civilization*, London; Routledge, 1989, pp. 120–24.

3. For these important distinctions, see M. Voigt, "The Goddess From Anatolia, an Archaeological Perspective," *Oriental Rug Review* 11.2 (1991), pp. 36–38.

4. C. Tilley, "Ideology and the Legitimization of Power in the Middle Neolithic of Southern Sweden," in D. Miller and C. Tilley (eds.), *Ideology, Power and Prehistory*, Cambridge: Cambridge University Press, 1984, pp. 111–46.

5. R. Blanton, "Anthropological Studies of Cities," in B. Siegal, A. Beals, and S. Tyler (eds.), *Annual Review of Anthropology* 5, Palo Alto, CA: Annual Reviews Inc., 1976, pp. 249–64.

6. Kemp, *Ancient Egypt. Anatomy of a Civilization*, London; Routledge, 1989, chap. 7.

## Chapter 5

1. B. Trigger, *Nubia Under the Pharaohs*, London: Thames and Hudson, 1976, p. 140.

2. Ibid., p. 144.

3. W. Adams, *Nubia Corridor to Africa*, London: Allen Lane, Penguin Books, 1977, pp. 256–59.

4. R. Morkot, "Nubia in the New Kingdom: the Limits of Egyptian Control," in W. Davies (ed.), *Egypt and Africa Nubia from Prehistory to Islam*, London: The British Museum Press, 1991, p. 294.

5. W. Adams, *Nubia Corridor to Africa*, London: Allen Lane, Penguin Books, 1977, pp. 240.

6. N. de G. Davies, *The Tomb of Rekh-mi-re' at Thebes*, New York: Metropolitan Museum of Art, 1943, Vol. I, pp. 33–36; Vol. II, Plates XXIX–XXXV.

7. C. Meillassoux, *The Anthropology of Slavery. The Womb of Iron and Gold*, transl. by A. Dasnois, Chicago: University of Chicago Press, 1991, p. 51.

8. The early Kurru graves are always described as "tumuli" in the literature, but Kendall has shown they were in reality "probably steep-sided cylindrical structures"; cf. T. Kendall, "The Origin of the Napatan State," to appear in *Meroitica* 6. I am grateful for permission to cite his conclusions here.

9. Kendall, *op. cit.*, has suggested the mastabas were actually bases for small, steep-sided pyramids; but has no directly relevant evidence for this until the time of Kashta, and even then it cannot be shown definitively that this was the case. In the present state of the evidence therefore I prefer the evolutionary picture suggested here.

## *Chapter 6*

1. Meroe, it is suggested, was the permanent royal residence of Napatan pharaohs from the beginning of the fifth century B.C., but archaeologically its Napatan aspects go back at least to the seventh century; cf. K.-H. Priese, "The Kingdom of Kush: the Napatan Period," in *Africa in Antiquity I. The Arts of Ancient Nubia and the Sudan, The Essays,* Brooklyn, NY: The Brooklyn Museum, 1978, pp. 77–78.

2. Cf. M. Horton, "Africa in Egypt: New Evidence from Qasr Ibrim," and L. Heidorn, "The Saite and Persian Period Forts at Dorginarti," both in W. V. Davies (ed.), *Egypt and Africa. Nubia from Prehistory to Islam,* London: The British Museum Press and Egyptian Exploration Society, 1991, pp. 264–77 and 205–19.

3. Horton, "Africa in Egypt: New Evidence from Qasr Ibrim," in W. V. Davies (ed.), *Egypt and Africa. Nubia from Prehistory to Islam,* London: The British Museum Press and Egyptian Exploration Society, 1991, p. 268.

4. W. Adams, *Nubia Corridor to Africa*, London: Allen Lane, Penguin Books, 1977, p. 354.

5. Quoted, with approval, in L. Török, *Economic Offices and Officials in Meroitic Nubia (A Study in Territorial Administration of the Late Meroitic Kingdom)*, Studia Aegyptiaca V; Études Publiées par les Chaires d'Histoire Ancienne de l'Université Loránd Eötvös de Budapest 26, Budapest, 1979, p. 60. Török's entire study forcefully argues the case for a relatively high level of administrative and political integration within the Meroitic kingdom.

6. D. Edwards, *Archaeology and Settlement in Upper Nubia in the 1st Millennium* A.D., Cambridge Monographs in African Archaeology 36, BAR International Series 537, 1989, p. 10.

7. Ibid., pp. 40–43.

8. S. Dafa'alla, "The Empire of Meroe and Its Antecedents," *Expedition* 35.2, 1993.

9. Bradley argues nomads were a significant component in the Meroitic population; but also notes large nomadic populations, active in the Butana, that lay outside of Meroitic control; cf. R. Bradley, *Nomads in the Archaeological Record. Meroitica* 13, S. Wenig (ed.), Humboldt-Universität zu Berlin, Institut für Sudan archäologie und Ägyptologie, Akademie-Verlag GmbH, Berlin, 1992, 213–215.

10. C. Meillassoux, *The Anthropology of Slavery. The Womb of Iron and Gold*, transl. by A. Dasnois, Chicago: University of Chicago Press, 1991, pp. 176 ff., especially 177–80.

11. S. Dafa'alla, "Succession in the Kingdom of Napata 900–300 B.C.," *The International Journal of African Historical Studies* 26.1 (1993), pp. 1–7.

12. On the processes of royal succession in the Napatan-Meroitic kingdom, see K.-H. Priese, "The Kingdom of Kush: the Napatan Period," in *Africa in Antiquity I. The Arts of Ancient Nubia and the Sudan, The Essays*, Brooklyn, NY: The Brooklyn Museum, 1978, pp. 83–86; F. Hintze, "The Kingdom of Kush: Meroitic Period," in *Africa in Antiquity I, The Arts of Ancient Nubia and the Sudan*, Brooklyn, NY: The Brooklyn Museum, 1978, p. 95; I. Hofmann, *Studien zum meroitischen konigtum*, Monographies Reine Élisabeth 2, Brussels: Fondation égyptologique reine Elisabeth, 1971, pp. 11–18.

13. N. Miller, "Meroitic Religion," in F. Hintze (ed.), *Meroitica 7. Meroitische Forschungen 1980*, Berlin: Akademie-Verlag, 1984, p. 116.

14. Ibid., p. 117.

15. Adams, *Nubia Corridor to Africa*, London: Allen Lane, Penguin Books, 1977, p. 360.

16. G. Reisner, *Excavations at Kerma Parts I–III*, Harvard African Studies, Vol. V, Cambridge, MA: Peabody Museum of Harvard University, 1923, p. 129.

## Chapter 7

1. B. Kemp, *Ancient Egypt. Anatomy of a Civilization*, London and New York: Routledge, 1989, Part III; D. O'Connor, "New Kingdom and Third Intermediate Period, 1552–664 B.C.," in B. Trigger, B. Kemp, D. O'Connor, and A. Lloyd, *Ancient Egypt A Social History*, Cambridge: Cambridge University Press, 1992, pp. 204–18.

2. L. Török, "Kush and the External World," in S. Donadoni and S. Wenig (eds.), *Meroitica 10. Studia Meroitica 1989*, Berlin: Akademie-Verlag, 1989, pp. 147–48.

3. A. M. Abdalla, "Meroitic Social stratification," in F. Hintze (ed.), *Meroitica 7. Meroitische Forschungen 1980*, Berlin: Akademie-Verlag, 1984, pp. 23–84.

4. It is also, however, alternatively identified as a palace; cf. W. Adams, *Nubia Corridor to Africa*, London: Allen Lane, Penguin Books, 1977, pp. 358–60.

## Chapter 8

1. N. Yoffee, "Orienting Collapse," in N. Yoffee and G. Cowgill (eds.), *The Collapse of Ancient States and Civilizations*, Tucson, AR: University of Arizona Press, 1991, pp. 11–19, especially 14–15.

2. On nomadic states in general, cf. A. Khazanov, *Nomads and the Outside World*, Cambridge Studies in Social Anthropology, Cambridge: Cambridge University Press, 1983, pp. 165–66, 198–228; on nomadic states among the ancient Libyans, distant neighbors of the Nubians, cf. D. O'Connor, "The Nature of Tjemhu (Libyan) Society in the Later New Kingdom," in A. Leahy (ed.), *Libya and Egypt c. 1300–750 B.C.*, School of African and Oriental Studies, Center of Near and Middle Eastern Studies, and the Society for Libyan Studies, University of London, London, 1990, pp. 106–108.

# Suggested Readings

## Chapter 1

Two books on ancient Nubia are particularly valuable: (1) W. Adams, *Nubia Corridor to Africa* (London: Allen Lane, Penguin Books, 1977), is a comprehensive review of Nubian history and culture from the Stone Age to modern times that is unrivaled in scope; (2) B. Trigger, *Nubia Under the Pharaohs* (London: Thames and Hudson, 1976), is an excellent introduction to Nubia from early times to the 25th Dynasty. The story is then taken up in another fine, short book, by P. Shinnie, *Meroe: A Civilization of the Sudan* (New York and Washington, DC: Praeger, 1967). An important complement to these studies is a two-volume work: S. Hochfield and E. Riefstahl (eds.), *Africa in Antiquity I. The Arts of Ancient Nubia and the Sudan, The Essays* (Brooklyn, NY: The Brooklyn Museum, 1978); and S. Wenig, *Africa in Antiquity II. The Arts of Ancient Nubia and the Sudan, The Catalogue* (Brooklyn, NY: The Brooklyn Museum, 1978). These two richly illustrated volumes provide a view of Nubia's artistic and cultural achievements from early times to the Christian period that is not easily available anywhere else.

Other introductory books still of value, although older and somewhat outdated, are A. Arkell, *A History of the Sudan From the Earliest Times to 1821* (London: University of London, Athlone Press, 1961); and W. B. Emery, *Egypt in Nubia* (London: Hutchinson, 1965). A more recent short overview is J. Taylor, *Egypt and Nubia* (London: The British Museum Press, 1991), and an important collection of up-to-date scholarly essays covering all periods of Nubian history has appeared as W. V. Davies (ed.), *Egypt and Africa Nubia from Prehistory to Islam* (London: The British Museum Press in association with the Egypt Exploration Society, 1991).

The fundamental study of relations between Egypt and Nubia in the Bronze Age remains T. Säve-Söderbergh, *Ägypten und Nubien, ein Beitrage zur Geschichte altägyptischen Aussenpolitik* (Lund: Haaken Ohlsson, 1941). This is now complemented by an important new study of the topic, K. Zibelius-Chen, *Die ägyptische Expansion nach Nubien eine Darlegung der Grundfaktoren*. Beihefte zum Tübinger Atlas des vorderen Orients Reihe B (Geisteswissenschaften) Nr. 78 (Wiesbaden: Ludwig Reichert, 1988).

Environment and settlement patterns are crucial aspects of the study of ancient civilization. A complete coverage of these topics so far as Nubia is concerned is not available, but two relevant works are notable. B. Trigger, *History and Settlement in Lower Nubia* (New Haven: Yale University Publications in Anthropology 69, 1965), covers the northern part of Nubia from early times into the Christian period; and D. Edwards, *Archaeology and Settlement in Upper Nubia in the 1st Millennium A.D.* (Cambridge Monographs in African Archaeology 36, BAR International Series 537, 1989), covers Upper and Southern Nubia, but not before 100 B.C. However, Edwards' observations on environment and subsistence economies are clearly applicable in part to earlier periods as well. On the history of the Saharan and Nubian environments, see K. Neumann, "Holocene Vegetation in the Eastern Sahara: Charcoal from Prehistoric Sites," *The African Archaeological Review* 7, 1989, pp. 97–116; and also A. Grove, "Africa's Climate in the Holocene," in T. Shaw, P. Sinclair, B. Andah and A. Okpoko (eds.), *The Archaeology of Africa Food, Metals and Towns*, Routledge, London and New York, 1993, 32–42.

An important study of the nomadic groups that often interacted with the Nubians should also be noted, namely, K. Sadr, *The Development of Nomadism in Ancient Northeast Africa* (Philadelphia: University of Pennsylvania Press, 1991).

The fundamental studies on the status of Nubians and other African people in Hellenistic and Roman times, and earlier, are F. Snowden, Jr., *Blacks in Antiquity, Ethiopians in the Greco-Roman Experience* (Cambridge, MA: Belknap Press of Harvard University Press, 1970), and F. Snowden, Jr., *Before Color Prejudice; The Ancient View of Blacks* (Cambridge, MA, and London: Harvard University Press, 1983). For a fascinating discussion of possible ethnographic parallels to the customs and life-styles of the ancient Nubians, see T. Kendall, "Ethnoarchaeology in Meroitic Studies," in S. Donadoni and S. Wenig (eds.), *Meroitica 10 Studia Meroitica 1984* (Berlin: Akademie-Verlag, 1989, pp. 625–745)

On Zimbabwe, see G. Connah, *African Civilizations. Precolonial Cities and States in Tropical Africa: An Archaeological Perspective* (Cambridge: Cambridge University Press, 1987, chap. 8).

## Chapter 2

On early Egypt and Nubia, see B. Trigger, "The Rise of Egyptian Civilization," in B. Trigger, B. Kemp, D. O'Connor, and A. Lloyd, *Ancient Egypt, A Social History* (Cambridge: Cambridge University Press, 1992, pp. 1–70). Early Nubia is

covered by B. Trigger, *Nubia Under the Pharaohs* (London: Thames and Hudson, 1976, chaps. II and III); and W. Adams, *Nubia Corridor to Africa* (London: Allen Lane, Penguin Books, 1977, chaps. 4 and 5). For the earliest, hitherto unrecognized phase of the A-Group see H. S. Smith, "The Development of the A-Group Culture in Northern Lower Nubia," in W. Davies (ed.), *Egypt and Africa Nubia from Prehistory to Islam* (London: The British Museum Press and the Egypt Exploration Society, 1991, pp. 92–111). For recent discussions of aspects of early Nubia, see articles by I. Caneva, J. Reinold, and A. Marks in W. V. Davies, ibid. The A-Group cemeteries analyzed in this chapter are published in H.-A. Nordstrom, *Neolithic and A-Group Sites, The Scandinavian Joint Expedition to Sudanese Nubia*, vol. 3, no. 2, Scandinavian University Books, 1972 (Denmark: Munksgaard, Copenhagen; Norway: Universitetsforlaget Oslo, Bergen, Tromso; Sweden: Läromedelsförlagen, Stockholm, Gothenburg, Lund). The distinctions between chiefdoms and states in general are discussed in depth in A. Johnson and T. Earle, *The Evolution of Human Societies* (Stanford, Calif.: Stanford University Press, 1987).

## Chapter 3

For these periods in Nubia, see B. Trigger, *Nubia Under the Pharaohs* (London: Thames and Hudson, chaps. IV–VI); W. Adams, *Nubia Corridor to Africa* (London: Allen Lane, Penguin Books, chaps. 6–8); B. Kemp, "Old Kingdom, Middle Kingdom and Second Intermediate Periods c. 2686–1552 B.C.," in B. Trigger, B. Kemp, D. O'Connor, and A. Lloyd, *Ancient Egypt, A Social History* (Cambridge: Cambridge

University Press, 1992, pp. 116–37, 160–74). The most detailed studies of the C-Group and Kerma-Group, respectively, are M. Bietak, *Studien zur Chronologie der nubischen C-Gruppe*, Österreichische Akademie der Wissenschaften Philosophisch-Historische Klasse Denkschriften 97 Band (Wien, 1968); and B. Gratien, *Les cultures Kerma essai de classification* (Publication de l'Université de Lille III, 1978). For revisionist discussions of the location of Nubian polities in Early and Middle Bronze Age Nubia, and of the process of early state formation in Nubia, see D. O'Connor, "The Locations of Yam and Kush and Their Historical Implications" (*Journal of the American Research Center in Egypt* 23, 1986, pp. 26–50); D. O'Connor, "Early States along the Nubian Nile," in W. Davies (ed.), *Egypt and Africa Nubia from Prehistory to Islam* (London: The British Museum Press and Egypt Exploration Society, 1991, pp. 145–65). See also L. Bell, *Interpreters and Egyptianized Nubians in Ancient Egyptian Foreign Policy* (Ph.D. diss., University of Pennsylvania, 1976); and J. Bourriau, "Egypt and Kerma," in W. V. Davies (ed.), *Egypt and African Nubia from Prehistory to Islam* (London: The British Museum Press and Egypt Exploration Society, 1991, 129–44).

## Chapter 4

The primary publication on Areika is D. Randall-MacIver and C. Woolley, *Areika* (Philadelphia: The University Museum, 1909). Two important new studies of the site are forthcoming: J. Wegner, *The Settlement of Areika, A Reanalysis* (in preparation) and *Egyptian and C-Group Ceramics from the Settlement at Areika* (in preparation). The best available introductions

to Kerma are C. Bonnet, *Kerma territoire et metropole* (Institut Français d'Archéologie Orientale du Caïre, Bibliothèque Générale, T. IX, Cairo, 1986); and C. Bonnet (ed.), *Kerma, royaume de Nubie* (Mission Archéologique de l'Université de Genève au Soudan, Genève, 1990). The Classic Kerma cemetery discussed in this chapter is published in G. Reisner, *Excavations at Kerma*, Parts I–III (Harvard African Studies, Vol. V); *Excavations at Kerma* Parts IV–V (Harvard African Studies Vol. VI) (Cambridge, MA: Peabody Museum of Harvard University, 1923). See also D. O'Connor, "Kerma and Egypt: the Significance of the Monumental Buildings Kerma I, II, and XI," *Journal of the American Research Center in Egypt* XXI (1984, pp. 65–108).

## Chapter 5

Nubia in the Late Bronze Age is covered in B. Trigger, *Nubia Under the Pharaohs* (London: Thames and Hudson, 1976, chap. VII); W. Adams, *Nubia Corridor to Africa* (London: Allen Lane, Penguin Books, 1977, chap. 9); and D. O'Connor, "New Kingdom and Third Intermediate Period, 1552–664 B.C.," in B. Trigger, B. Kemp, D. O'Connor, and A. Lloyd, *Ancient Egypt A Social History* (Cambridge: Cambridge University Press, 1992, pp. 252–71). The important evidence on the princedom of Tekhet is published in T. Säve-Söderbergh and L. Troy, *New Kingdom Pharaonic Sites. The Finds and the Sites* (The Scandinavian Joint Expedition to Sudanese Nubia, Vol. 5:2 [Text and Plate volumes], 1991).

More specialized studies of significance are B. Kemp, "Imperialism and Empire in New Kingdom Egypt (c. 1575–1087 B.C.)," in P.

Garnsey and C. Whittaker (eds.), *Imperialism in the Ancient World* (Faculty of Classics, Cambridge University, 1978, pp. 7–57); D. O'Connor, "The Location of Irem" (*Journal of Egyptian Archaeology* 73, 1987, pp. 99–136); and R. Morkot, "Nubia in the New Kingdom: The Limits of Egyptian Control," in W. V. Davies (ed.), *Egypt and Africa Nubia from Prehistory to Islam* (London: The British Museum Press and Egypt Exploration Society, 1991, pp. 294–301). On the tomb of Huy, see N. de G. Davies, *The Theban Tomb Series, Vol. 4: The Tomb of Huy* (London: Egypt Exploration Society, 1926).

## Chapter 6

For the Napatan-Meroitic period in general, see P. Shinnie, *Meroe, A Civilization of the Sudan* (New York and Washington DC: Praeger, 1967); and W. Adams, *Nubia Corridor to Africa* (London: Allen Lane, Penguin Books, 1977, chaps. 10–12). More specialized but valuable studies are N. Millet, "Social and Political Organization in Meroe" (*Zeitschrift für ägyptische Sprache und Altertumskunde* 108, 1981, 124–41); L. Török, *Economic Offices and Officials in Meroitic Nubia (A study in Territorial Administration of the Late Meroitic Kingdom)*, Studia Aegyptiaca V (Études publiée par les Chaires d'Histoires Ancienne de l'Université Lorand Eötvös de Budapest 26, Budapest, 1979); and L. Török, *Der meroitische Staat 1*, Meroitica 9 (Berlin: Akademie-Verlag, 1986). A useful introduction to the Meroitic religion is N. Millet, "Meroitic Religion," in F. Hintze (ed.), *Meroitica 7* (*Meroitische Forschungen* 1980, Berlin: Akademie-Verlag 1984, pp. 111–21); and to Meroitic architecture, W. Adams, "Meroitic Architecture," in F. Hintze

(ed.), ibid., pp. 255–79. An important study of Meroitic kingship is I. Hofmann, *Studien zum meroitischen Königtum* (Monographies Reine Elisabeth 2, Brussels: Fondation égyptologique Reine Elisabeth, 1971).

## Chapter 7

The basic publication of Karanog consists of C. L. Woolley and D. Randall-MacIver, *Karanog. The Romano-Nubian Cemetery*, 2 vols. (Philadelphia: The University Museum, 1911); C. L. Woolley, *Karanog. The Town* (Philadelphia: The University Museum, 1911); F. L. Griffith, *Karanog. The Meroitic Inscriptions of Shablul and Karanog* (Philadelphia: The University Museum, 1911). For an important discussion of the socio-economic picture presented by the cemetery, see A. M. Abdalla, "Meroitic Social Stratification," in F. Hintze (ed.), *Meroitica 7* (*Meroitische Forschungen* 1980, Berlin: Akademie-Verlag, 1984, pp. 23–84, especially 46 ff.). See also I. Hofmann, "Zu Sozialstruktur einer spät-meroitischen Stadt in Unternubien" (*Anthropos* 72, 1977, pp. 193–224).

## Chapter 8

For the post-Meroitic period in general, see W. Adams, *Nubia Corridor to Africa* (London: Allen Lane, Penguin Books, 1977, chap. 13); and D. N. Edwards, *Archaeology and Settlement in Upper Nubia in the 1st Millennium A.D.* (Cambridge Monographs in African Archaeology 36, BAR International Serires 537, 1989, chap. 5). Important observations on Nubia at this time are found in L. Török, "The Historical Background: Meroe, North and South," in T. Hägg (ed.), *Nubian Culture Past and Present: Main Papers Presented at the Sixth International Conference for Nubian Studies in Uppsala 11–16 August, 1986* (Konferenser/Kungl. Vitterhets, historie och antikvitetsw akademien, 17; Stockholm: Almquist and Wiksell International, 1987, pp. 176–93); and in L. Török, *Late Antique Nubia* (Antaeus 16, Budapest, 1987). On the cemetery at Hobagi, see P. Lenoble and Nigm ed Din Mohammed Sharif, "Barbarians at the Gates? The Royal Mounds of El Hobagi and the End of Meroe" (*Antiquity* 66, 1992, pp. 626–35).

On the Christian period, see W. Adams, *Nubia Corridor to Africa* (London: Allen Lane, Penguin Books, 1977, chaps. 14–16).

# Compendium of Objects in Exhibition

*T*he compendium section of this volume includes a photographic and documentary record of each of the 319 objects in the traveling exhibition "Ancient Nubia: Egypt's Rival in Africa." All the material in this exhibition is from the collections of the Egyptian Section of The University Museum of Archaeology and Anthropology.

The compendium is organized chronologically from the Prehistoric (beginning ca. 3700 B.C.) through the Christian Period (ending in the 6th century A.D.). The basic subdivision is by cultural grouping; within each group the pottery (which includes the majority of the objects) is listed first followed by artifacts of other materials (stone, shell, bronze, etc.). The entries are numbered consecutively from 1–234; some entries contain multiple objects. Each entry includes a black-and-white photograph and documentation for the artifact(s). The information is as follows: specific type designation, cultural group, date, provenience, acquisition information, Museum accession number, measurements, and material.

All Egyptian objects acquired by the Museum prior to 1929 have accession numbers comprised of a capital "E" followed by a series of digits. All Museum objects acquired after 1929 have a tripartite numbering system. The first two digits designate the year the object was obtained; the middle digit(s) define the object's group association, therefore all objects acquired during a given year from a single source have the same middle digit(s); the third set of digits identify the object's number within its acquisition group.

The majority of the artifacts in the exhibition come from excavations sponsored by the Museum—the Coxe Expeditions of 1907–1911 to Areika, Buhen, Aniba, Karanog, and Shablul and the joint Yale-Pennsylvania Expedition of 1961–1962. A second group of important material was acquired in 1992 through reciprocal exchange of Nubian objects with the Boston Museum of Fine Arts; these pieces are identifiable by the "2" as the central digit in their acquisition numbers.

The objects in this exhibition present a comprehensive overview of the rich and complex civilization of Ancient Nubia.

1

2

3

**Black-Topped Jar**
*Early A-Group (Nagada II).*
*ca. 3700–3400 B.C.*

Khor Bahan, Cemetery 17, Tomb 68.

Archaeological Survey of Nubia,
1907–1908

92-2-1  H: 23.2; D: 10.1 cm
Ceramic

**Wavy Handled Jar**
*Terminal A-Group (Nagada III).*
*ca. 3200–3000 B.C.*

Amadeh Cemeteries.

Coxe Expedition 1907

E 15051  H: 22.0; D: 12.2 cm
Ceramic

**Decorated Bowl**
*Classic–Terminal A-Group.*
*ca. 3100–2900 B.C.*

Amadeh Cemeteries, Am 206.

Coxe Expedition 1907

E 16035  H: 17.6; D: 18.8 cm
Ceramic

4

5

6

**Conical Eggshell Ware
Bowl**
*Terminal A-Group.*
*ca. 3000–2900 B.C.*

Nag Wadi, Cemetery 142.

Archaeological Survey of Nubia,
1910–1911

92-2-2  H: 18.6; D: 16.7 cm
Ceramic

**Deep Eggshell Ware Bowl**
*Terminal A-Group.*
*ca. 3000–2900 B.C.*

Nag Wadi, Cemetery 142, Tomb 9.

Archaeological Survey of Nubia,
1910–1911

92-2-5  H: 16.4; D: 19.8 cm
Ceramic

**Incised Roughware Jar**
*A-Group.*
*ca. 3400–3000 B.C.*

Sayala, Cemetery 136, Tomb 1.

Archaeological Survey of Nubia,
1910–1911

92-2-6  H: 14.6; D: 10.7 cm
Ceramic

7

8

**Rhomboid Palette**
*A-Group.*
*ca. 3400–3000 B.C.*

Nag Wadi, Cemetery 142, Tomb 1.

Archaeological Survey of Nubia,
1910–1911

92-2-8  W: 7.3; L: 14.8; T: 0.6 cm
White quartz

**Grinder**
*A-Group.*
*ca. 3400–3000 B.C.*

Sayala, Cemetery 137, Tomb 1.

Archaeological Survey of Nubia,
1910–1911

92-2-9  W: 7.5; L: 15.0; T: 2.8 cm
Speckled porphyry

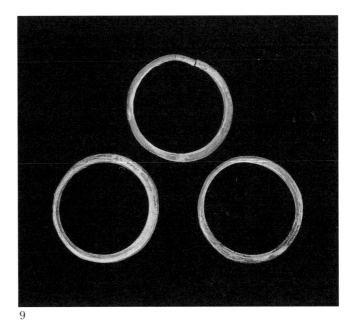

9

**Group of Three Bracelets**
*A-Group.*
*ca. 3400–3000 B.C.*

Meris-Markos, Cemetery 41, Tomb 402.

Archaeological Survey of Nubia, 1907–1908

92-2-11-1 D: 5.8; T: 0.6 cm
92-2-11-2 D: 5.9; T: 0.6 cm
92-2-11-3 D: 5.8; T: 0.5 cm
Shell

10

11

12

**Large Storage Jar**
*Transitional A-Group/C-Group.*
*ca. 2900–2400 B.C.*

Aniba Region.

Coxe Expedition 1910

92-10-3  H: 34.4; D: 36.7 cm
Ceramic

**Polished Incised Bowl**
*C-Group, phase IIA.*
*ca. 1900–1700 B.C.*

Dakka, Cemetery 101, Tomb 51.

Archaeological Survey of Nubia,
1909–1910

92-2-12  H: 8.5; D: 11.0 cm
Ceramic

**Roughware Jar with
Incised Decoration**
*C-Group, phase IIA/B.*
*ca. 2000–1600 B.C.*

Dakka, Cemetery 101, Tomb 360.

Archaeological Survey of Nubia,
1909–1910

92-2-17  H: 17.5; D: 16.0 cm
Ceramic

13

14

15

**Incised Black-Topped
Bowl**
*C-Group, phase IIA.*
*ca. 2000–1800 B.C.*

Dakka, Cemetery 101, Tomb 451.

Archaeological Survey of Nubia,
1909–1910

92-2-14  H: 6.0; D: 13.1 cm
Ceramic

**Black-Topped Red
Polished Bowl**
*C-Group, phase IIA/B.*
*ca. 1900–1600 B.C.*

Amadeh Cemeteries, Am 13.

Coxe Expedition 1910

E 11256  H: 6.5; D: 11.0 cm
Ceramic

**Black-Topped Red
Polished Bowl**
*C-Group, phase IIA/B.*
*ca. 2000–1600 B.C.*

Dakka, Cemetery 101, Tomb 59.

Archaeological Survey of Nubia,
1909–1910

92-2-13  H: 9.0; D: 12.0 cm
Ceramic

16

**Roughware Jar**

*C-Group, phase IIA/B.*
*ca. 1900–1550 B.C.*

Aniba Region.

Coxe Expedition 1910

E 8777  H: 18.2; D: 15.2 cm
Ceramic

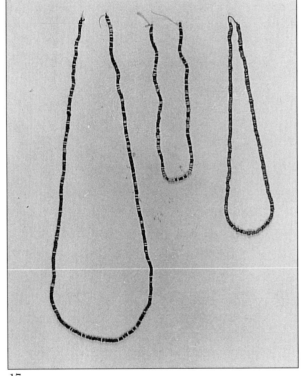

17

**Necklaces**

*C-Group.*
*ca. 2000–1600 B.C.*

Aniba, Cemetery N, Tombs 553 and 655.

Coxe Expedition 1910

92-2-15   L: 47.0; D: 3.0 cm (bead)    Tomb 553
92-2-16b L: 34.6; D: 2.0 cm (bead)    Tomb 655
92-2-16a L: 75.6; D: 3.0 cm (bead)    Tomb 655
Faience, shell and carnelian

18

19

20

**Incised Houseware Vessel**

*C-Group, phase IIA/B.*
*ca. 1900–1550 B.C.*

Areika.

Coxe Expedition 1907

E 4102   W: 14.5; L: 18.8; T: 0.4 cm
E 4197   W: 11.6; L: 14.7; T: 2.0 cm
E 4442   W: 11.8; L: 12.2; T: 0.7 cm
Ceramic

**Sherd of a Black-Topped Jar**

*C-Group, phase IIA/B.*
*ca. 1900–1550 B.C.*

Areika.

Coxe Expedition 1907

92-10-1   W: 18.7; L: 15.6; T: 0.4 cm
92-10-2   W: 5.5; L: 7.7; T: 0.4 cm
E 4119   W: 8.3; L: 11.6; T: 0.6 cm
Ceramic

**Decorated Roughware Jar**

*C-Group, phase IIA.*
*ca. 1900–1700 B.C.*

Areika.

Coxe Expedition 1907

E 4139  H: 5.5; W: 9.3; L: 11.7; T: 0.5 cm
E 4141  H: 6.9; W: 10.6; L: 16.2; T: 1.0 cm
Ceramic

21

22

23

**Sherd of a Globular Incised Marlware Jar**

*Egyptian, Mid–Late Dynasty 12.*
*ca. 1900–1800 B.C.*

Areika.

Coxe Expedition 1907

E 4232   H: 2.2; W: 8.8; L: 8.1; T: 0.9 cm
E 4161   H: 2.2; W: 5.5; L: 8.1; T: 0.8 cm
E 4257   W: 6.4; L: 12.7; T: 0.8 cm
E 4327   W: 7.8; L: 10.6; T: 0.4 cm
E 4221   W: 8.6; L: 14.4; T: 0.9 cm
E 4501   W: 11.1; L: 12.9; T: 1.5 cm
E 4334   W: 6.6; L: 3.3; T: 0.8 cm
Ceramic

**Sherd of a Black Polished Incised Bowl**

*C-Group, phase IIA/B.*
*ca. 1900–1550 B.C.*

Areika.

Coxe Expedition 1907

E 4181   W: 7.7; L: 6.1; T: 1.0 cm
E 4182   W: 4.6; L: 7.2; T: 0.9 cm
Ceramic

**Sherd of a Decorated Roughware Jar**

*C-Group, phase IIA.*
*ca. 1900–1700 B.C.*

Areika.

Coxe Expedition 1907

E 4466   W: 5.6; L: 8.3; T: 0.8 cm
E 4496   W: 11.2; L: 15.9; T: 1.3 cm
E 4642   W: 6.2; L: 9.6; T: 1.0 cm
Ceramic

24

25

### Animal and Human Figurines

*C-Group, phase IIA/B.*
*ca. 1900–1550 B.C.*

Areika.

Coxe Expedition 1907

E 4009   H: 3.4; W: 2.6; L: 6.2 cm
E 4022   W: 3.2; L: 7.3; T: 2.4 cm
E 4021   W: 2.2; L: 5.7; T: 2.4 cm
Ceramic

### Figurine Fragments

*C-Group, phase IIA/B.*
*ca. 1900–1550 B.C.*

Areika.

Coxe Expedition 1907

E 4025   W: 4.1; L: 4.3; T: 3.8 cm
E 4026   H: 6.9; W: 3.3; L: 8.9 cm
E 4030   H: 6.2; W: 2.4; L: 4.4 cm
Ceramic

26

### Objects

*C-Group, phase IIA/B.*
*ca. 1900–1550 B.C.*

Areika.

Coxe Expedition 1907

E 4071   W: 3.2; L: 6.6; T: 0.7 cm
E 4097   W: 8.5; L: 8.9; T: 1.7 cm
E 4072   W: 4.2; L: 7.1; T: 0.9 cm
E 4073   W: 5.0; L: 7.6; T: 2.5 cm
Ceramic

27

28

29

**Black-Topped Bowl**
*Early Kerma.*
*ca. 2300–2000 B.C.*

Kerma, Cemetery N, Tomb 60.

Museum of Fine Arts Expedition,
1915–1916

92-2-18  H: 7.5; D: 13.0 cm
Ceramic

**Black-Topped Incised
Bowl**
*Early Kerma.*
*ca. 2300–2000 B.C.*

Kerma, Cemetery N, Tomb 60.

Museum of Fine Arts Expedition,
1915–1916

92-2-20  H: 11.5; D: 16.0 cm
Ceramic

**Black-Topped Bowl with
Incised Rim**
*Early Kerma.*
*ca. 2300–2000 B.C.*

Kerma, Cemetery N, Tomb 173.

Museum of Fine Arts Expedition,
1915–1916

92-2-21  H: 19.0; D: 32.2 cm
Ceramic

30

31

32

**Black-Topped Bowl**
*Early Kerma.*
*ca. 2300–2000 B.C.*

Kerma, Cemetery N, Tomb 60.

Museum of Fine Arts Expedition,
1915–1916

92-2-19  H: 8.0; D: 13.5 cm
Ceramic

**Black-Topped
Hemispherical Jar**
*Middle Kerma.*
*ca. 2000–1650 B.C.*

Kerma, Cemetery M, Tomb 6.

Museum of Fine Arts Expedition,
1914–1915

92-2-24  H: 12.3; D: 25.4 cm
Ceramic

**Globular Roughware Jar**
*Middle Kerma (Middle Kingdom).*
*ca. 2000–1650 B.C.*

Kerma, Cemetery M, Tomb 6.

Museum of Fine Arts Expedition,
1914–1915

92-2-27  H: 15.4; D: 12.0 cm
Ceramic

33

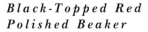

34

35

**Black-Topped Red
Polished Beaker**

*Classic Kerma.
ca. 1650–1550 B.C.*

Kerma, Cemetery S, Tumulus KIV,
Grave 425.

Museum of Fine Arts Expedition,
1912–1913

92-2-37  H: 13.0; D: 15.2 cm
Ceramic

**Black-Topped Red
Polished Beaker**

*Classic Kerma.
ca. 1650–1550 B.C.*

Kerma, Cemetery S, Tumulus KIV,
Grave 425.

Museum of Fine Arts Expedition,
1912–1913

92-2-40  H: 12.1; D: 14.5 cm
Ceramic

**Black-Topped Red
Polished Beaker**

*Classic Kerma.
ca. 1650–1550 B.C.*

Kerma, Cemetery S, Tumulus KIV,
Grave 425.

Museum of Fine Arts Expedition,
1912–1913

92-2-41  H: 11.0; D: 14.1 cm
Ceramic

36

37

38

**Black-Topped Red
Polished Beaker**

*Classic Kerma.
ca. 1650–1550 B.C.*

Kerma, Cemetery S, Tumulus KIV,
Grave 425.

Museum of Fine Arts Expedition,
1912–1913

92-2-46  H: 11.6; D: 14.7 cm
Ceramic

**Black-Topped Red
Polished Beaker**

*Classic Kerma.
ca. 1650–1550 B.C.*

Buhen, Tomb J33.

Coxe Expedition 1909

E 10611  H: 11.6; D: 14.9 cm
Ceramic

**Spouted Black-Topped
Red Polished Beaker**

*Classic Kerma.
ca. 1650–1550 B.C.*

Buhen, Tomb J33.

Coxe Expedition 1909

E 10614  H: 12.5; D: 19.8 cm
Ceramic

39

40

41

**Black-Topped Red
Polished Bowl**
*Classic Kerma.*
*ca. 1650–1550 B.C.*
Buhen, Tomb J33.
Coxe Expedition 1909
E 10615  H: 7.5; D: 18.0 cm
Ceramic

**Black-Topped Roughware
Jar**
*Classic Kerma.*
*ca. 1650–1550 B.C.*
Buhen, Tomb J33.
Coxe Expedition 1909
E 10848  H: 33.3; D: 28.0 cm
Ceramic

**Black-Topped Red
Polished Beaker**
*Classic Kerma.*
*ca. 1650–1550 B.C.*
Kerma, Cemetery S, Tumulus KIV,
Grave 425.
Museum of Fine Arts Expedition,
1912–1913
92-2-39  H: 11.5; D: 14.0 cm
Ceramic

42

43

44

**Black-Topped Red
Polished Beaker**
*Classic Kerma.*
*ca. 1650–1550 B.C.*
Kerma, Cemetery S, Tumulus KIV,
Grave 425.
Museum of Fine Arts Expedition,
1912–1913
92-2-42  H: 13.1; D: 13.5 cm
Ceramic

**Black-Topped Red
Polished Beaker**
*Classic Kerma.*
*ca. 1650–1550 B.C.*
Kerma, Cemetery S, Tumulus KIV,
Grave 425.
Museum of Fine Arts Expedition,
1912–1913
92-2-35  H: 12.3; D: 14.2 cm
Ceramic

**Black-Topped Red
Polished Beaker**
*Classic Kerma.*
*ca. 1650–1550 B.C.*
Kerma, Cemetery S, Tumulus KIV,
Grave 425.
Museum of Fine Arts Expedition,
1912–1913
92-2-44  H: 12.1; D: 14.4 cm
Ceramic

45

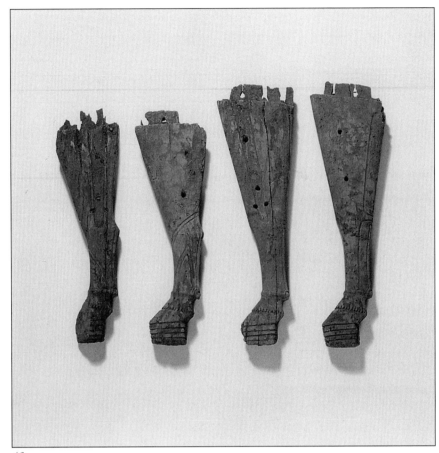

**Pendant**

*Early Kerma.*
*ca. 2300–2000 B.C.*

Kerma, Cemetery N, Tomb 185.

Museum of Fine Arts Expedition, 1915–1916

92-2-22  D: 8.5 cm
Pierced shell

46

**Bed Legs**

*Classic Kerma.*
*ca. 1650–1550 B.C.*

Kerma, Cemetery S, Tumulus KIV, Grave 425.

Museum of Fine Arts Expedition 1912–1913

92-2-48 A   W: 11.1; L: 36.7; T: 4.1 cm
92-2-48 B   W: 10.4; L: 36.4; T: 3.4 cm
92-2-48 C   W: 12.4; L: 41.4; T: 3.5 cm
92-2-48 D   W: 12.3; L: 40.8; T: 3.8 cm
Wood

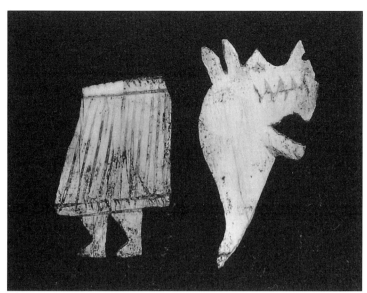

47

48

**Thueris Figures, Lower and Upper Bodies**

*Classic Kerma.*
*ca. 1650–1550 B.C.*

Kerma, Cemetery S.

Museum of Fine Arts Expedition, 1912–1913

92-2-49   W: 3.6; L: 5.2; T: 0.4 cm
92-2-50   W: 4.3; L: 7.0; T: 0.4 cm
Ivory

**Group of Four Pins**

*Classic Kerma.*
*ca. 1650–1550 B.C.*

Kerma, Cemetery S.

Museum of Fine Arts Expedition,
1912–1913

92-2-53   W: 1.5; L: 14.9; T: 0.8 cm
92-2-54   W: 2.1; L: 12.3; T: 1.4 cm
92-2-55   W: 1.5; L: 14.1; T: 1.2 cm
92-2-56   W: 1.3; L: 11.5; T: 0.9 cm
Worked bone

49

50

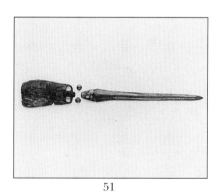

51

**Bead Necklace**

*Classic Kerma.*
*ca. 1650–1550 B.C.*

Kerma, Cemetery S.

Museum of Fine Arts Expedition,
1912–1913

92-2-58  L: 20.7; D: 0.5 (bead); T: 0.4
cm (bead)
Blue glazed quartz

**Decorative Fly**

*Second Intermediate Period/Classic*
*Kerma.*
*ca. 1650–1550 B.C.*

Buhen, Tomb J33.

Coxe Expedition 1909

E 10347 A  W: 6.0; L: 11.5;T: 1.6 cm
Ivory, bronze and electrum

**Sword**

*Second Intermediate Period/Classic*
*Kerma.*
*ca. 1650–1550 B.C.*

Buhen, Tomb J33.

Coxe Expedition 1909

E 10341  Blade W: 3.4; L: 31.2;
Handle: L 14.1, W: 6.8; Studs: D: 1.3,
H: 1.8 cm
Bronze with riveted ivory handle

52

53

54

**Hemispherical Cup**
*Egyptian, Late Dynasty 12.*
*ca. 1850–1800 B.C.*

Buhen, Cemetery K, Tomb 5.

Coxe Expedition 1909

E 15103  H: 7.5; D: 13.3 cm
Ceramic

**Tell el-Yahudiyeh Juglet**
*Egyptian, Late Second Intermediate*
*Period.*
*ca. 1600–1550 B.C.*

Buhen, Tomb J9.

Coxe Expedition 1909

E 10765  H: 16.0; D: 9.5 cm
Ceramic

**Stirrup-Shaped Finger**
**Rings**
*New Kingdom, Egyptian.*
*1550–1100 B.C.*

Buhen, Cemetery J, Tombs 13 and 15.

Coxe Expedition 1909

E 10135  H: 1.0; D: 2.4 cm   Tomb 13
E 10138  H: 1.0; D: 2.3 cm   Tomb 15
Blue and green faience

55

56

57

**Duck Shaped Vessel**
*Early Dynasty 18.*
*ca. 1500 B.C.*

Buhen, Tomb J28.

Coxe Expedition 1909

E 10603  H: 8.9; W: 6.8; L: 20.0 cm
Ceramic

**Duck Shaped Vessel**
*Early Dynasty 18.*
*ca. 1500 B.C.*

Buhen, Tomb J28.

Coxe Expedition 1909

E 10604a  H: 9.0;  W: 7.5;  L: 20.0 cm
Ceramic

**Jug**
*Egyptian, Dynasty 18.*
*ca. 1550–1300 B.C.*

Buhen, Tomb J30.

Coxe Expedition 1909

E 10605  H: 18.6; D: 13.7 cm
Ceramic

58

59

60

**Bowl**
*Egyptian, Dynasty 18.*
*ca. 1550–1300 B.C.*

Buhen, Tomb J4.

Coxe Expedition 1909

E 10624  H: 5.9; D: 14.3 cm
Ceramic

**Trumpet-Mouth Jar**
*Egyptian, Late Dynasty 18–Dynasty 19.*
*ca. 1400–1200 B.C.*

Buhen, Tomb K13.

Coxe Expedition 1909

E 10789  H: 19.0; D: 13.6 cm
Ceramic

**Jug**
*Egyptian, Dynasty 19.*
*ca. 1350–1200 B.C.*

Aniba, Tomb SA 31.

Coxe Expedition 1910

E 11317  H: 12.3; D: 10.1 cm
Ceramic

61

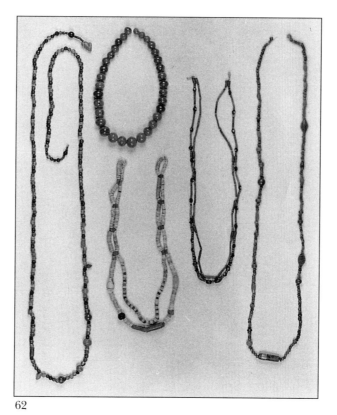

62

**Jug**
*Egyptian, Dynasty 18.*
*ca. 1550–1300 B.C.*

Buhen.

Coxe Expedition 1909

E 16041  H: 17.5; D: 12.7 cm
Ceramic

**Necklaces**

*Egyptian, New Kingdom.*
*ca. 1550–1100 B.C.*

Buhen, Tomb K13.

Coxe Expedition 1909

E 10780  L: 54.0 cm
E 16050  L: 41.0 cm

E 10786   L: 33.0 cm
E 16051 b L: 50.5 cm
E 15784   L: 42.0 cm
Carnelian, amethyst and garnet;
shell, faience, quartz and alabaster;
carnelian; blue faience beryl and
glazed composition; carnelian, gold
and red glazed composition

63

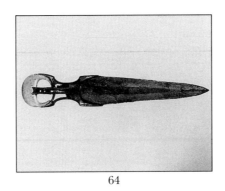

64

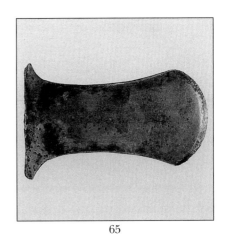

65

**Heart Scarab On Horus Headed Pectoral**
*Egyptian, Dynasty 20.*
*ca. 1200–1100 B.C.*

Aniba, Tomb SA 38.

Coxe Expedition 1910

E 11061 H: 3.2; W: 9.3; L: 6.0 cm
Steatite

**Dagger**
*Egyptian, Early Dynasty 18.*
*ca. 1550 B.C.*

Aniba, Tomb SA 16.

Coxe Expedition 1910

E 11104 W: 4.3; L: 27.2; T: 1.0 cm
Bronze

**Axehead**
*Egyptian, Early Dynasty 18.*
*ca. 1550–1500 B.C.*

Aniba, Tomb SA 29.

Coxe Expedition 1910

E 11152 W: 6.7; L: 11.5; T: 0.2 cm
Bronze

66

67

68

**Shawabti**
*Egyptian, Dynasty 19–20.*
*ca. 1300–1100 B.C.*

Aniba, Tomb SA 14.

Coxe Expedition 1910

E 11098 h H: 9.2; W: 1.8; L: 2.9 cm
Blue-green faience

**Shawabti**
*Egyptian, Dynasty 19–20.*
*ca. 1300–1100 B.C.*

Aniba, Tomb SA 14.

Coxe Expedition 1910

E 11098 t H: 15.2; W: 6.0; L: 3.0 cm
Green faience

**Shawabti**
*Egyptian, Late Dynasty 19–Dynasty 20.*
*ca. 1250–1150 B.C.*

Aniba, Tomb SA 34.

Coxe Expedition 1910

E 11197 c W: 3.1; L: 10.8; T: 2.2 cm
White faience

69

**Shawabti**

> *Dynasty 18.*
> *ca. 1350 B.C.*
>
> Toshka, Tomb of Hekanefer.
>
> Yale-Pennsylvania Expedition, 1966
>
> 66-11-1  H: 11.2; W: 8.7; T: 5.0 cm
> Painted limestone

70

**Shawabti**

> *Egyptian, Dynasty 20.*
> *ca. 1200–1070 B.C.*
>
> Aniba, Tomb of Pennut.
>
> Coxe Expedition 1910
>
> E 92-10-4  H: 11.3; W: 3.8; T: 2.4 cm
> White faience

71

72

73

**Shawabti of King Taharka**
*Napatan Period.*
*690–664 B.C.*

Nuri, Pyramid 1.

Harvard University-Boston Museum of Fine Arts Egyptian Expedition

92-2-66  H: 26.3; W: 8.8; T: 5.2 cm
Alabaster

**Shawabti of King Taharka**
*Napatan Period.*
*690–664 B.C.*

Nuri, Pyramid 1.

Harvard University-Boston Museum of Fine Arts Egyptian Expedition

92-2-67  H: 32.7; W: 10.2; T: 7.3 cm
Syenite

**Shawabti of King Senkamenisken**
*Napatan Period.*
*643–623 B.C.*

Nuri, Pyramid 3.

Harvard University-Boston Museum of Fine Arts Egyptian Expedition

92-2-69  H: 17.0; W: 5.5; T: 4.0 cm
Serpentine

74

75

**Shawabti of King Anlemani**
*Napatan Period.*
*623–593 B.C.*

Nuri, Pyramid 6.

Harvard University-Boston Museum of Fine Arts Egyptian Expedition

92-2-70  H: 26.0; W: 8.6; T: 5.7 cm
Faience

**Shawabti of a Queen (Amanimalel?)**
*Napatan Period.*
*623–593 B.C.*

Nuri, Pyramid 22.

Harvard University-Boston Museum of Fine Arts Egyptian Expedition

92-2-71  H: 14.8; W: 4.5; T: 3.1 cm
Faience

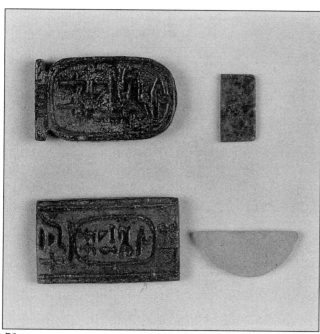

76

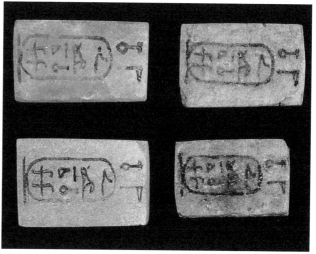

77

**Foundation Deposit Plaques**
*Napatan Period.*
*555–542 B.C.*

Nuri, Pyramid 5, southeast corner.

Harvard University-Boston Museum of Fine Arts
Egyptian Expedition

92-2-84   W: 2.1; L: 3.7; T: 0.6 cm
92-2-77   W: 0.9; L: 1.6; T: 0.2 cm
92-2-74   W: 2.1; L: 3.7; T: 0.6 cm
92-2-78   W: 1.1; L: 2.7; T: 0.3 cm
Gold, bronze, faience, alabaster, green beryl, red
jasper, lapis lazuli

**Foundation Deposit Plaques**
*Napatan Period.*
*555–542 B.C.*

Nuri, Pyramid 5, southeast corner.

Harvard University-Boston Museum of Fine Arts
Egyptian Expedition

92-2-75   W: 1.4; L: 2.6; T: 0.5 cm
92-2-76   W: 1.6; L: 2.4; T: 0.4 cm
92-2-83   W: 1.6; L: 2.5; T: 0.5 cm
92-2-82   W: 1.4; L: 2.2; T: 0.4 cm
Gold, bronze, faience, alabaster, green beryl, red
jasper, lapis lazuli

78

**Foundation Deposit Plaques**
*Napatan Period.*
*555–542 B.C.*

Nuri, Pyramid 5, southeast corner.

Harvard University-Boston Museum of Fine Arts
Egyptian Expedition

92-2-81   W: 1.7; L: 2.6; T: 0.2 cm
92-2-79   W: 1.2; L: 3.5; T: 0.1 cm
92-2-80   W: 1.7; L: 2.9; T: 0.2 cm
Gold, bronze, faience, alabaster, green beryl, red
jasper, lapis lazuli

79

80

**Cosmetic Jar**
*Napatan Period.*
*555-542 B.C.*

Nuri, Pyramid 5.

Harvard University-Boston Museum of
Fine Arts Egyptian Expedition

92-2-94  H: 19.5; D: 6.5 cm
Alabaster

**Cosmetic Jar**
*Napatan Period.*
*700–660 B.C.*

Meroe Tomb W 643, No. 5.

Harvard University-Boston Museum of
Fine Arts Egyptian Expedition

92-2-95  H: 13.0; D: 8.5 cm
Alabaster

81

82

**Canopic Jar and lid of Queen
Alakhebasken**
*Napatan Period.*
*690–664 B.C.*

Nuri, Pyramid 35.

Harvard University-Boston Museum of Fine
Arts Egyptian Expedition

92-2-92-2  H: 13.2; D: 10.5 cm  Lid
92-2-92-1  H: 31.5; D: 16.5 cm  Jar
Alabaster

**Amulet**
*Napatan Period.*
*800–700 B.C.*

Kurru, grave 51.

Harvard University-Boston Museum of Fine Arts Egyptian
Expedition

92-2-97  W: 6.0; L: 9.1; T: 0.8 cm
Faience

83

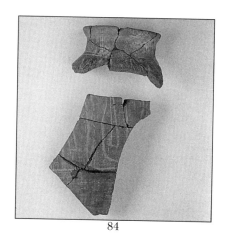

84

85

**Jar From Tomb of Queen Saka'aye**
*Napatan Period.*
*463–435 B.C.*

Nuri 31.

Harvard University-Boston Museum of Fine Arts Egyptian Expedition

92-2-101  H: 30.8; D: 13.4 cm
Ceramic

**Jar Sherds**
*Napatan Period.*
*ca. 870 B.C.*

Kurru, Tumulus 6.

Harvard University-Boston Museum of Fine Arts Egyptian Expedition

92-2-102.a  W: 15.2; H: 10.6; T: 1.1 cm
92-2-102.b  W: 25.5; L: 15.1; T: 1.8 cm
Ceramic

**Bottle**
*Napatan Period.*
*ca. 700–300 B.C.*

Kurru 701.

Harvard University-Boston Museum of Fine Arts Egyptian Expedition

92-2-103  H: 24.1; D: 20.5 cm
Ceramic

86

87

88

**Jar Stand**
*Meroitic Period.*
*40 B.C.–A.D. 114*

Meroe, West Cemetery No. 324.

Harvard University-Boston Museum of Fine Arts Egyptian Expedition

92-2-105  H: 23.6; D: 35.7 cm
Ceramic

**Footed Bowl**
*Meroitic Period.*
*463–431 B.C.*

Meroe, Tomb S 97.

Harvard University-Boston Museum of Fine Arts Egyptian Expedition

92-2-107  H: 11.9; D: 20.1 cm
Ceramic

**Bottle**
*Meroitic Period.*
*40 B.C.–A.D. 114*

Meroe, Tomb W 450/1.

Harvard University-Boston Museum of Fine Arts Egyptian Expedition

92-2-108  H: 19.9; D: 16.3 cm
Ceramic

89

90

91

**Funerary Statue Head**
*Meroitic Period.*
*100 B.C.–A.D. 300*
Shablul, grave 29.
Coxe Expedition 1907
E 5015  H: 18.0; D: 11.5; T: 10.9 cm
Sandstone

**Funerary Statue**
*Meroitic Period.*
*A.D. 240–260*
Karanog, grave 203.
Coxe Expedition 1908
E 7000  H restored: 80.0; H original:
58.0 W: 23.0; L: 46.0 cm
Sandstone

**Funerary Statue Head**
*Meroitic Period.*
*A.D. 225–275*
Karanog, grave 183.
Coxe Expedition 1908
E 7001  H: 18.4; W: 14.3; T: 16.2 cm
Sandstone

92

93

94

**Funerary Statue**
*Meroitic Period.*
*100 B.C.–A.D. 300*
Karanog.
Coxe Expedition 1908
E 7003  H: 59.0; W: 14.5; L: 35.5 cm
Sandstone

**Funerary Statue**
*Meroitic Period.*
*100 B.C.–A.D. 300*
Karanog, grave 133.
Coxe Expedition 1908
E 7004  H: 69.5; W: 18.5; L: 50.5 cm
Sandstone

**Funerary Statue**
*Meroitic Period.*
*100 B.C.–A.D. 300*
Karanog, grave 182.
Coxe Expedition 1908
E 7005  H: 76.4; W: 53.0; L: 54.0 cm
Sandstone

95

96

97

**Funerary Statue**
*Meroitic Period.*
*100 B.C.–A.D. 300*
Karanog.
Coxe Expedition 1908
E 7018  H: 72.0; W: 15.0; L: 40.5 cm
Sandstone

**Funerary Statue**
*Meroitic Period.*
*100 B.C.–A.D. 300*
Karanog.
Coxe Expedition 1908
E 7032  H: 39.5; W: 18.0; L: 37.5 cm
Sandstone

**Head of a Funerary Statue**
*Meroitic Period.*
*100 B.C.–A.D. 300*
Karanog.
Coxe Expedition 1908
E 7037  H: 26.5; D: 14.5; T: 12.5 cm
Sandstone

98

99

100

**Funerary Statue Head**
*Meroitic Period.*
*100 B.C.–A.D. 300*
Karanog.
Coxe Expedition 1908
E 7038  H: 17.9; D: 12.1; T: 10.7 cm
Sandstone

**Funerary Statue Head**
*Meroitic Period.*
*100 B.C.–A.D. 300*
Karanog.
Coxe Expedition 1908
E 7070  H: 13.2; D: 13.5; T: 9.9 cm
Sandstone

**Stela**
*Meroitic Period.*
*100 B.C.–A.D. 300*
Karanog.
Coxe Expedition 1908
E 7081  H: 34.0; W: 22.5; T: 5.0 cm
Sandstone

101

102

103

***Offering table***
*Meroitic Period.*
*100 B.C.–A.D. 300*

Karanog, grave 82.

Coxe Expedition 1908

E 7088  W: 44.5; L: 47.0 cm
Sandstone

***Offering Table***
*Meroitic Period.*
*100 B.C.–A.D. 300*

Karanog, grave 701.

Coxe Expedition 1908

E 7095  W: 45.3; L: 46.5; T: 7.8 cm
Sandstone

***Offering Table***
*Meroitic Period.*
*100 B.C.–A.D. 300*

Karanog, grave 285.

Coxe Expedition 1908

E 7097  W: 25.9; L: 34.5; T: 6.9 cm
Sandstone

104

105

106

***Stela***
*Meroitic Period.*
*100 B.C.–A.D. 300*

Karanog, grave 180.

Coxe Expedition 1908

E 7100  W: 34.2; L: 41.0 cm
Sandstone

***Door jamb***
*Meroitic Period.*
*100 B.C.–A.D. 300*

Arminna West.

Yale-Pennsylvania Expedition 1961-62

66-11-42  W: 20.0; L: 92.6; T: 9.5 cm
Sandstone

***Ostrakon***
*Meroitic Period.*
*100 B.C.–A.D. 300*

Karanog.

Coxe Expedition 1908

E 8953  H: 9.2; L: 12.0; T: 0.8 cm
Ceramic

107

108

***Ostrakon***
*Meroitic Period.*
*100 B.C.–A.D. 300*

Karanog.

Coxe Expedition 1908

E 8954   H: 5.4; L: 5.9; T: 0.8 cm
Ceramic

***Ostrakon***
*Meroitic Period.*
*100 B.C.–A.D. 300*

Karanog (north end of cemetery).

Coxe Expedition 1908

E 8956   H: 14.8; L: 11.1; T: 0.9 cm
Ceramic

109

110

***Strings of Beads***
*Meroitic Period.*
*100 B.C.–A.D. 300*

Karanog, graves 312, 783, 779

Coxe Expedition 1908

E 7794   L: 36.0 cm   grave 312
E 7932   L: 30.5 cm   grave 783
E 7934   L: 23.5 cm   grave 779
Glass, stone, paste and faience

***Strings of Beads***
*Meroitic Period.*
*100 B.C.–A.D. 300*

Karanog, graves 26, 45, 83, 300, 229, 242.

Coxe Expedition 1908

E 7755    L: 28.0 cm   grave 26
E 7759    L: 17.5 cm   grave 45
E 7765    L: 21.5 cm   grave 83
E 7840 b  L: 24.2 cm   grave 300
E 7816    L: 17.5 cm   grave 229
E 7819    L: 12.0 cm   grave 242
Glass, stone, paste and faience

111

### Strings of Beads

*Meroitic Period.*
*100 B.C.–A.D. 300*

Karanog, graves 712, 307, 361

Coxe Expedition 1908

E 7920    L: 37.8 cm    grave 712
E 7849    L: 34.0 cm    grave 307
E 7847    L: 49.7 cm    grave 307
E 7877    L: 61.0 cm    grave 361
E 7868    L: 47.5 cm    grave 361
Glass, stone, paste and faience

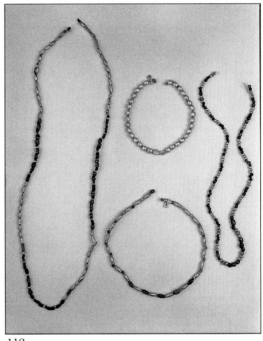

112

### Strings of Beads

*Meroitic Period.*
*100 B.C.–A.D. 300*

Karanog, graves 755, 527, 726, 488

Coxe Expedition 1908

E 7928    L: 29.2 cm    grave 755
E 7871    L: 20.0 cm    grave 527
E 7922    L: 40.3 cm    grave 726
E 7905    L: 60.0 cm    grave 488
Carnelian, glass, gold, hematite and paste

113

### Strings of Beads

*Meroitic Period.*
*100 B.C.–A.D. 300*

Karanog, graves 523, 307

Coxe Expedition 1908

E 7759     L: 17.5 cm    grave 523
E 7791B    L: 33.5 cm    grave 307
92-10-5    L: 44.5 cm
92-10-6    L: 27.3 cm
Glass, paste, stone

114

115

**Ring with Engraved Bezel**

*Meroitic Period.*
*100 B.C.–A.D. 300*

Karanog, graves 647.

Coxe Expedition 1908

E 8046  W: 1.4; L: 2.6; D: 1.7 cm
Iron, bronze

**Ring with Engraved Bezel**

*Meroitic Period.*
*100 B.C.–A.D. 300*

Karanog, graves 324.

Coxe Expedition 1908

E 8054  W: 1.5; L: 2.6; D: 1.7 cm
Iron, bronze

116

117

**Ring with Engraved Bezel**

*Meroitic Period.*
*100 B.C.–A.D. 300*

Karanog, graves 723.

Coxe Expedition 1908

E 8068  W: 1.3; L: 2.5; D: 2.8 cm
Iron, bronze

**Ring with Engraved Bezel**

*Meroitic Period.*
*100 B.C.–A.D. 300*

Karanog, graves 241.

Coxe Expedition 1908

E 8077  W: 1.3; L: 2.6; D: 1.8 cm
Iron, bronze

118

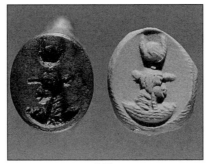

119

120

**Ring with Engraved Bezel**
*Meroitic Period.*
*100 B.C.–A.D. 300*
Karanog, graves 331.
Coxe Expedition 1908
E 8084  W: 1.2; L: 2.5; D: 1.8 cm
Iron, bronze

**Ring with Engraved Bezel**
*Meroitic Period.*
*100 B.C.–A.D. 300*
Karanog, graves 683.
Coxe Expedition 1908
E 8105  W: 1.5; L: 2.6; D: 1.9 cm
Iron, bronze

**Ring with Engraved Bezel**
*Meroitic Period.*
*100 B.C.–A.D. 300*
Karanog, graves 161.
Coxe Expedition 1908
E 8110  W: 1.6; L: 2.4; D: 1.8 cm
Iron, bronze

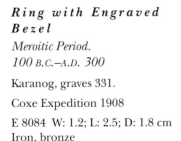

121

122

123

**Ring with Engraved Bezel**
*Meroitic Period.*
*100 B.C.–A.D. 300*
Karanog, graves 711.
Coxe Expedition 1908
E 8114  W: 1.6; L: 3.3; D: 1.7 cm
Iron, bronze

**Ring with Engraved Bezel**
*Meroitic Period.*
*100 B.C.–A.D. 300*
Karanog, graves 521.
Coxe Expedition 1908
E 8126  W: 1.6; L: 2.4; D: 1.9 cm
Iron, bronze

**Kohl Tube**
*Meroitic Period.*
*100 B.C.–A.D. 300*
Karanog, graves 45.
Coxe Expedition 1908
E 7514  H: 17.8; D: 4.3 cm
Wood, ivory

124

**Kohl Tube**
*Meroitic Period.*
*100 B.C.–A.D. 300*
Karanog, graves 293.
Coxe Expedition 1908
E 7515 a-b  H: 26.0; D: 4.9 cm
Wood, ivory

125

**Kohl Tube**
*Meroitic Period.*
*100 B.C.–A.D. 300*
Karanog, graves 521.
Coxe Expedition 1908
E 7602 a-b  H: 16.0; D: 3.5 cm
Wood, ivory

126

**Kohl Tube**
*Meroitic Period.*
*100 B.C.–A.D. 300*
Karanog, graves 361.
Coxe Expedition 1908
E 7618 a-c  H: 16.1; D: 3.6 cm
Wood, ivory

127

**Box**
*Meroitic Period.*
*100 B.C.–A.D. 300*
Karanog, grave 45.
Coxe Expedition 1908
E 7519  H: 28.1; W: 26.9; T: 23.1 cm
Wood, ivory

128

**Bottle**
*Meroitic Period.*
*100 B.C.–A.D. 300*
Karanog, grave 278.
Coxe Expedition 1908
E 7339  H: 13.0; W: 4.8; T: 5.5 cm
Glass

129

**Flask**
*Meroitic Period.*
*A.D. 275–325*
Karanog, grave 384.
Coxe Expedition 1908
E 7340  H: 9.9; D: 8.0 cm
Glass

130

131

132

**Bottle**

*Meroitic Period.*
A.D. *1–300*

Karanog, grave 314.

Coxe Expedition 1908

E 7342  H: 17.4; D: 6.7 cm
Glass

**Bowl**

*Meroitic Period.*
A.D. *275–325*

Karanog, grave 384.

Coxe Expedition 1908

E 7343  H: 5.5; D: 7.8 cm
Glass

**Oil Flask**

*Meroitic Period.*
*100 B.C.–A.D. 300*

Karanog, grave 355.

Coxe Expedition 1908

E 7348  H: 7.8; D: 7.3 cm
Glass

133

134

135

**Oil Flask**

*Meroitic Period.*
*100 B.C.–A.D. 300*

Karanog, grave 330.

Coxe Expedition 1908

E 7353  H: 15.7; D: 12.5 cm
Glass

**Cup**

*Meroitic Period.*
*100 B.C.–A.D. 300*

Karanog, grave 139.

Coxe Expedition 1908

E 7366  H: 8.5; D: 8.5 cm
Faience

**Lamp**

*Meroitic Period.*
A.D. *225–275*

Karanog, grave 187.

Coxe Expedition 1908

E 7147  H: 35.0; W: 10.4 cm
Bronze

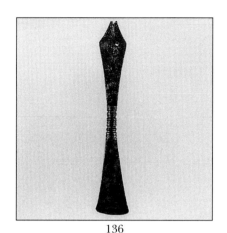

136

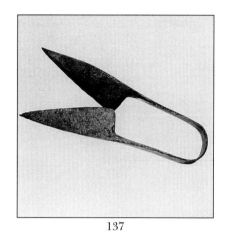

137

138

**Chisel**
*Meroitic Period.*
*100 B.C.–A.D. 300*

Karanog, grave 585.

Coxe Expedition 1908

E 7301  W: 2.0; L: 11.4; T: 0.5 cm
Iron

**Shears**
*Meroitic Period.*
*100 B.C.–A.D. 300*

Karanog, grave 585.

Coxe Expedition 1908

E 7303  W: 5.5; L: 14.5; T: 1.4 cm
Bronze

**Chisel**
*Meroitic Period.*
*100 B.C.–A.D. 300*

Karanog, grave 254.

Coxe Expedition 1908

E 7367  W: 3.4; L: 18.7; T: 1.7 cm
Iron

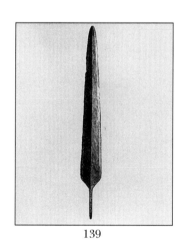

139

140

**Spearhead**
*Meroitic Period.*
*100 B.C.–A.D. 300*

Karanog, grave 141.

Coxe Expedition 1908

E 7368  W: 2.3; L: 20.3; T: 0.4 cm
Iron

**Anklet**
*Meroitic Period.*
*100 B.C.–A.D. 300*

Karanog, grave 8.

Coxe Expedition 1908

E 7379  D: 7.4; T: 1.1 cm
Iron

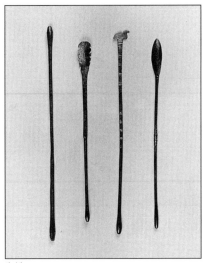

141

142

143

**Kohl Sticks**

*Meroitic Period.*
*100–1 B.C.*

Karanog, graves 315, 131, 467,
and 304.

Coxe Expedition 1908

E 7387  W: 1.0; L: 16.4 cm  grave 315
E 7388  W: 0.5; L: 18.5 cm  grave 131
E 7392  W: 1.5; L: 17.6 cm  grave 467
E 7396  W: 1.3; L: 15.5 cm  grave 304
Bronze, iron

**Spoon**

*Meroitic Period.*
*A.D. 225–275*

Karanog, grave 187.

Coxe Expedition 1908

E 7420  W: 4.0; L: 21.0 cm
Bronze

**Spoon**

*Meroitic Period.*
*A.D. 225–275*

Karanog, grave 187.

Coxe Expedition 1908

E 7422  W: 4.2; L: 19.0 cm
Wood

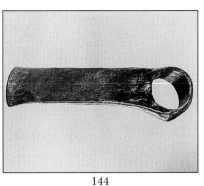

144

145

**Adze**

*Meroitic Period.*
*100 B.C.–A.D. 300*

Karanog, grave 672.

Coxe Expedition 1908

E 7459  H: 3.9; L: 18.0 cm
Iron

**Ring**

*Meroitic Period.*
*A.D. 225–275*

Karanog, grave 187.

Coxe Expedition 1908

E 7570  H: 2.3; D: 4.5 cm
Wood

146

147

148

**Spindle Whorl**
*Meroitic Period.*
*100 B.C.–A.D. 300*

Karanog, graves 293.

Coxe Expedition 1908

E 7678 b  H: 2.1; D: 3.4 cm
Wood

**Spindle Whorl**
*Meroitic Period.*
*100 B.C.–A.D. 300*

Karanog, graves 217.

Coxe Expedition 1908

E 7679  H: 2.4; D: 4.0 cm
Wood

**Archer's Thumb Ring**
*Meroitic Period.*
*100 B.C.–A.D. 300*

Karanog, grave 488.

Coxe Expedition 1908

E 7682 a  H: 2.8; D: 3.0 cm
Stone

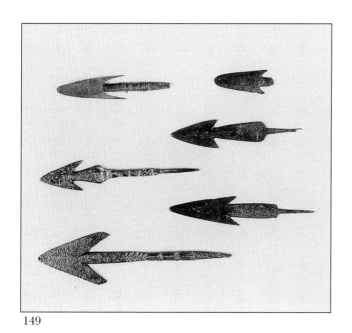

149

150

**Arrowheads**
> *Meroitic Period.*
> *100 B.C.–A.D. 300*
>
> Karanog, graves 254, 324, 607, 778.
>
> Coxe Expedition 1908

| E 7230 | W: 0.9; L: 3.4; T: 0.1 cm | grave 254 |
| E 7270 | W: 1.7; L: 7.6; T: 0.2 cm | grave 254 |
| E 7272 | W: 1.6; L: 8.3; T: 0.2 cm | grave 254 |
| E 7280 | W: 1.6; L: 9.2; T: 0.4 cm | grave 324 |
| E 7292 | W: 2.9; L: 11.0; T: 0.6 cm | grave 607 |
| E 7419 | W: 1.5; L: 6.5; T: 0.2 cm | grave 778 |

Iron

**Arrowheads**
> *Meroitic Period.*
> *100 B.C.–A.D. 300*
>
> Karanog, graves 141, 254.
>
> Coxe Expedition 1908

| E 7198 | W: 1.4; L: 6.3; T: 0.2 cm | grave 141 |
| E 7203 | W: 1.9; L: 9.3; T: 0.3 cm | grave 141 |
| E 7204 | W: 1.7; L: 10.0; T: 0.1 cm | grave 141 |
| E 7206 | W: 2.0; L: 9.9; T: 0.2 cm | grave 141 |
| E 7207 | W: 1.9; L: 9.1; T: 0.2 cm | grave 141 |
| E 7260 | W: 2.1; L: 11.7; T: 0.15 cm | grave 254 |

Iron

151

152

### Arrowheads

*Meroitic Period.*
*100 B.C.–A.D. 300*

Karanog, graves 141, 254, 324.

Coxe Expedition 1908

| | | |
|---|---|---|
| E 7202 | W: 1.3; L: 7.8; T: 0.2 cm | grave 141 |
| E 7237 | W: 0.6; L: 5.0; T: 0.5 cm | grave 254 |
| E 7238 | W: 1.6; L: 6.2; T: 0.2 cm | grave 254 |
| E 7260 | W: 2.1; L: 11.7; T: 0.15 cm | grave 254 |
| E 7266 | W: 2.3; L: 10.7; T: 0.3 cm | grave 254 |
| E 7279 | W: 0.6; L: 7.2; T: 0.5 cm | grave 324 |

Iron

### Arrowheads

*Meroitic Period.*
*100 B.C.–A.D. 300*

Karanog, graves 141, 254, 324.

Coxe Expedition 1908

| | | |
|---|---|---|
| E 7180 | W: 1.9; L: 8.8; T: 0.2 cm | grave 141 |
| E 7181 | W: 2.0; L: 8.2; T: 0.1 cm | grave 141 |
| E 7226 | W: 1.6; L: 5.5; T: 0.2 cm | grave 254 |
| E 7276 | W: 2.1; L: 13.6; T: 0.3 cm | grave 324 |

Iron

153

### Human Vertebra with Embedded Arrowhead

*Meroitic Period.*
*100 B.C.–A.D. 300*

Karanog, grave 628.

Coxe Expedition 1908

E 7726  H: 6.0; W: 6.3; L: 9.9 cm
Bone, bronze

154

155

156

**Bowl**
*Meroitic Period.*
*100 B.C.–A.D. 300*
Karanog, grave 331.
Coxe Expedition 1908
E 7129  H: 6.5; D: 9.5 cm
Bronze

**Bowl**
*Meroitic Period.*
*100 B.C.–A.D. 300*
Karanog, grave 270.
Coxe Expedition 1908
E 7130  H: 6.3; D: 11.6 cm
Bronze

**Cup**
*Meroitic Period.*
*100 B.C.–A.D. 300*
Karanog, grave 394.
Coxe Expedition 1908
E 7132  H: 7.2; D: 9.2 cm
Bronze

157

158

159

**Cup**
*Meroitic Period.*
*100-1 B.C.*
Karanog, grave 712.
Coxe Expedition 1908
E 7133  H: 7.0; D: 8.6 cm
Bronze

**Cup**
*Meroitic Period.*
*100 B.C.–A.D. 300*
Karanog, grave 671.
Coxe Expedition 1908
E 7134  H: 7.0; D: 7.2 cm
Bronze

**Three-Footed Bowl**
*Meroitic Period.*
*100 B.C.–A.D. 300*
Karanog, grave 45.
Coxe Expedition 1908
E 7137  H: 11.2; D: 13.5 cm
Bronze

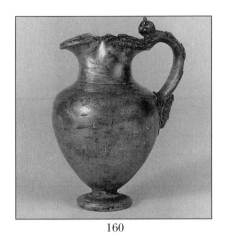

160

**Pitcher**
*Meroitic Period.*
A.D. *225–275*

Karanog, grave 187.

Coxe Expedition 1908

E 7512  H: 14.0; D: 5.5 cm
Bronze

161

**Jar**
*Meroitic Period.*
*100 B.C.–A.D. 300*

Shablul.

Coxe Expedition 1907

E 6598  H: 7.0; D: 3.1 cm
Ceramic

162

**Jar**
*Meroitic Period.*
*100 B.C.–A.D. 300*

Shablul, grave 101(?).

Coxe Expedition 1907

E 5331  H: 22.5; D: 16.2 cm
Ceramic

163

**Jar**
*Meroitic Period.*
A.D. *75–125*

Karanog, grave 528.

Coxe Expedition 1908

E 8154  H: 38.7; D: 22.0 cm
Ceramic

164

**Jar**
*Meroitic Period.*
*100–1 B.C.*

Karanog, grave 712.

Coxe Expedition 1908

E 8157  H: 28.9; D: 28.1 cm
Ceramic

165

**Jar**
*Meroitic Period.*
*100–1 B.C.*

Karanog, grave 542.

Coxe Expedition 1908

E 8162  H: 31.0; D: 11.6 cm
Ceramic

166

167

168

**Jar**
*Meroitic Period.*
*100 B.C.–A.D. 300*

Karanog, grave 301.

Coxe Expedition 1908

E 8168  H: 33.6; D: 17.2 cm
Ceramic

**Jar**
*Meroitic Period.*
*100 B.C.–A.D. 300*

Karanog, grave 112.

Coxe Expedition 1908

E 8170  H: 30.7; D: 12.9 cm
Ceramic

**Amphora**
*Meroitic Period.*
*A.D. 1–50*

Karanog, grave 626.

Coxe Expedition 1908

E 8173  H: 45.6; D: 10.0 cm
Ceramic

169

170

171

**Jar**
*Meroitic Period.*
*100 B.C.–A.D. 300*

Karanog.

Coxe Expedition 1908

E 8176  H: 22.2; D: 19.7 cm
Ceramic

**Jar**
*Meroitic Period.*
*100–1 B.C.*

Karanog, grave 566.

Coxe Expedition 1908

E 8183  H: 34.0; D: 29.4 cm
Ceramic

**Jar**
*Meroitic Period.*
*A.D. 75–125*

Karanog, grave 129.

Coxe Expedition 1908

E 8192  H: 31.0; D: 26.7 cm
Ceramic

172

173

174

**Jar**
*Meroitic Period.*
*100 B.C.–A.D. 300*
Karanog, grave 535.
Coxe Expedition 1908
E 8193  H: 36.5; D: 19.9 cm
Ceramic

**Jar**
*Meroitic Period.*
*A.D. 225–275*
Karanog, grave 181.
Coxe Expedition 1908
E 8197  H: 21.3; D: 12.0 cm
Ceramic

**Jar**
*Meroitic Period.*
*A.D. 75–125*
Karanog, grave 112.
Coxe Expedition 1908
E 8216  H: 30.7; D: 16.9 cm
Ceramic

175

176

177

**Jar**
*Meroitic Period.*
*100 B.C.–A.D. 300*
Karanog, grave 134.
Coxe Expedition 1908
E 8218  H: 32.5; D: 26.0 cm
Ceramic

**Jar**
*Meroitic Period.*
*100 B.C.–A.D. 300*
Karanog, grave 550.
Coxe Expedition 1908
E 8237  H: 16.0; D: 16.3 cm
Ceramic

**Jar**
*Meroitic Period.*
*A.D. 75–125*
Karanog, grave 271.
Coxe Expedition 1908
E 8257  H: 27.5; D: 22.0 cm
Ceramic

178

179

180

**Jar**
*Meroitic Period.*
*100 B.C.–A.D. 300*

Karanog.

Coxe Expedition 1908

E 8261  H: 26.0; D: 18.8 cm
Ceramic

**Jar**
*Meroitic Period.*
*100 B.C.–A.D. 300*

Karanog, grave 735.

Coxe Expedition 1908

E 8270  H: 16.8; D: 16.5 cm
Ceramic

**Jar**
*Meroitic Period.*
*A.D. 1–50*

Karanog, grave 530.

Coxe Expedition 1908

E 8275  H: 20.5; D: 18.2 cm
Ceramic

181

182

183

**Jar**
*Meroitic Period.*
*100 B.C.–A.D. 300*

Karanog, grave 73.

Coxe Expedition 1908

E 8276  H: 16.8; D: 7.0 cm
Ceramic

**Jar**
*Meroitic Period.*
*100 B.C.–A.D. 300*

Karanog, grave 221.

Coxe Expedition 1908

E 8284  H: 23.5; D: 20.0 cm
Ceramic

**Jug**
*Meroitic Period.*
*100 B.C.–A.D. 300*

Karanog, grave 295.

Coxe Expedition 1908

E 8290  H: 21.2; D: 14.2 cm
Ceramic

184

**Jar**
*Meroitic Period.*
A.D. *75–125*

Karanog, grave 162.

Coxe Expedition 1908

E 8293  H: 37.0; D: 19.5 cm
Ceramic

185

**Pot**
*Meroitic Period.*
A.D. *25–75*

Karanog, grave 543.

Coxe Expedition 1908

E 8310  H: 14.0; D: 13.5 cm
Ceramic

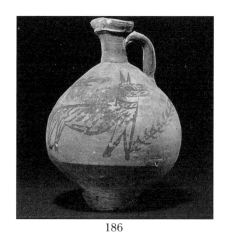

186

**Pitcher**
*Meroitic Period.*
*100* B.C.–A.D. *300*

Karanog, grave 634.

Coxe Expedition 1908

E 8334  H: 13.5; D: 10.0 cm
Ceramic

187

**Jar**
*Meroitic Period.*
*100* B.C.–A.D. *300*

Karanog, grave 741.

Coxe Expedition 1908

E 8550  H: 20.0; D: 21.5 cm
Ceramic

188

**Jar**
*Meroitic Period.*
*100* B.C.–A.D. *300*

Karanog, grave 118.

Coxe Expedition 1908

E 8565  H: 26.5; D: 26.1 cm
Ceramic

189

**Amphora**
*Meroitic Period.*
A.D. *75–125*

Karanog, grave 112.

Coxe Expedition 1908

E 8571  H: 53.1; D: 16.2 cm
Ceramic

190

191

192

**Jug**
*Meroitic Period.*
*100 B.C.–A.D. 300*

Karanog, grave 638.

Coxe Expedition 1908

E 8577  H: 15.0; D: 10.7 cm
Ceramic

**Table Amphora**
*Meroitic Period.*
*100 B.C.–A.D. 300*

Karanog, grave 729.

Coxe Expedition 1908

E 8596  H: 28.3; D: 19.9 cm
Ceramic

**Jar**
*Meroitic Period.*
*100 B.C.–A.D. 300*

Karanog, grave 210.

Coxe Expedition 1908

E 8811  H: 14.0; D: 10.1 cm
Ceramic

193

194

195

**Pot With Lid**
*Meroitic Period.*
*100 B.C.–A.D. 300*

Karanog, grave 549.

Coxe Expedition 1908

E 8967  H: 15.7; D: 12.6 cm
Ceramic

**Jar**
*Meroitic Period.*
*100 B.C.–A.D. 300*

Buhen, grave H 4.

Coxe Expedition
1909-1910

E 10435  H: 24.0; D: 21.0 cm
Ceramic

**Cup**
*Meroitic Period.*
*100 B.C.–A.D. 300*

Shablul.

Coxe Expedition 1907

E 5252  H: 7.0; D: 7.2 cm
Ceramic

196

197

198

***Cup***
*Meroitic Period.*
*100 B.C.–A.D. 300*
Shablul.
Coxe Expedition 1907
E 5271  H: 8.5; D: 8.7 cm
Ceramic

***Cup***
*Meroitic Period.*
*100 B.C.–A.D. 300*
Karanog, grave 304.
Coxe Expedition 1908
E 8437  H: 8.0; D: 9.8 cm
Ceramic

***Cup***
*Meroitic Period.*
*100 B.C.–A.D. 300*
Karanog, grave 549.
Coxe Expedition 1908
E 8447  H: 8.3; D: 9.2 cm
Ceramic

199

200

201

***Cup***
*Meroitic Period.*
*100 B.C.–A.D. 300*
Karanog, grave 189.
Coxe Expedition 1908
E 8451  H: 7.8; D: 9.7 cm
Ceramic

***Cup***
*Meroitic Period.*
*100 B.C.–A.D. 300*
Karanog, grave 284.
Coxe Expedition 1908
E 8453  H: 9.0; D: 8.3 cm
Ceramic

***Cup***
*Meroitic Period.*
*100 B.C.–A.D. 300*
Karanog, grave 325.
Coxe Expedition 1908
E 8469  H: 8.0; D: 9.8 cm
Ceramic

202

203

204

***Cup***
*Meroitic Period.*
*100 B.C.–A.D. 300*
Karanog, grave 377.
Coxe Expedition 1908
E 8472  H: 8.2; D: 8.8 cm
Ceramic

***Bowl***
*Meroitic Period.*
*100 B.C.–A.D. 300*
Karanog, grave 304.
Coxe Expedition 1908
E 8478  H: 2.4; D: 9.5 cm
Ceramic

***Cup***
*Meroitic Period.*
*100 B.C.–A.D. 300*
Karanog, grave 665.
Coxe Expedition 1908
E 8483  H: 7.6; D: 8.6 cm
Ceramic

205

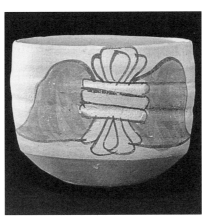

206

207

***Carinated Bowl***
*Meroitic Period.*
*100 B.C.–A.D. 300*
Karanog.
Coxe Expedition 1908
E 8602  H: 8.5; D: 12.5 cm
Ceramic

***Cup***
*Meroitic Period.*
*100–1 B.C.*
Karanog, grave 566.
Coxe Expedition 1908
E 8628  H: 7.0; D: 9.0 cm
Ceramic

***Cup***
*Meroitic Period.*
*100 B.C.–A.D. 300*
Karanog, grave 615.
Coxe Expedition 1908
E 8631  H: 8.0; D: 9.0 cm
Ceramic

208

209

210

***Cup***
*Meroitic Period.*
A.D. *225–275*

Karanog, grave 181.

Coxe Expedition 1908

E 8638  H: 9.1; D: 11.1 cm
Ceramic

***Cup***
*Meroitic Period.*
*100* B.C.–A.D. *300*

Karanog, grave 400.

Coxe Expedition 1908

E 8645  H: 9.9; D: 10.4 cm
Ceramic

***Cup***
*Meroitic Period.*
A.D. *275–325*

Karanog, grave 384.

Coxe Expedition 1908

E 8671  H: 7.3; D: 8.5 cm
Ceramic

211

212

213

***Cup***
*Meroitic Period.*
*100* B.C.–A.D. *300*

Karanog, grave 154.

Coxe Expedition 1908

E 8672  H: 8.0; D: 8.9 cm
Ceramic

***Cup***
*Meroitic Period.*
A.D. *525–575*

Karanog, grave 579.

Coxe Expedition 1908

E 8704  H: 7.1; D: 8.3 cm
Ceramic

***Cup***
*Meroitic Period.*
A.D. *1–50*

Karanog, grave 655.

Coxe Expedition 1908

E 8724  H: 8.3; D: 9.1 cm
Ceramic

214

215

216

**Cup**
*Meroitic Period.*
*100 B.C.–A.D. 300*
Karanog, grave 292.
Coxe Expedition 1908
E 8734  H: 5.0; D: 10.5 cm
Ceramic

**Cup**
*Meroitic Period.*
*100 B.C.–A.D. 300*
Karanog, grave 743.
Coxe Expedition 1908
E 8735  H: 5.2; D: 8.4 cm
Ceramic

**Box Lid**
*Meroitic Period.*
*A.D. 1-50*
Karanog, grave735.
Coxe Expedition 1908
E 8737  H: 3.9; W: 9.7; L: 17.0 cm
Ceramic

217

218

219

**Bowl**
*Meroitic Period.*
*100 B.C.–A.D. 300*
Karanog.
Coxe Expedition 1908
E 8851  H: 11.0; D: 15.4 cm
Ceramic

**Footed Cup**
*Meroitic Period.*
*100 B.C.–A.D. 300*
Karanog, grave 591.
Coxe Expedition 1908
E 8875  H: 5.3; D: 10.1 cm
Ceramic

**Cup**
*Meroitic Period.*
*100 B.C.–A.D. 300*
Karanog, grave 189.
Coxe Expedition 1908
E 8876  H: 7.0; D: 7.7 cm
Ceramic

220

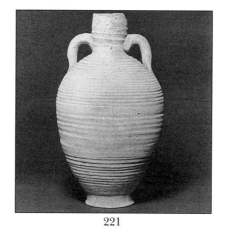

221

222

***Jar***
*X-Group Period.*
A.D. *320–550*

Karanog, grave 267.

Coxe Expedition 1908

E 8892  H: 23.7; D: 20.5 cm
Ceramic

***Jar***
*X-Group Period.*
A.D. *320–550*

Toshka West.

Yale-Pennsylvania Expedition 1961-62

66-11-71  H: 33.5; D: 19.0 cm
Ceramic

***Vase***
*X-Group Period.*
A.D. *320–550*

Toshka West.

Yale-Pennsylvania Expedition 1961-62

66-11-72  H: 23.6; D: 21.3 cm
Ceramic

223

224

225

***Jar***
*X-Group Period.*
A.D. *320–550*

Toshka West.

Yale-Pennsylvania Expedition 1961-62

66-11-74  H: 27.7; D: 18.8 cm
Ceramic

***Jar***
*X-Group Period.*
A.D. *320–550*

Toshka West.

Yale-Pennsylvania Expedition 1961-62

66-11-77  H: 39.7; D: 28.0 cm
Ceramic

***Bowl***
*X-Group Period.*
A.D. *320–550*

Karanog, grave 422.

Coxe Expedition 1908

E 8698  H: 10.0; D: 12.3 cm
Ceramic

226

227

*C u p*

> *X-Group Period.*
> A.D. *320–550*
> Karanog, grave 648.
> Coxe Expedition 1908
> E 8702  H: 6.9; D: 9.3 cm
> Ceramic

*C u p*

*X-Group Period.*
A.D. *320–550*
Toshka West.
Yale-Pennsylvania Expedition 1961-62
66-11-55  H: 7.4; D: 10.1 cm
Ceramic

228

229

230

*B o w l*
*X-Group Period.*
A.D. *320–550*
Toshka West.
Yale-Pennsylvania Expedition 1961-62
66-11-60  H: 11.0; D: 9.3 cm
Ceramic

*C u p*
*X-Group Period.*
A.D. *320–550*
Toshka West.
Yale-Pennsylvania Expedition 1961-62
66-11-61  H: 12.0; D: 9.0 cm
Ceramic

*C u p*
*X-Group Period.*
A.D. *320–550*
Toshka West.
Yale-Pennsylvania Expedition 1961-62
66-11-62  H: 8.4; D: 10.8 cm
Ceramic

231

232

**Jar Sherd**
*Christian Period.*
A.D. *540–1550*

Arminna West.

Yale-Pennsylvania Expedition 1961-62

66-11-50  H: 10.5; L: 15.0; T: 1.6 cm
Ceramic

**Funerary Stela**
*Christian Period.*
A.D. *921*

Arminna West.

Yale-Pennsylvania Expedition 1961-62

66-11-48  W: 23.5; L: 37.0; T: 3.7 cm
Ceramic

233

234

**Censer**
*Christian Period.*
A.D. *540–1550*

Arminna West.

Yale-Pennsylvania Expedition 1961-62

66-11-52  H: 26.9; D: 8.0 cm
Bronze

**Lamp**
*Christian Period.*
A.D. *540–1550*

Toshka West.

Yale-Pennsylvania Expedition 1961-62

66-11-53  H: 5.9; W: 8.5; L: 11.5 cm
Ceramic

# Concordance

| MUSEUM NO. | COMPENDIUM NO. | MUSEUM NO. | COMPENDIUM NO. | MUSEUM NO. | COMPENDIUM NO. |
|---|---|---|---|---|---|
| 66-11-1 | 69 | 92-2-55 | 48 | E 4197 | 18 |
| 66-11-42 | 105 | 92-2-56 | 48 | E 4221 | 21 |
| 66-11-48 | 231 | 92-2-58 | 49 | E 4232 | 21 |
| 66-11-50 | 232 | 92-2-66 | 71 | E 4257 | 21 |
| 66-11-52 | 233 | 92-2-67 | 72 | E 4327 | 21 |
| 66-11-53 | 234 | 92-2-69 | 73 | E 4334 | 21 |
| 66-11-55 | 227 | 92-2-70 | 74 | E 4442 | 18 |
| 66-11-60 | 228 | 92-2-71 | 75 | E 4466 | 23 |
| 66-11-61 | 229 | 92-2-74 | 76 | E 4496 | 23 |
| 66-11-62 | 230 | 92-2-75 | 77 | E 4501 | 21 |
| 66-11-71 | 221 | 92-2-76 | 77 | E 4642 | 23 |
| 66-11-72 | 222 | 92-2-77 | 76 | E 5015 | 89 |
| 66-11-74 | 223 | 92-2-78 | 76 | E 5252 | 195 |
| 66-11-77 | 224 | 92-2-79 | 78 | E 5271 | 196 |
| 92-2-1 | 1 | 92-2-80 | 78 | E 5331 | 162 |
| 92-2-2 | 4 | 92-2-81 | 78 | E 6598 | 161 |
| 92-2-5 | 5 | 92-2-82 | 77 | E 7000 | 90 |
| 92-2-6 | 6 | 92-2-83 | 77 | E 7001 | 91 |
| 92-2-8 | 7 | 92-2-84 | 76 | E 7003 | 92 |
| 92-2-9 | 8 | 92-2-92-1 | 81 | E 7004 | 93 |
| 92-2-11-1 | 9 | 92-2-92-2 | 81 | E 7005 | 94 |
| 92-2-11-2 | 9 | 92-2-94 | 79 | E 7018 | 95 |
| 92-2-11-3 | 9 | 92-2-95 | 80 | E 7032 | 96 |
| 92-2-12 | 11 | 92-2-97 | 82 | E 7037 | 97 |
| 92-2-13 | 15 | 92-2-101 | 83 | E 7038 | 98 |
| 92-2-14 | 13 | 92-2-102.a | 84 | E 7070 | 99 |
| 92-2-15 | 17 | 92-2-102.b | 84 | E 7081 | 100 |
| 92-2-16a | 17 | 92-2-103 | 85 | E 7088 | 101 |
| 92-2-16b | 17 | 92-2-105 | 86 | E 7095 | 102 |
| 92-2-17 | 12 | 92-2-107 | 87 | E 7097 | 103 |
| 92-2-18 | 27 | 92-2-108 | 88 | E 7100 | 104 |
| 92-2-19 | 30 | 92-10-1 | 19 | E 7129 | 154 |
| 92-2-20 | 28 | 92-10-2 | 19 | E 7130 | 155 |
| 92-2-21 | 29 | 92-10-3 | 10 | E 7132 | 156 |
| 92-2-22 | 45 | 92-10-4 | 70 | E 7133 | 157 |
| 92-2-24 | 31 | 92-10-5 | 113 | E 7134 | 158 |
| 92-2-27 | 32 | 92-10-6 | 113 | E 7137 | 159 |
| 92-2-35 | 43 | E 4009 | 24 | E 7147 | 135 |
| 92-2-37 | 33 | E 4021 | 24 | E 7180 | 152 |
| 92-2-39 | 41 | E 4022 | 24 | E 7181 | 152 |
| 92-2-40 | 34 | E 4025 | 25 | E 7198 | 150 |
| 92-2-41 | 35 | E 4026 | 25 | E 7202 | 151 |
| 92-2-42 | 42 | E 4030 | 25 | E 7203 | 150 |
| 92-2-44 | 44 | E 4071 | 26 | E 7204 | 150 |
| 92-2-46 | 36 | E 4072 | 26 | E 7206 | 150 |
| 92-2-48 A | 46 | E 4073 | 26 | E 7207 | 150 |
| 92-2-48 B | 46 | E 4097 | 26 | E 7226 | 152 |
| 92-2-48 C | 46 | E 4102 | 18 | E 7230 | 149 |
| 92-2-48 D | 46 | E 4119 | 19 | E 7237 | 151 |
| 92-2-49 | 47 | E 4139 | 20 | E 7238 | 151 |
| 92-2-50 | 47 | E 4141 | 20 | E 7260 | 150 |
| 92-2-53 | 48 | E 4161 | 21 | E 7260 | 151 |
| 92-2-54 | 48 | E 4181 | 22 | E 7266 | 151 |
| | | E 4182 | 22 | E 7270 | 149 |

| Museum No. | Compendium No. | Museum No. | Compendium No. | Museum No. | Compendium No. |
|---|---|---|---|---|---|
| E 7272 | 149 | E 7928 | 112 | E 8645 | 209 |
| E 7276 | 152 | E 7932 | 109 | E 8671 | 210 |
| E 7279 | 151 | E 7934 | 109 | E 8672 | 211 |
| E 7280 | 149 | E 8046 | 114 | E 8698 | 225 |
| E 7292 | 149 | E 8054 | 115 | E 8702 | 226 |
| E 7301 | 136 | E 8068 | 116 | E 8704 | 212 |
| E 7303 | 137 | E 8077 | 117 | E 8724 | 213 |
| E 7339 | 128 | E 8084 | 118 | E 8734 | 214 |
| E 7340 | 129 | E 8105 | 119 | E 8735 | 215 |
| E 7342 | 130 | E 8110 | 120 | E 8737 | 216 |
| E 7343 | 131 | E 8114 | 121 | E 8777 | 16 |
| E 7348 | 132 | E 8126 | 122 | E 8811 | 192 |
| E 7353 | 133 | E 8154 | 163 | E 8851 | 217 |
| E 7366 | 134 | E 8157 | 164 | E 8875 | 218 |
| E 7367 | 138 | E 8162 | 165 | E 8876 | 219 |
| E 7368 | 139 | E 8168 | 166 | E 8892 | 220 |
| E 7379 | 140 | E 8170 | 167 | E 8953 | 106 |
| E 7387 | 141 | E 8173 | 168 | E 8954 | 107 |
| E 7388 | 141 | E 8176 | 169 | E 8956 | 108 |
| E 7392 | 141 | E 8183 | 170 | E 8967 | 193 |
| E 7396 | 141 | E 8192 | 171 | E 10135 | 54 |
| E 7419 | 149 | E 8193 | 172 | E 10138 | 54 |
| E 7420 | 142 | E 8197 | 173 | E 10341 | 51 |
| E 7422 | 143 | E 8216 | 174 | E 10347 A | 50 |
| E 7459 | 144 | E 8218 | 175 | E 10435 | 194 |
| E 7512 | 160 | E 8237 | 176 | E 10603 | 55 |
| E 7514 | 123 | E 8257 | 177 | E 10604a | 56 |
| E 7515 a-b | 124 | E 8261 | 178 | E 10605 | 57 |
| E 7519 | 127 | E 8270 | 179 | E 10611 | 37 |
| E 7570 | 145 | E 8275 | 180 | E 10614 | 38 |
| E 7602 a-b | 125 | E 8276 | 181 | E 10615 | 39 |
| E 7618 a-c | 126 | E 8284 | 182 | E 10624 | 58 |
| E 7678 b | 146 | E 8290 | 183 | E 10765 | 53 |
| E 7679 | 147 | E 8293 | 184 | E 10780 | 62 |
| E 7682 a | 148 | E 8310 | 185 | E 10786 | 62 |
| E 7726 | 153 | E 8334 | 186 | E 10789 | 59 |
| E 7755 | 110 | E 8437 | 197 | E 10848 | 40 |
| E 7759 | 110 | E 8447 | 198 | E 11061 | 63 |
| E 7759 | 113 | E 8451 | 199 | E 11098 h | 66 |
| E 7765 | 110 | E 8453 | 200 | E 11098 t | 67 |
| E 7791B | 113 | E 8469 | 201 | E 11104 | 64 |
| E 7794 | 109 | E 8472 | 202 | E 11152 | 65 |
| E 7816 | 110 | E 8478 | 203 | E 11197 c | 68 |
| E 7819 | 110 | E 8483 | 204 | E 11256 | 14 |
| E 7840 b | 110 | E 8550 | 187 | E 11317 | 60 |
| E 7847 | 111 | E 8565 | 188 | E 15051 | 2 |
| E 7849 | 111 | E 8571 | 189 | E 15103 | 52 |
| E 7868 | 111 | E 8577 | 190 | E 15784 | 62 |
| E 7871 | 112 | E 8596 | 191 | E 16035 | 3 |
| E 7877 | 111 | E 8602 | 205 | E 16041 | 61 |
| E 7905 | 112 | E 8628 | 206 | E 16050 | 62 |
| E 7920 | 111 | E 8631 | 207 | E 16051 b | 62 |
| E 7922 | 112 | E 8638 | 208 | | |

# *Index*

# Index